D1078853

below.

in General Practice

Edited by

Michael Drury

Radcliffe Medical Press

Radcliffe Medical Press Ltd
18 Marcham Road, Abingdon, Oxon OX14 1AA

British Library Cataloguing in Publication Data

A catalogue record for this book is available from the British Library.

ISBN 1 85775 367 4

Typeset by Acorn Bookwork, Salisbury, Wiltshire
Printed and bound by TJ-International Ltd, Padstow, Cornwall

Contents

List of contributors

Stuart Carne CBE MB FRCGP HonFRCPCH HonFRNZCGP
Senior Forensic Medical Examiner
Past President, Royal College of General Practitioners
Past Senior Tutor in General Practice, Royal Postgraduate Medical School

Simon Dinnick BA
Partner
Le Brasseur J Tickle
London

Mark Drury MB ChB MRCGP DRCOG
General Practitioner, Wantage
Part-time Research Fellow, Imperial Cancer Research Fund
Department of Public Health and Primary Care
University of Oxford

Sir Michael Drury OBE FRCP FRCGP FRACGP HonFRCPCH
Past President, Royal College of General Practitioners
Emeritus Professor of General Practice, University of Birmingham

John R Griffiths BA (Oxon) LLB WS
Partner, Shepherd & Wedderburn WS
Chairman, Law Society of Scotland's Panel for accrediting solicitors as specialists in the law of medical negligence

Nigel Ineson MB BS FRCGP DRCOG DFFP
Partner in a five-doctor teaching practice
Partner in his own medico-legal practice

Fiona MF Paterson LLB Dip Legal Practice
Assistant Solicitor to John R Griffiths, Shepherd & Wedderburn WS
Acts for members of the Medical & Dental Defence Union of Scotland

John Pickering LLB
Head of Personal Injury Department
Irwin Mitchell Solicitors, Sheffield

Antony Townsend BA (Oxon)
Director of Standards and Education, General Medical Council

List of case studies

Glossary

Old terminology	New terminology
pleadings	statements of case
action	claim
summons	claim form
writ	claim form
particulars/statement of claim	particulars of claim
plaintiff	claimant
defendant	defendant
defence	defence
reply	reply
rejoinder/rebutter	(abolished)
counterclaim	Part 20 claim
third party proceedings	Part 20 claim

Acknowledgements

It is a pleasure to express my thanks to so many collaborators and friends who have made this book a possibility. All of them were convinced from the outset of the importance of the topic and the mixture of lawyers and doctors, with their differing viewpoints and approaches, has provided a forum which we have all found stimulating and challenging. Authors have shown great tolerance of my badgering and requests for additional material, and have been forthcoming with ideas. In particular, John Griffiths and John Pickering have given very helpful editorial advice. Heidi Allen, commissioning editor, and all of the staff at Radcliffe Medical Press have demonstrated once again their patience and efficiency, making my task an enjoyable one.

Introduction

This book has been written to help doctors and solicitors respond to two important features of modern practice, namely the steady rise in the number of allegations of clinical negligence made against doctors in general practice (and almost every other branch of medicine), and the enormous changes to civil law resulting from the Access to Justice Report produced by Lord Woolf in 1996. Both of these have resulted in many anxieties, two of which seem paramount. Will general practitioners be forced to become progressively more defensive, to the detriment of good and cost-effective patient care? And will faster and cheaper legal process increase or lessen access to just compensation for damaged patients?

The book is not only concerned with the mechanisms that exist for handling complaints of all sorts, but also attempts to explore their place in helping to maintain standards. Unless the increase in the number of complaints is reversed – an unlikely event – doctors have to adapt in good conscience to complaints by seeing them as opportunities to improve standards and minimise errors. Errors will occur in even the best-regulated practices, but they carry the obligation to learn from them and to be accountable for them. Indeed, clinical freedom depends to a large extent on how the profession responds to moves seeking to make doctors more accountable. The ultimate test is the best interest of the patient, and this has to be open to the scrutiny of the courts. It is at this point that the interests of doctors and lawyers coincide.

The intention of the authors is to produce practical guidelines that enable both professions to understand better the processes within which general practice and the law operate. The book has been written by a team of doctors and lawyers experienced in the field who have taken the opportunity to achieve realism by including a large number of actual cases. The first chapter sets out to provide an overview of the topic and briefly analyses some of the causes and effects of the increased number of complaints. The next two chapters set allegations of clinical negligence in the context of the other two areas in which complaints against general practitioners may be dealt with, namely the National Health Service and the General Medical Council. In both chapters detailed descriptions of how the various mechanisms operate are given. The law of negligence and the process of the law are covered in two chapters by lawyers experienced in this field, although we have to add the caveat that it is still too early to be sure how the new Civil Procedure Rules will operate in England and Wales. One of the changes derived from the 'Woolf' reforms has been to alter the nomenclature of parts of the legal process. For example, the person making the complaint was known as the 'plaintiff', which has now been changed to the 'claimant'. We have used the latter word even when we are describing cases that occurred before the change took place, for reasons of simplicity, unless it forms part of a quotation.

Chapter 6 explores the difficult subject of limitation – that is, the time after an event during which a case can be launched. It is a large subject and differs in Scotland from the rest of the UK, but we have tried to set out the main principles in a way that can be readily understood. Chapter 7 describes a large number of cases in which clinical negligence has been alleged against general practitioners, and attempts to draw lessons from these which will help the practitioner to avoid some of the pitfalls. The role of the medical defence organisations has changed very greatly with the establishment of Crown Indemnity for National Health Service hospital doctors, but there have been many other changes and these are explored in Chapter 8. The responses which should be expected from a general practitioner against whom an allegation is made are drawn together in Chapter 9, and Chapter 10 outlines the duties and responsibilities expected of those general practitioners who work as medical experts in this area. The last two chapters detail fatal accident inquiries in Scotland and some of the differences in Scottish civil law.

It is hoped that the information in this book will help lawyers to understand the medical process and doctors to understand the legal process, thus demystifying much that occurs. It is also hoped that it will make a contribution towards altering the attitudes of doctors so that the response to a complaint is recognised as part of the normal process of accountability, rather than a stigma upon a whole professional career.

Michael Drury
April 2000

Editor's Note

Indemnity insurance

General practitioners must, of course, take care to carry indemnity for their negligent acts with one of the appropriate Medical Defence Organisations. They are also responsible, vicariously, for the negligent acts of those they employ. Whilst not responsible for the negligent acts of their partners in the events of a partner being uninsured or otherwise unable to pay any compensation awarded against him, the partnership may be held liable for that debt, thus it is important for a practice to ensure that the indemnity cover of each partner is up-to-date.

A locum is an independent practitioner and must be separately insured. A practice will not be held to be responsible for their negligent acts. If they are employed by an outside body then that body may also be held to be resposible.

The position of a trainee is more obscure and has not been tested in the Courts. Generally, it is believed, they would be held responsible for their own actions but in the event of them being supervised by a trainer in a particular case, it is possible that the trainer would also be held to be responsible.

CHAPTER ONE

Cause and effect

Michael Drury

Increasing numbers of complaints

The past 50 years have seen remarkable changes in medical care. The range of effective treatments available has expanded enormously, and their accessibility to almost the whole of the population has increased proportionately. It has been a half century of great medical success, so it is somewhat of a paradox that the number of complaints made against doctors in every field of work has grown greatly during this time. The level of public dissatisfaction with the systems for monitoring medical standards has increased, exemplified dramatically by a number of high-profile cases, such as the paediatric cardiac surgery cases originating in Bristol, which ultimately came before the General Medical Council. Moreover, as therapies have become more powerful, their possible adverse effects have become more pronounced and the public now seeks protection by more ambitious and more punishing litigation.

During the decade from 1988 to 1998 the number of complaints notified to the medical defence organisations increased more than tenfold, and the average cost of compensation more than doubled. The highest award increased from £132 000 in 1977 to £1.6 million in 1998 (awarded to the family of a child who died after the general practitioner failed to diagnose meningitis). Between 1988 and 1997 the number of complaints about doctors received by the General Medical Council more than tripled, and the number in which action was taken more than doubled. The UK legal aid bill increased from £166 million in 1990 to over £600 million in 1996, and the cost to the NHS of providing indemnity rose by over 300% during that period.

Although the number of complaints and the size of awards has increased dramatically, the proportion of successful claims in the courts has not increased. Less than 2% of the cases in which legal action is started still actually reach court, and of those that do, only in 17% of cases is judgement given against the doctor. However, this is not to say that the other cases were trivial or the litigation vexatious. It would be incorrect to assume that because a minority of complaints are upheld in any forum the others should not have been brought. There are probably more patients with a genuine cause for grievance who do not sue than there are patients with spurious claims who do.

The cause of failure of actions is complex, as this book will show. In many complaints there will be genuine misunderstanding or misinterpretation of what can actually be shown to have taken place. At other times it will not be possible to show that the actions complained of caused the damage to the patient and yet, at other times, although a mistake occurred it happened despite care, and it is probable that other thoughtful and careful doctors would have made the same error.

Sometimes the damage alleged to have been done by some treatment, or failure to treat, will launch a high-profile class action, as occurred with drugs such as thalidomide, lorazepam and the oral contraceptives, or from the misinterpretation of cervical smears. One in four complaints against general practitioners follows a patient's death. Here the emotional issues surrounding such an event make good communication between doctors and relatives particularly important. A breakdown of trust is particularly unforgiving even if there was no error in care. Then clearly there are also a minority of people who have a long history of unhappiness with doctors and of personal difficulties, and even some who believe it might be possible to supplement their income by their interpretation of events – and in some of these cases it is possible to find a pattern of similar attempts in the past. It is therefore of some comfort to know that judges will essentially only find a doctor to be negligent if his or her peers say so.

Fifty years ago, newly qualified doctors could look forward to a lifetime without a single serious complaint being levelled at them, and their subscription to a Defence Society would have been covered by a few hours' work. Today a new graduate must expect to have to respond to a number of formal complaints during their time in practice and several weeks of work will be needed to pay the annual subscription. However, it is worth noting that even though doctors are more likely to be complained against now than in the past, no greater proportion is likely to be found negligent than in earlier years. Of course this rise in the number of complaints is not peculiar either to this country or to the medical profession. In North America the rise in the number of complaints against all professions has been even greater, and some doctors will pay six-figure professional indemnity fees, all of which are ultimately paid by the patient. Even in this country, lawyers, accountants, financial advisers and members of almost every other profession are experiencing a similar degree of apparent disenchantment. It may be salutary to note in passing that in the case of mistakes made by lawyers, it is usually they themselves that draw attention to the error – a policy which should be adopted by the medical profession (*see* Chapter 5, p. 77).

The fear is often expressed that the situation in the UK will eventually be the same as that in the USA. It is suggested that if this were to happen, we would become overwhelmed by a tide of litigation, to the detriment of both our professional relationships and our standards of care, because of the need to practise defensively and the time involved in responding to unsuccessful claims. However, this is unlikely to happen because the systems in the two countries are very different, and different factors exist to influence behaviour. One of these is the fact that medical care in the USA is within the private sector to a much greater extent, so a higher proportion of the cost of repairing any damage caused by medical negligence falls upon the patient. Another factor is that the amount of damages in the USA is assessed by a jury and not by the judge, and juries are notoriously more generous. Furthermore, in the USA a jury has the power to add 'punitive' damages to 'cost' damages, and these can result in huge sums being paid out. In the USA there are more lawyers than there are in all the rest of the world put together. There is one lawyer to every 300 or so citizens, whereas in the UK there is about one to every 1200 citizens. The legal services are also different, and whilst they will undoubtedly change in the UK, the practice of charging contingency fees, no win – no payment, by the legal services is not yet well established and is likely to be carefully controlled. Despite this there is still a view expressed[1] that lawyers will find 'ways of suing for almost any injury or slight however trivial' and accusations about 'ambulance chasing' still exist. Finally, cultural patterns within the two societies are still very different, and most people within the UK are more diffident with regard to complaining about anything, and consider it 'un-British' to do so.

Causes

The causes of the rise in the number of complaints are numerous and complex. Undoubtedly there is now a greater level of general knowledge among patients about technical matters. There is also a much higher level of expectation about what can – and therefore should – be provided. Sometimes the media encourage an unreal expectation about what medicine can or should do, and frequently this goes unchallenged – doctors themselves have contributed to the presence of unreal expectations both within the private consultation and by public statements that they have made. Sometimes this stems from attitudes based more on hope than on reality.

There always was, as Rudolf Klein wrote in one of the early studies on this subject,[2] 'good reason to examine the power of Kings and Ministers, bureaucrats and businessmen.' He added 'Now, however, it seems equally relevant – perhaps more so – to examine the power of professional people, of doctors and lawyers, town planners and social workers'. Here we have to recognise that it is not only the power that medicine as a science now has but, perhaps more importantly, the patient appears before the doctor stripped of bodily and emotional cover, and it is impossible to overstate the power that this vulnerability gives to the doctor 'n the transaction.

Thus there is now not as much of the traditional tolerance ai d patience with less than best practice by the medical profession is there was in the past. This change, allied to more efficie it mechanisms for receiving complaints, and fewer barriers to making dissatisfaction known, is sometimes perceived as a positi ve encouragement to complain. If something has gone wrong in medical care, there is now a widespread belief that someone must be to blame. As society has become more litigious, it follows that lawsuits against doctors have increased. There is also a widespread feeling that doctors – and other professionals – have been insufficiently regulated for too long, and that too much has been expected of self-governance. This has been exemplified by a series of high-profile cases, culminating in 1998 with the widespread concern resulting from the high incidence of deaths among babies operated on for heart disease in Bristol, the apparent technical incompetence of a Kent gynaecologist and the perceived limitations of the subsequent General Medical Council (GMC) investigations.

Effects

The power and cost of medicine have increased enormously in many ways over the past 50 years, due largely to modern technology, but so has the cost of failure. In the days before effective antibiotics, the failure to visit a patient with pneumonia may have done little harm, but today it may be the cause of their death. The treatment of malignancy has now improved to the point that any delay in referring appropriately can lose all the gains made in treatment, and delay in investigating appropriately can become literally a life-or-death decision. Family doctors now have the power to prevent the birth of many babies who would otherwise be born with gross handicaps. Here not only are there major human costs and ethical issues involved, but it may also mean that the neglect of a simple test costing a few pounds can result in the birth of a handicapped baby for whom the parents require tens of thousands of pounds each year to maintain the best quality of life for the child and for those who care for him or her. Failure to prescribe properly can result in children with meningitis becoming brain-damaged, adults becoming dependent on hypnotics or sedatives, and patients being left with permanent disabilities due to a failure to monitor long-term treatment carefully. The development of more complex care within the community requires teamwork and careful co-ordination, and here the failure to communicate properly and keep adequate records can result in devastating problems. Indeed, a common cause of failure identified in many cases in this book stems from the fragmentation of modern medical care, resulting in delivery by different people from different disciplines, often working in different buildings and failing to communicate well. This could well turn out to be the major problem facing medical care in the twenty-first century.

Later in this book cases are described illustrating all of these problems and we deal in more depth, for example, with what constitutes an adequate record. Here it is sufficient to recognise that busy general practitioners do not usually have the luxury of time and space in which to expand their records as they would wish. Other situations occur where a failure to examine a patient adequately may lead to pathology being missed, and failure to listen adequately to patients and their relatives is perhaps the commonest origin of a complaint. It can be seen from this that the issues of most concern are those of a deficiency in normal good practice and usual standards of good care, and not a failure

to recognise abstruse clinical syndromes or provide esoteric therapies.

We shall consider the matter of general complaints in more detail
later. Suffice it to say here that one study[3] identified four major
reasons, namely concerns about standards of care, the need for
explanation, the desire for compensation and the belief that doctors
are accountable. Simanowitz[4] wrote that 'The vast majority of the
victims of medical accidents do not initially seek financial compensation but want an explanation for what went wrong, sympathetic
treatment and, if appropriate, an apology,' and this is the experience of most of us.

Although the rise in the number of complaints is not peculiar to
this profession, the medical community does find itself more disadvantaged than some others in being exposed to triple or even
quadruple jeopardy for one complaint – contractual matters scrutinised by the health authority, professional standards by the GMC,
personal liability claims within civil law and complaints upheld by
the Health Services Ombudsman. Finally, criminal law can become
involved by way of a manslaughter charge when gross negligence
is alleged. We shall touch upon this, too, later in this book.

Another curious anomaly is that, although the number of
complaints against doctors is increasing, the profession of medicine
remains top, or nearly so, in public esteem in any popularity poll of
the professions. A MORI poll conducted in 1998 concluded that
doctors were the most popular of all the professions. This perhaps
mirrors the often repeated sentiment that 'doctors in general are
awful but my doctor is wonderful'.

Part of the explanation for this apparent conflict may lie in the
particular relationship that exists between doctor and patient.
Much of this depends upon trust, a concept which protects either
side from exploitation by the other. Of course, a client will trust
their solicitor in the same way, and will praise them if they serve
well or sack them if they do a bad job, but the relationship will
rarely be characterised by the same intensity of feeling that
develops between doctor and patient. This is because many of the
issues that arise between the doctor and his or her patient will
involve sensitive ethical or moral concerns. There may be confi-
dences about other members of their family, or about friends or
colleagues at work. Some issues may touch upon sexual
weaknesses, moral or character failures or other intensely personal
and private matters. Not infrequently the issues concern matters of
life or death or may involve problems that will cause permanent
handicap. If the doctor serves the patient and the family well,

affection and admiration will grow between them, but one lapse or careless slip can, due to a sense of breach of trust, transform these feelings into hatred. For this reason, the cost of a single momentary error can be so high that the efforts required to avoid it must, at times, seem disproportionately great.

However great the consequences of the breakdown of trust can be upon the patient, they may be almost as devastating to the doctor. His or her investment over months or years in developing this relationship is blown away by a single complaint. An allegation of negligence relating to a single incident will not only be deeply felt but may also reflect adversely upon a lifetime of conscientious professionalism. Lord Denning said in one judgement[5] that for a doctor 'it was comparable to having a dagger plunged into his back'. Yet every doctor will be aware of times when they have fallen below the high standards they have set themselves and, as they read of the troubles of others, will silently say, as did John Bradford in the sixteenth century whilst watching criminals on their way to execution, 'There but for the Grace of God go I'.

Maintenance of standards

A fundamental tenet of 'professional practice' has been the under-taking to maintain the quality of service provided, and for many years both profession and public have been content to leave it so. For much of the past 50 years this was implicit in the mere fact of being a member of that profession, without having to demonstrate the steps taken to maintain it. However, there has now developed a general acceptance of the need to make this aspiration for quality explicit to both the 'employer' and the 'consumer'. Initially, regular attendance at continuing education sessions, first in a voluntary capacity and then linked to financial reward, appeared to be suffi-cient, but gradually the notion that performance has to be tested against a standard arose. Audit was seen as one way into this challenging and potentially threatening arena – the systematic recording of performance so that it can be measured against standards either created internally or drawn from outside. However, to be effective, medical audit has to be a way of searching for error. If it is only a system for measuring one's practice against a set of norms established from outside then, as Marinker states,[6] 'it has little to do with science and quality'.

With the acceptance of this concept, the medical profession has moved towards a notion that, given errors will inevitably occur, the least that can be done is to identify the cause of error and put into place patterns of behaviour to avoid such occurrences in future. This can be the only positive outcome of a complaint, and it can provide the doctor with the means of gaining some professional and intellectual advantage from what would otherwise be an entirely negative experience.

Acknowledging an error is difficult enough in the privacy of an audit or in the setting of a peer group which provides a guarantee against breach of confidentiality. Any anxiety is compounded when the results of an audit are to be exposed, even in an educational arena, to a wider group of people. Where exposure is concerned with assessing compensation for the victim of that error or – even worse – when it is concerned with blame and the approach is punitive, the worry increases greatly. Yet errors will occur. In one case, Lord Justice Donaldson[7] said 'There are very few professional men who will assert that they have never fallen below the high standards rightly expected of them. That they have never been negligent. If they do, it is unlikely that they should be believed. And this is as true of lawyers as it is of medical men.' It is within the sense of this judgement that civil litigation can be seen as part of the mechanism for maintaining professional standards. It is about compensation and not about blame. It is about trying to repay a patient in financial terms, difficult though that often is, for what has been lost. One tenable view is to regard it as only natural justice and as a part of the mechanism for maintaining standards. Perhaps this can help to make such confrontations bearable.

We refer in a number of places in this book to 'standards' and how these have become the touchstone in any medical negligence action. There is an increasing tendency for 'Guidelines' and 'Protocols' to be written in order to help doctors to manage relatively common situations, and some doctors may believe that they are a safe haven from criticism. However, most doctors recognise that guidelines are just what they say, and are not a rigid set of rules that apply to every case – and the courts also recognise this. Just because a protocol exists, this does not mean that following it would be reasonable in every set of circumstances, or that failing to follow it would be evidence of substandard care. As Brian Hurwitz says,[8] 'Clinical guidelines cannot offer doctors thought-proof mechanisms for improving medical care.' A faulty guideline would make a clinician who followed it more liable to charges of negligence, rather than less so, and as we have seen, acceptable standards of care derive from good clinical practice and not from outside rules. In any case, a protocol introduced into a legal case is not subject to cross-examination, so the court will always regard it as *hearsay evidence*. However, often an expert witness will introduce one in support of their view of what an acceptable standard of care is, and this may be accepted by the court. This suggests that if a guideline or protocol exists, a medical practitioner should at least have a good reason for not following it in a particular case, otherwise it may be difficult to justify. For example, Lord Goff, in a judgement[9] concerning a patient in a persistent vegetative state following the Hillsborough football disaster, supported the fact that a doctor treating such a patient would not be negligent if he followed the guidelines laid down by the BMA Medical Ethics Committee. The issues surrounding these are discussed much more fully by Dr Brian Hurwitz in his book on clinical guidelines and the law.[10] We shall refer more to this and to the notion of risk management later in this book.

Of course an allegation has to be defended if there is defence – if the doctor is convinced there was no error. This has to be tested, but if damage has followed the error of a doctor, the patient is as entitled to compensation as is the doctor him- or herself from the errors of a careless motorist, plumber or flight engineer.

In some ways, taking these ideas on board will reduce the stress on a doctor against whom a complaint is made – but not completely, of course. It is a normal response to defend oneself in such a situation, and as we have said this may be exacerbated by the nature of the relationship between patient and doctor and the sense of betrayal that can arise.

Principles

There can be no doubt that the receipt of a formal allegation of negligence will send a shiver down the spine of the most confident and rational person, yet the process of civil litigation in this country can also be a strong defender of the practitioner. The recent seismic changes made to the process of the law in England and Wales have not altered the basic rules. The standard against which the practitioner is measured is not some abstract set of guidelines or academic rules, but is the ordinary competent and current practice of his or her peers of equal standing. It is also fundamental to note that in law it is not for the doctor to prove that he or she has not been guilty of substandard care. It is for the claimant to show that he or she was failed by the doctor and that the damage complained of was caused by this failure.

In Chapter 4 of this book we shall deal in more detail with the 'Bolam' principle, which is the touchstone in assessing whether or not a medical man has been negligent. We shall also repeat some of the words spoken in the case, because of their importance. Suffice it to say here that in a landmark judgement[11] concerning the case of a Mr Bolam, who was given electroconvulsive therapy, during which he sustained a fracture of the vertebra, Mr Justice McNair, in his direction to the jury said:

> How do you test whether this act or failure is negligent? In an ordinary case it is generally said you judge it by the action of the man in the street. He is the ordinary man. In one case it has been said you judge it by the conduct of the man on the top of a Clapham omnibus. He is the ordinary man. But where you get a situation which involves the use of some special skill or competence, then the test as to whether there has been negligence or not is not the test of the man on the top of a Clapham omnibus, because he has not got this special skill. The test is the standard of the ordinary skilled man exercising and professing to have that special skill. A man need not possess the highest expert skill; it is well established by law that it is sufficient if he exercises the ordinary skill of an ordinary competent man exercising that particular art.

The jury found the doctor not guilty of negligence because he acted, as Mr Justice McNair said, 'in accordance with a practice accepted as proper by a responsible body of medical men skilled in that area'. This judgement has been interpreted and expanded by further rulings, but the principle holds good that the standard is that set by ordinary doctors and does not have to be the most expert, or even the best, but is entrenched in law as 'the accepted medical practice'. Thus a general practitioner making an assessment of a surgical condition does not have to perform to the standard of a surgeon but to that of a competent general practitioner. The judge has to decide whether he or she has reached that standard or fallen below it, but will be guided by the evidence of experienced general practitioners in making that decision. The law has thus opted for a subjective assessment of competence rather than for any objective test, and whilst the courts are there to test the patient's rights and, to a lesser extent, his or her responsibilities, they are also concerned not only with the doctor's responsibilities but also with his or her rights, too.

Blowing the whistle

For the greater part of this century, the notion that a doctor could criticise the actions of a professional colleague was unthinkable. Practising doctors saw examples of medical work with which the great majority of their colleagues would have been profoundly uncomfortable, to say the least. At that time there was no mechanism for reporting professional anxiety about such matters, and there existed some pressure upon the doctor not to do so. One important lesson then taught to newly qualifying doctors was that a doctor never did or said anything that might belittle or demean a colleague. The 'whistleblower' was unacceptable. The rationale for this was the perceived need to maintain a patient's confidence in his or her doctor, and the confidence of the public at large with the medical profession. This seemed very important at a time when maintaining confidence was perhaps the most effective weapon in the doctor's armamentarium. This was, like many other things in those days, an ethic which effectively protected the doctor more than his or her patient, whatever might be said to the contrary. This ethic has now changed. The issue of protecting the patient is now seen as paramount, and 'whistleblowing' has become acceptable although, unfortunately, not always without peril for the whistleblower. Mechanisms exist by which these professional anxieties can be properly aired. However, great care must still be exercised, as an unguarded critical remark made in the hearing of the patient, often without the time or facts with which to make a reasoned judgement, is not infrequently the cause of much unnecessary heartache and anxiety for doctor and patient alike, and has to be eschewed. Nowadays a significant number of complaints arise from the profession itself, or from sister professions. These have implications for professional boundaries and issues, such as trust and confidentiality, which are beyond the remit of this book to discuss in detail, but must at least be recognised. In this context there is also the discomfort sometimes expressed by colleagues at the actions of the medical expert in court criticising another member of his or her discipline. Only a few moments of consideration will be required to recognise that the courts, and through them the claimant, are entitled to seek to obtain an impartial view of the care given, and the profession has a responsibility to provide this. The expert is not a 'hired gun'. He or she is explicitly employed to advise the court, and not to be an advocate for either side.

Richard Baker, in an editorial in the *British Medical Journal*,[12] made the point that if the failures of people and systems are to be corrected, a complaints system alone will not be sufficient. It has to be linked to a range of other strategies, including continuing professional development, audit, risk management and critical incident reporting. Only if this is done will the likelihood of learning from mistakes and reducing the number of failures be increased.

References

1   *Sunday Times*. **17 November 1996**.

2   Klein R (1973) *Complaints Against Doctors*. Charles Knight & Co, London.

3   Vincent C, Young M, Phillips A (1994) Why do patients sue their doctors? A study of patients and their relatives taking legal action. *Lancet*. **343**: 1609–13.

4   Simanowitz A (1986–87) In P Byrne (ed) *Medicine in Contemporary Society*. Kings College Studies, London.

5   Hatcher v Black (1954) *The Times*. **2 July.**

6   Marinker M (ed) (1990) *Medical Audit and General Practice*. BMJ Publications, London.

7   Whitehouse v Jordan (1981) 1 *All ER* 267, WLR 246, 125 *Sol Jo*, 167, HL.

8   Hurwitz B (1999) Legal and political considerations of clinical practice guidelines. *BMJ*. **318**: 661 -4.

9   Airedale NHS Trust v Bland (Guardian *ad litem*) (1993) 1 *All ER*: 821–96.

10 Hurwitz B (1998) *Clinical Guidelines and the Law*. Radcliffe Medical Press, Oxford.

11 Bolam v Friern HMC (1957) 2 *All ER* 118, 1 *WLR* 582, 587–8.

12 Baker R (1999) Learning from complaints about general practitioners. *BMJ*. **318**: 1567–8.

CHAPTER TWO

Complaints and the National Health Service

Mark Drury

One of the few achievements of the NHS complaints procedures before 1996 was to unite demoralised adversaries in a sense of frustration and exhaustion. Doctors' representatives at Local Medical Committee conferences and patients' organisations had expressed discontent over a period of many years. Where they existed, the complaints procedures were obscure, difficult and regarded by both patients and doctors as potentially unfair. Rising numbers of allegations of clinical negligence at the time may, in part, have reflected patients' sense of obfuscation. However, the continuation of this trend, since changes in the system that have been introduced since 1996, is more difficult to explain.

Complaints in the National Health Service

In 1993, evidence of dissatisfaction with the complaints system was presented in over 250 submissions to an Independent Review Committee under the chairmanship of Professor Alan Wilson. The National Association of Health Authorities and Trusts, the Medical Defence Union and the Health Service Ombudsman were unanimous in their view that the existing processes were confusing and laborious. The BMA set up a working group to study the problem, and their report was presented as evidence on behalf of doctors. This report supported the view of the Consumers' Association, representing the patients, that a new system should be 'visible, transparent, fast, impartial, effective and flexible with the right to appeal'.

It was agreed that the primary function of any new system should be to address the concerns of the complainant. One survey[1] had shown that these concerns included the following:

- the desire to prevent similar incidents
- the wish for a full explanation, and
- the identification of an accountable individual or organisation.

This survey also showed that lack of honesty, a reluctance to apologise, the feeling of being treated as neurotic, and unclear and uninformative explanations contributed to the decision to pursue complaints as far as litigation. At the same time, another audit[2] of complaints to a health board showed that timely and comprehensive responses reduced the likelihood of litigation.

Recognising and dealing with these types of issues at the earliest possible stage is the aim of a complaints procedure and, when successful, may reduce the likelihood of both patient and practitioner submitting to a lengthy and arduous legal process. This chapter does not attempt a comprehensive review of procedures, but some understanding of them may allow the reader recourse to this book out of interest rather than necessity. A more detailed description of existing complaints procedures can be found elsewhere.[3]

The impetus to improve complaint procedures was not solely driven by the need to satisfy customers. There was recognition that complaints had the potential to improve the quality of the service. In 1983 the Griffiths Report[4] endorsed quality assurance as a crucially important tool in the National Health Service, and emphasised that patients' perceptions of the service were essential information for health authorities. This was accepted by the Government of the time in 1989 who, in the White Paper entitled *Working for Patients*,[5] were able to recommend that the service should from now onward be more concerned with customers' views. A plethora of patient satisfaction surveys were reported and generally interpreted as evidence of good service but, curiously, complaints received little attention.

It is now clear that the relatively low level of complaints in the early 1990s was not an indicator of a good service. First, despite a diffident national character, they had risen in number by a factor of 10 between 1980 and 1992, and over 30% had been demonstrated to be proper and justified. Second, the low incidence of complaints was more likely to reflect patients' perceptions that the complaints system was antipathetic, and that the National Health Service was indifferent and monolithic.

These attitudes have gradually changed. The Patients' Charter, the more active role of Community Health Councils and the change to the NHS internal market have been factors contributing to this. The system is now less inflexible. General practitioners, and by association their patients, are now customers of the hospital service and able to take their business elsewhere. Changes to the registration systems have meant that patients can transfer from one general practitioner to another much more easily. However, despite the attention that is now paid to patient satisfaction, it is certainly true that the clear and direct relationship that exists in the business world between customer satisfaction and business success is more tenuous and less clear-cut in the National Health Service.

The Wilson Report

The Wilson Committee reported its findings in May 1994, and recommended the adoption of a common system for investigating all complaints throughout the NHS with the sole aim of resolving the complaint whilst specifically excluding any disciplinary function. Key objectives for which the new system was designed included responsiveness (that is, the aim of satisfying complainants as to the process but not necessarily the outcome), accessibility to all, simplicity, impartiality, cost-effectiveness and speed.

The report recognised the potential for information gleaned from complaints to enhance the quality of the service by identifying problems and developing solutions, and the need for clear lines of accountability which led, ultimately, to chairmen and non-executive members of trusts. Undoubtedly the system is now less complex, but possibly it is still more so than patients would wish. Confusingly, both detractors and enthusiasts can point to a substantial rise in the number of complaints heard in support of their arguments. Despite the resources required to run it, dissatisfaction with the system itself remains high, and the wider impact on quality of care is still unclear.

Many of the concerns about its implementation focused on fears that such a consumer-orientated system would necessarily both increase the number of complaints and encourage the practice of defensive medicine. However, the boundary that exists between the potential losses produced by defensive medicine and the gains of good and enhanced practice is far from clear. In questionnaire surveys[6,7] before the introduction of new procedures, positive as well as negative consequences of any increase in complaints were identified. The former included more detailed note-taking, better explanations of procedures, increased concentration upon screening and audit. There was also the potential for enhancement of consumer satisfaction activities and fuller consultations resulting in increased clinical vigilance. Negative effects might include more and unnecessary prescribing, and potentially more patients being removed from the doctor's list with consequent erosion of the relationship. Effects less easily categorised as beneficial or harmful could include higher referral rates, longer follow-up and increased diagnostic testing.

Complaints procedures and local resolution

After the beginning of April 1996 general practitioners were required by their terms of service to operate practice complaints procedures which complied with nationally agreed criteria (*see* Appendix 2.1). The change from an adversarial process to a conciliatory one was an acknowledgement that errors will always occur. It was designed to offer general practitioners an opportunity to admit them, to explain and to apologise without implicitly accepting a breach in their terms of service and the possibility of disciplinary action. The highly significant importance of this concept is that such local resolution is not incompatible with the adversarial legal system and must cease when legal action is started.

In managing local resolution good practice should include the following:

1 *Information* on local procedures should be provided, for example, in posters, leaflets and the practice brochure. It should include the name of a 'complaints administrator' (and a deputy for periods of absence), as well as information on how to complain which emphasises the advisability of early action. A number of ways into the system should be described – for example, by appointment, by telephone, by the use of a standard form or by a free text letter. None of these should preclude common sense, and if a complaint is relatively trivial and can be dealt with at the time then that should be done. The initial response to a complaint is very important, and here training in handling complaints should be offered to staff, together with an agreement to participate in the practice procedure included in staff

contracts. The impact of wider dissemination of information about complaints procedures was demonstrated in an audit 6 months after their introduction.[8] Practices using two methods to advertise their scheme were up to three times more likely to receive a complaint than those using one, and practices using three methods were four times more likely to receive a complaint.

2 *Acknowledgement* of all complaints must be made within 3 days. Initially it is only necessary to confirm receipt, but written acknowledgements could usefully include a phrase about being sorry for the distress felt, and reassurance that it will be looked into as a matter of urgency. There is no need for artifice or unnecessary rigidity. If at all possible, an explanation should be offered at the time of acknowledgement.

3 *Investigation* of a complaint should normally be completed within 10 days. The more rapid the response the less likely are positions to become entrenched, but thoroughness and fairness should not be sacrificed to speed. Confidentiality for staff and patient is essential, and written consent should be obtained if the complainant is not the patient directly involved. If a meeting is necessary, consideration should be given to involving a conciliator from the health authority or a Community Health Council representative. The conduct of a meeting should aim to promote listening and learning and avoid lecturing. Written records of the process should always be kept and should be separated from patients' records.

4 A *response* should consist of a written summary of the outcome, a résumé of the facts, an explanation, an expression of sympathy and an apology, with reassurance that corrective action has been taken when appropriate. This should end with the hope that it is now resolved, but that if it is not then complaints to the health authority should be made within 28 days.

Case 1: In-house management of a complaint

The following letter to a practice manager was received on 1 April 1998:

Dear Mrs H,
I am writing to express my concern at the way my 6-year-old son was treated when he came to see Dr A. The receptionist asked me when I wanted the appointment for and I said as soon as possible so I brought him that afternoon.

When I explained that when he exercises he gets breathless, the doctor said 'Do you think this is an emergency?'. I was very shocked by her attitude. She prescribed an inhaler anyway and said to bring him back to the clinic but to run him round the car park 2–3 times before coming in to do another breath test. I have never dealt with asthma before, so I asked for some leaflets. Dr A said there would be one with the inhaler, but when I asked the pharmacist he was shocked that the doctor hadn't told me beforehand about it. My son has been prescribed an inhaler for a potentially life-threatening condition about which I know nothing. I understand from a friend I should have been given something called a volumatic. I am very disappointed about the way I was treated, being made to feel I was time-wasting. It is inexcusable to prescribe for a child without any guidance being given. I have never complained before, but on this occasion I do feel I was treated in an unacceptable manner.

The following letter was sent from the practice manager to the complainant on 3 April 1998:

Dear Mrs B,
Thank you for your letter of 1 April 1998. I would first of all like to apologise for the distress that has been caused to you. I was quite upset to read your letter, and it is clear that the practice failed in its management and a series of misunderstandings resulted in an unsatisfactory consultation. We have not yet had an opportunity to discuss this with Dr A or the reception staff, but they will be made aware of your complaint, and I shall write to you again to tell you of the outcome and the action we propose to take. In the meantime, if you would like to discuss any aspect of this with Dr B (senior partner) or myself please do ring me. Once again I am very sorry and thank you for bringing it to my attention.

Report of discussion with receptionist on 3 April 1998:

I met with Ms C [receptionist] who received Mrs B's request for an appointment. Ms C said her recollection of events was unclear, but she did remember that the conversation included Mrs B telling her that her son had been breathless and asking for an appointment as soon as possible. It was for these reasons that an appointment was offered as an emergency. She agreed that the matter could be discussed anonymously with reception staff and partners.

Written summary received from Dr A on 5 April 1998:

I saw Mrs B and her son on 1 April 1998 as an emergency at the end of morning surgery. She told me that Thomas had been short of breath after sports for some months. After taking a history and an examination, including a normal peak-flow reading, I concluded that he was likely to be suffering from mild asthma induced by exertion.

I pointed out that Mrs B had an emergency appointment and that this did not allow the fuller assessment I felt he needed and that he should be brought back to the asthma clinic for this to be done. I prescribed a salbutamol inhaler with verbal instructions on its use, if required, as a short-term measure.

I regret any failure on my part to explain my conclusions and actions adequately, but would point out that, in the context of an emergency appointment, I believe I acted in a safe and appropriate manner. Adequate consultation time provided by a well-run appointments system is critical to offering good care to patients with asthma, and depends upon the co-operation of patients. I apologise if my attempts to explain this to Mrs B were in any way distressing.

Matter raised at regular receptionists meeting on 12 April 1998 (see report).
Discussed at partnership meeting on 15 April 1998 (see report).
Response sent from complaints manager to Mrs B on 20 April 1998:

Dear Mrs B,
I have now carefully looked into the matter of your complaint and, as promised, am writing to let you know the outcome.

Firstly the practice would like to offer an apology for the distress you were caused. Several points have arisen in the course of the investigation.

It was clearly a misunderstanding on the part of our staff that led you to receive an emergency rather than a routine appointment. In an emergency, appointment time is very limited and Dr A has asked me to apologise for any distress the necessary brevity caused you. I believe you have now had an opportunity to attend the asthma clinic, where I hope you found that the additional time allowed was sufficient to give you a full explanation of your son's condition and treatment.

It will now be a matter of practice policy always to confirm the nature of the appointment to patients receiving an emergency appointment. We have also asked our patient involvement group to publicise the difference between emergency and routine appointments in their next newsletter, as well as revising the advice offered in our practice brochure.

We do feel that the practice offers a high standard of care for patients with asthma, and we hope that, following your clinic appointment, your confidence in us is re-established. If you should remain unhappy please do let me know. If you wish, you are able to pursue your complaint by contacting the health authority (tel. 123456), but this must be done within 28 days. I enclose a leaflet about this process.

In general, local resolution of complaints has been judged to be a success, with most cases being settled to the satisfaction of both the general practitioner and the complaining patient.

The independent review

To pursue a complaint beyond local resolution, a written or oral request has to be made to the health authority within 28 days. Within the following 20 days a convenor must decide whether to establish a complaints panel. He or she will obtain a written statement from the complainant, inform the doctor concerned of the details, and advise him or her to contact the Secretary of the Local Medical Committee for help in responding. The convenor is assisted by the complaints officer, the independent lay-panel chairman, appointed by the health authority, and a doctor nominated by the Local Medical Committee, to give independent medical advice. This is mandatory in matters of clinical judgement. The convenor can refuse a request for a review, and may refer the complaint back to the local resolution process or suggest the involvement of a conciliator. He or she is not obliged to resolve the complaint, but must make an appropriate response.

The review panel will consist of the convenor, the independent lay chairman and a lay person. Either party to the complaint can enlist the help of an 'independent clinical assessor', whose role is to advise the panel about matters relating to clinical judgement, from a list of names held by the Local Medical Committee. The assessor may wish to make enquiries of staff and other witnesses, interview the parties to the complaint and, whenever matters of clinical judgement are at issue, will be present at all meetings of the panel.

Review panels have no disciplinary function and are constrained by the terms of reference developed by the convenor. A full and accurate record of the process has to be kept, and may have to withstand scrutiny by the ombudsman at a later date. It is the chairman's responsibility to set out the panel's views in a report, and he or she must include the comments made by the medical assessors. A draft may be offered to both complainant and doctor for comment. The report is sent to the chairman of the health authority, who will decide whether disciplinary action is necessary. It must be sent to the complainant within 5 working days of the chief executive receiving it, together with a letter advising them of their right to refer it to the ombudsman if they remain dissatisfied. It is probably true to say that at present the independent review has failed to gain the confidence of general practitioners.

Conciliation

The effect upon both the complainant and the respondent of managing a complaint can be very significant, with potentially damaging effects upon work, all the more so when local procedures fail. In primary care, complaints are often set in the context of a continuing relationship between a professional and a patient in which trust is the currency. The breakdown of this trust tends to polarise attitudes, and it may be particularly difficult for staff and doctors in the practice to achieve and convey the neutrality necessary to achieve a shared understanding with complainants. Complaints are more likely to be resolved before attitudes become entrenched. Establishing an open, honest, neutral atmosphere in which the complainant's concerns are heard quickly and taken seriously reduces the likelihood of litigation. The early involvement of a conciliator may help to achieve these objectives.

The new complaints procedures of 1996 identified a service offering conciliation as an important way of supporting a non-adversarial system. The involvement of a lay conciliator can be requested from the health authority by the practice, a convenor or the patient, and they can operate at both practice and review panel levels. In one survey, two-thirds of patients expressed a preference to take a complaint about their general practitioner to the health authority rather than the practice itself. Complainants' access to conciliation at this level is therefore particularly important. Usually conciliators will interview all parties individually before arranging a meeting, and may require access to independent clinical advisers nominated by the Local Medical Committee.

When litigation has begun, a matter of wider public interest is at stake, or when complaints are aired publicly conciliation is less likely to be appropriate.

Conciliation offers an opportunity for both parties to meet in a neutral, non-judgemental atmosphere, to review the issues and to develop a dialogue that addresses the problem rather than each other.

The health service commissioner (ombudsman)

A health services commissioner has been in place for several years, but when the complaints procedure was altered in 1996, the commissioner's role was widened to include matters previously excluded, namely clinical practice and the actions of general practitioners. There is no automatic right to take a complaint to the commissioner and all other procedures must have been exhausted. There is a time limit of 12 months, and if a remedy can reasonably be sought legally or the matter concerns disciplinary procedures, or other processes such as conciliation would be more appropriate, the commissioner may decide not to take up the issue. A report that is the sole responsibility of the commissioner will be produced. In preparation, advice can be sought from any appropriate individual, including an employed GP adviser. The annual report of the commissioner for 1997–1998[9] states that 38 093 written complaints were received about general medical and dental services and health services administration, but only 331 of these were referred to an independent review panel. During that year, 27 investigations into complaints about general practitioners were started by the commissioner.

More general practitioners are now facing independent reviews, and there has been an increase of 55% since 1996. There has been a dramatic rise in complaints to the ombudsman since 1996 (93% of which have been upheld), and litigation is increasing. These

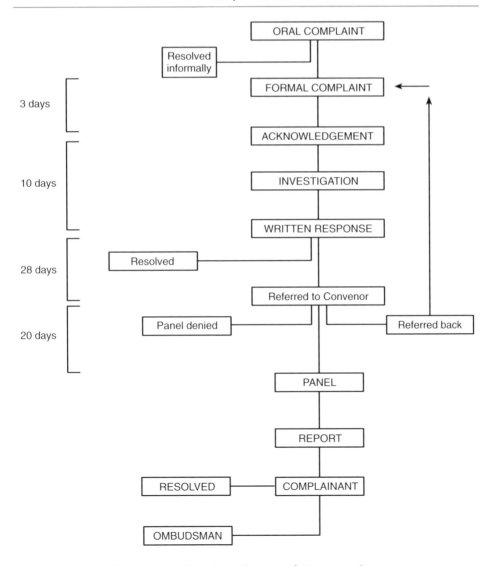

Figure 2.1: Flowchart for complaint procedure.

trends may all be indicators of the failure of the Wilson Report to meet its objectives, or indeed signs that the system is working well at least in one of its primary aims of improving the quality of service.

In 1999, in minutes of evidence submitted to the Select Committee on Public Administration by the Association of Community Health Councils, representing patients' concerns, it was acknowledged that the current system was more accessible but felt to be neither particularly visible nor speedy and patients remained concerned about its impartiality. The report of an independent review on current complaints practice in the NHS is expected in 2000.

In general, consumerist reforms in the NHS are still in their infancy and, far from being led by patients, could be criticised as paternalistic and driven by practitioners themselves. Nevertheless, a simpler, speedier, accessible and non-adversarial complaints procedure is now in place. Although separate from disciplinary processes, defensive attitudes among practitioners may take much longer to change. Dependent upon their demise is the development of a culture in which complaints become part of the process of improving quality and containing litigation.

References

1   Vincent C, Young M and Phillips A (1994) Why do people sue doctors? A study of patients and relatives taking legal action. *Lancet.* **343**: 1609–13.

2   Powell PV (1995) An audit of the handling of medical negligence complaints by a health board. *Health Bull.* **53**: 96–205.

3   Pickersgill D and Stanton T (1997) *Making Sense of the NHS Complaints and Disciplinary Procedures.* Radcliffe Medical Press, Oxford.

4   Department of Health and Social Security (1983) *National Health Service Management Inquiry* (Griffiths Report). HMSO, London.

5   Department of Health (1989) *Working for Patients.* HMSO, London.

6   Mulcahy L and Selwood M (1995) Consultants' response to clinical complaints (letter). *BMJ.* **310**: 1200.

7   Summerton N (1995) Positive and negative factors in defensive medicine: a questionnaire study of general practitioners. *BMJ.* **310**: 27–8.

8   Combes D and Lewis C (1997) Six months' experience of the new practice-based complaints procedure (letter). *Br J Gen Pract.* **47**: 461.

9   Health Service Commissioner (1999) *Annual Report 1997–98.* Department of Health, London.

Appendix 2.1: In-house complaints procedures; terms of service requirements

1 All practices must have and operate a complaints procedure for and on behalf of patients and former patients.

2 The procedure applies to complaints to do with any matter reasonably connected with the provision of general medical services and within the responsibility or control of any doctor in the practice whether partner, employee, former partner or member of staff employed by the doctors.

3 Complaints can be made on behalf of a patient or former patient with their consent or
   (a) where the patient is a child, by the parent, guardian or local authority or voluntary organisation under the Provisions of the Children Act, or
   (b) where the patient is incapable of making a complaint, by a relative or other adult person who has an interest in the patient's welfare.

4 Where the patient has died, the complaint may be made by a relative or other adult person with an interest.

5 Practice-based procedures require that the doctor must specify a person either by name or job title to be responsible for receiving and investigating all complaints. All complaints must be recorded in writing, acknowledged orally or in writing within three days, and properly investigated.

6 The complainant must be given a written summary of the investigation and its conclusions within 10 days of the receipt of the complaint.

7 Where the investigation requires access to the medical record, the complaints administrator must inform the patient or person acting on his behalf if the investigation will involve disclosure of information in those records to a person other than the doctor or a partner, a deputy or employee of the doctor.

8 The doctor must keep a record of all complaints and copies of all correspondence relating to complaints, but such records must be kept separate from the patient's records.

9 A doctor must inform patients about the practice-based complaints procedure which the practice operates and the name or title of the person administering the process.

CHAPTER THREE

The role of the General Medical Council

Antony Townsend

Negligence and fitness to practise

Why should doctors be punished twice if they make mistakes – once by the courts, and again by the General Medical Council (GMC)? Sometimes doctors see themselves as being at the mercy of increasingly merciless legal processes, driven by increasingly unforgiving patients.

However understandable this feeling may be, it is based upon a misconception of the respective roles of the courts and the GMC. To understand the differences between those roles, and why some medical accidents may result in action in the courts and also at the GMC, it is necessary to consider the purposes of the GMC's procedures. It is also helpful to see how those procedures have evolved, and are continuing to evolve, in response to changing expectations both within and outside the profession.

The GMC's role – different from that of the courts

Despite the complexity of the legal framework which governs the GMC, its role is simple to define. It has a duty to protect patients, and to guide doctors, by:

- setting and assuring the educational standards required for entry to the register
- keeping up-to-date registers of qualified doctors

- issuing guidance to the profession and the public about the standards expected of registered doctors
- dealing firmly and fairly with doctors whose fitness to practise is in doubt.

This list of the GMC's duties illustrates the fundamental difference between its role and that of the courts in a negligence case (*see* Table 3.1).

Although both the courts and the GMC may legitimately take into account the deterrent effect of any penalty which they impose, the courts' primary consideration is how to remedy past wrongs, balancing the rights of the patient and the doctor, whereas the GMC considers how to protect patients (not just the particular complainant) in the future, judging the public interest in the context of the doctor's right to a fair hearing.

Table 3.1: The role of the courts and the GMC

Function	The courts' role in litigation	The GMC's role in complaints
Type of judgement	To make a judgement between the cases of two parties on the balance of probabilities	To consider whether an allegation is proved beyond reasonable doubt
Aim	To supply the claimant (patient) with redress for a past wrong	To consider whether a doctor should be allowed to practise (remain registered) in the future, and what action is required to prevent recurrence by this, or another, doctor
Sanction	Financial compensation	Restriction or removal of registration

Doctors' accountability for their performance

The possible penalties available to the GMC's Professional Conduct Committee, which used to be confined to the ultimate sanction of erasure, have been extended to include suspension and the imposition of conditions upon practice. This suggests that the offence [of serious professional misconduct] was intended to include serious cases

> of negligence … the public has higher expectations of doctors and members of other self-governing professions. Their governing bodies are under a corresponding duty to protect the public against the genially incompetent as well as the deliberate wrongdoers. (Judgement of the Judicial Committee of the Privy Council in the case of *David Noel McCandless v The General Medical Council*, 1995)

This judgement sounds like a statement of the obvious – of course doctors must be competent, and of course professional bodies should ensure that patients' reasonable expectations of quality are met. However, as recently as the late 1960s, only about 5% of the hearings at the GMC had anything to do with the delivery of clinical care to patients. For the first 100 years of the GMC's existence, the Council's fitness-to-practise procedures – the mechanism by which the GMC can remove unsuitable doctors from the register – were deployed almost exclusively against the fraudster and the cad, supplying the tabloids and their predecessors with a steady stream of stories which exposed greed and lust behind the façade of professional respectability.

Why was there this absence of GMC proceedings relating to quality of care? Was it due to a reluctance among patients to challenge their doctors' professionalism? Was it due to an absence of legal powers to enable the GMC to tackle the problem? Was it due to a reluctance within the profession to open a Pandora's box of substandard practice, or to a comfortable assumption that any properly qualified medical man (and it was only men that they talked about) could be left to his own clinical devices?

A changing climate

It was probably a combination of these factors. Actions for negligence against doctors have, as explained in Chapter 1, risen dramatically. At the same time, the GMC's practices and procedures have changed – and are continuing to change – dramatically. Behind these changes lies the assumption – not peculiar to the medical profession – that the patient (client) is an educated consumer of services, entitled to make decisions and to expect a certain quality of service, and also the assumption that, if that expectation is not met, the professional must justify his or her performance before the courts and/or the professional regulator.

What has changed in professional regulation?

It is only within the last 20 to 30 years that there has been a significant overlap between civil proceedings relating to professional negligence, and professional proceedings. Gradually the number of doctors appearing before the GMC's Professional Conduct Committee (and its predecessor, the Disciplinary Committee) has increased from around 40 a year in the late 1970s to around 150 a year in the late 1990s. The striking change has been that, whereas 30 years ago cases almost invariably concerned the character of the doctor, today more than half of the cases being heard involve allegations relating to the standards of care delivered.

This process has been partly piecemeal, evolutionary and arguably subconscious; and partly consciously revolutionary, marked by significant legal and structural change.

The landmarks

As in most processes of change, a continuum of external and internal events has been punctuated by milestones which have, psychologically or practically, been seen as critical in prompting change. Arguably one of the most important of these was the case of Dr Oliver Archer in 1983.

Case 2: The 'Archer' case

Dr Archer was in effect brought before the GMC on a charge of serious negligence. The facts found in the case were that Dr Archer, in visiting a child patient, had:

1 failed adequately to examine him
2 failed adequately to treat him, and
3 failed to arrange hospital treatment for him

when respectively his condition so required.

What marked out this case was not the circumstances alleged against Dr Archer, but the unusual terms of the GMC Disciplinary Committee's judgement. The Committee said:

> The Committee are seriously concerned by the evidence which has been adduced before them in this case. They are disturbed not only by your failure to arrange appropriate specialist treatment for a seriously ill boy who was your

patient, but also by the poor standard of courtesy which you extended towards the patient's parents. The Committee regard such behaviour as below the standard which can be regarded as acceptable in a medical man.

The Committee have nevertheless felt able to take account of your expression of regret and the representations made on your behalf. The Committee have accordingly determined that in all the circumstances you are not guilty of serious professional misconduct in relation to the facts found proved against you in the charge.

It is interesting to compare that judgement with the Judicial Committee's judgement in *McCandless*, quoted at the beginning of this chapter. In *Archer* the Disciplinary Committee's judgement was in effect an admission of the gap between the historically narrow definition of 'serious professional misconduct' (the legal phrase which frames all allegations of misconduct against doctors, and against which doctors are judged in disciplinary proceedings) and acceptable behaviour. Despite being 'seriously concerned' about the lack of examination and treatment for a 'seriously ill' boy, and acknowledging that that standard was unacceptable, serious professional misconduct was not found.

By contrast, the Judicial Committee's judgement in *McCandless* some 12 years later, upholding the GMC's verdict of serious professional misconduct against Dr McCandless, explicitly endorsed the notion that 'serious professional misconduct' encompasses quality-of-care issues, not just matters of character.

The case of Dr Archer was one of the catalysts for change. It was widely quoted as illustrating the inadequacies of the profession's regulatory regime, and it led to several attempts, led by Nigel Spearing MP, to amend the Medical Act to enable the GMC to take action against doctors who, while not guilty of *serious* professional misconduct in the then understood sense of the term, were guilty of misconduct which merited some form of action in the public interest.

The major changes at the GMC

Over the 15 years which elapsed between the Archer case and the introduction of new GMC procedures to deal with poorly performing doctors, there were a number of developments.

Shifting definition of 'serious professional misconduct'

First, as described above, there was the subtle change in the interpretation of 'serious professional misconduct'. In practice, complaints about poor performance by doctors increasingly reached the final stage of public hearings, and the Professional Conduct Committee showed itself willing to find charges of that kind proved.

Publication of new guidance on good medical practice

Secondly, the Council's published advice to the profession – traditionally statements describing 'ungentlemanly' behaviour such as sexual relations with a patient, fraud, advertising or 'bringing the profession into disrepute', matters which could lead to erasure from the register – began to talk also of standards of care. In 1985, the first step was taken when a new edition of the *Blue Book*, the Council's then guidance to the profession, included two paragraphs on standards of care (in a 30-page document).

This process culminated in the publication in 1995 of *Good Medical Practice* (second edition published by the GMC in 1998) which replaced the *Blue Book*. *Good Medical Practice* set out, for the first time, a statement of the key duties and attributes of the good doctor. It combined the requirements of technical competence, quality assurance, professional duties and ethical behaviour. In place of the old list of offences, it established the qualities which patients could expect of all doctors on the register (Box 3.1).

Box 3.1

Patients must be able to trust doctors with their lives and well-being. To justify that trust, we as a profession have a duty to maintain a good standard of practice and care and to show respect for human life. In particular as a doctor you must:
- make the care of your patient your first concern
- treat every patient politely and considerately
- respect patients' dignity and privacy
- listen to patients and respect their views
- give patients information in a form that they can understand
- respect the rights of patients to be fully involved in decisions about their care

- keep your professional knowledge and skills up to date
- recognise the limits of your professional competence
- be honest and trustworthy
- respect and protect confidential information
- make sure that your personal beliefs do not prejudice your patients' care
- act quickly to protect patients from risk if you have good reason to believe that you or a colleague may not be fit to practise
- avoid abusing your position as a doctor, and
- work with colleagues in the ways that best serve patients' interests.

The *Duties of a Doctor* conspicuously places the patient's needs at the centre of the picture, and it is no coincidence that between 1979 and 1996 the proportion of lay members on the Council increased from 10% to 25%.

Performance procedures

While the evolving interpretation of 'serious professional miscon-duct', backed by the principles articulated in *Good Medical Practice*, was enabling the Council to deal with some cases of grossly substandard care through the traditional procedures, it was clear that many doctors whose poor performance placed patients at risk were still not being dealt with adequately.

For that reason, the GMC developed new legal procedures to tackle poor performance. The development and implementation of these procedures took most of the 1990s. The GMC concluded that the solution to the problem was not to lower the threshold for the kinds of misconduct with which it could deal, but to introduce a new allegation of 'seriously deficient performance', and a new set of procedures which would enable the Council to undertake an in-depth assessment of the practice of doctors whose performance was causing concern. Unlike the evidence generated by an individual complaint, this assessment would provide comprehensive evidence on the basis of which adequate action could be taken to protect patients.

The new performance procedures were enacted by Parliament in 1995, with all-party support, and came into force in 1997. The first assessments, and the first decisions under the new procedures to suspend poorly performing doctors from the register, occurred in 1998. A description of the performance procedures is given below.

Revalidation

In February 1999, the Council decided that all registered doctors must be able to demonstrate on a regular basis that they are fit to practise in their chosen field, and that this should be linked to continuing registration. This decision marks a radical departure from the current system of registration, which is based on the assumption that doctors will continue to be registered, and therefore entitled to practise, unless they are subject to an adverse report.

The details of new procedures to implement the Council's decision are still in development, but it is clear that doctors will soon be obliged periodically to produce evidence of their continuing fitness to practise. This new process, which has been called 'revalidation', represents the logical culmination of the historical trend described above, under which doctors have become increasingly accountable both to the courts and to their professional regulator for the quality of care that they deliver.

Summary

The GMC has moved from being a regulator setting out examples of misconduct, concentrating on offences of poor behaviour, and waiting for complaints before taking action, to being a regulator setting standards of good practice, and holding doctors to account for poor performance. Increasingly, the GMC's fitness-to-practise procedures (including the new performance procedures) are dealing with substandard care.

The GMC's role in relation to complaints about doctors' practice is to assess whether, in the interests of patients in the future, a doctor's conduct or poor performance merits restriction or removal of registration. The GMC's role is not to provide redress to an individual.

How the GMC's fitness-to-practise procedures work

There are three fitness-to-practise procedures operated by the GMC. The *health procedures* (which are not described in any detail in this chapter) deal with information which suggests that a doctor's fitness to practise is seriously impaired by illness (usually addiction or mental conditions). The *conduct procedures* deal with criminal convictions and allegations of serious professional misconduct. The *performance procedures* consider evidence of seriously deficient performance.

What happens when information about a doctor is received?

Information about doctors' conduct and performance comes to the GMC from a number of sources, including the following:

- patients complaining about an episode or episodes of care, or about the doctor's behaviour (sometimes reporting the outcome of court proceedings)
- employing or contracting authorities reporting misconduct or concerns about performance, sometimes following the outcome of local complaints and disciplinary procedures
- colleagues reporting concerns
- other authorities (e.g. the police routinely report convictions of registered medical practitioners).

Following checks to ensure that the information relates to a registered medical practitioner, and that it could raise a matter of serious professional misconduct or seriously deficient performance, a medical member of the GMC reviews the evidence to decide whether any further action is warranted.

Cases in which no further action by the GMC is justified

If no further action appears to be necessary because no question of serious professional misconduct or seriously deficient performance arises, the opinion of a lay member of Council is sought. If he or she agrees, the complainant is informed, as is the doctor. Information of this kind is usually retained by the GMC for three years so that it can be revived if there is further evidence which, taken with the original evidence, suggests that the GMC should act.

Cases in which further action is considered necessary

If the medical member considers that a question of serious professional misconduct or seriously deficient performance has arisen, he or she must then decide:

- whether further evidence is needed before a decision can be taken. If so, further inquiries are made, which may involve interviews with potential witnesses, inquiries of a health authority, health board or Trust, and the obtaining of records
- whether the evidence is in a form which can be used by the GMC. If the information comes from an individual as distinct from a public authority, it has to be supported by a sworn statement
- whether a question of serious professional misconduct has arisen, in which case the conduct procedures are used, or whether the case should be dealt with under the performance procedures as potentially seriously deficient performance.

Sometimes the GMC may consider a complaint while proceedings in the criminal or civil courts, or local disciplinary procedures, are in train. The existence of proceedings by another authority will not necessarily deter the GMC from acting simultaneously, if the protection of patients requires it.

Conduct or performance?

Some kinds of case (e.g. improper relationships with patients, fraud, violence) are clearly matters of conduct. However, others may be less clear-cut. Potentially dangerous prescribing might raise a question of *seriously deficient performance*, but particularly if there was evidence that the doctor ignored warnings from colleagues, or persisted without seeking help despite evidence that patients were suffering ill effects a question of serious professional misconduct might arise.

   Every case is assessed on its own merit, but it is important to understand that a case which involves poor performance may none the less be dealt with under the conduct procedures if there are incidents which might amount to serious professional misconduct.

Cases dealt with under the conduct procedures

If it is decided that a case should be dealt with as a conduct matter, it is referred to the Preliminary Proceedings Committee (PPC). The doctor is informed of the matters which appear to raise a question of serious professional misconduct, is sent copies of the available evidence, and is given at least 28 days in which to submit a written response.

   The Preliminary Proceedings Committee consists of five medical members and two lay members, is advised by a senior lawyer (legal assessor) and meets in private at the GMC's offices.

Unless interim suspension or conditional registration is being contemplated by the GMC (see below), the doctor does not appear before the PPC. The Committee considers the papers which have been sent to the doctor, and any explanation which the doctor may wish to give (doctors often make use of their medical defence organisations or legal advisers to prepare an explanation). The Committee's options are as follows:

- to take no further action on the grounds that there is no issue of serious professional misconduct
- to adjourn for further information (either further evidence of the events in question, or for information about the doctor's state of health if a question of impairment of fitness to practise on health grounds arises)
- to issue a letter of advice to the doctor (in effect, a caution) – this option is sometimes used in cases where a doctor admits to failings, and the Committee is satisfied that formal action to affect registration is not required
- to refer the case to the Professional Conduct Committee for a formal public hearing
- to refer the case to the Health Committee for a private hearing to consider whether the doctor's fitness to practise is seriously impaired on health grounds.

Interim suspension and conditional registration

If, on referring a case to the PPC, the GMC considers that it may be necessary to suspend, or place conditions upon, a doctor's registration pending a formal hearing of the case by the PCC (or Health Committee), the doctor will be given the opportunity to attend the meeting of the PPC (and/or to be legally represented) in order to present arguments *in relation to the question of the interim order only*. The PPC can only consider the question of an interim order *after* they have made a decision to refer a case to the PCC (or Health Committee), and the doctor is entitled to attend only that part of the discussion which relates to the imposition of the order. Any explanation in relation to the merits of the case itself must therefore be sent in writing in advance.

Referral of cases to the Professional Conduct Committee (PCC)

If a case is referred to the PCC, the doctor receives a formal Notice of Inquiry setting out the details of the matters which are alleged to raise a question of serious professional misconduct, and giving at least 4 weeks' notice of the hearing.

The PCC sits in public, usually in the GMC's Council Chamber at 44 Hallam Street, London W1. Panels of the PCC are made up as follows:

In hearings by the Professional Conduct Committee, cases are usually heard by at least five members, one or more of whom must be a lay member, and the PCC is advised by a senior lawyer (legal assessor). The GMC (or the complainant) is legally represented, and the doctor is entitled to be legally represented.

The main stages of a PCC hearing, which are very similar to those of a criminal trial, are as follows:

1 The charge is read, and legal applications may be made at this and later stages to have the charge amended or parts of the charge dropped. The charge comprises one or more facts which, in total, are alleged to amount to serious professional misconduct.

2 Lawyers acting for the GMC (or sometimes acting for an individual complainant) set out the case and call witnesses (who may be cross-examined by the doctor or the doctor's lawyers).

3 At the end of the case against the doctor, the doctor or the doctor's lawyers may argue that:
   • there is insufficient evidence to find some or all of the facts alleged against the doctor proved beyond reasonable doubt; and/or
   • the facts alleged against the doctor would not, even if proved, amount to serious professional misconduct.

4 If part or all of the first of these submissions is successful, the relevant facts are found to be not proved. If the second submission is successful, the case is concluded.

5 If the case continues beyond this stage, the doctor – or lawyers on his or her behalf – present the doctor's case, calling evidence as necessary. The doctor may choose to give evidence in his or her defence.

6 At the end of the doctor's case, after each side has summed up their arguments, the panel considers whether the doctor is guilty of any or all of the facts alleged. The panel uses the criminal standard of proof – beyond reasonable doubt – in reaching its findings. If none of the facts is found to be proved, the case is concluded.

7 If any of the facts is found to be proved, the panel then considers whether those facts found to be proved could amount

to serious professional misconduct. If they could not, the case also ends. If they could, the case proceeds.

8 If the case proceeds, the Council's (or complainant's) lawyers make further submissions about the circumstances and gravity of the facts found proved, and the doctor or lawyers can make submissions about whether the facts found proved amount to serious professional misconduct, and whether there are mitigating circumstances, including the doctor's previous character.

9 The panel then consider in private whether the doctor is guilty of serious professional misconduct and, if so, whether to reprimand the doctor, place conditions upon the doctor's registration, suspend registration, or erase the doctor from the register.

10 Conditions can be placed upon registration for up to three years. These may include restrictions on the type of practice which the doctor may undertake, and requirements for training. If the doctor breaches any of the conditions, suspension or erasure may be ordered. At the end of the period of conditions, the Committee may resume hearing the case and, if it wishes, impose new conditions for further periods of up to a year at a time.

11 Suspension may be imposed for up to a year at a time and may, if the panel directs, be renewed (or replaced by conditional registration or erasure) at a resumed hearing at the end of the period.

12 Erasure is indefinite. A doctor may apply for restoration to the register 10 months after erasure has taken effect, and every 10 months thereafter. However, the onus is on the erased doctor to satisfy the panel that he or she is fit to be restored to the register. There is no expectation of restoration, and most doctors are never restored.

Cases dealt with under the performance procedures

In cases where, following consideration of a complaint (*see* above), it is decided that the performance procedures should be used, the GMC writes to the doctor with details of the complaint, and gives the doctor an opportunity to argue why the performance procedures should not be instituted. Doctors may, at this stage, seek the advice of their medical defence organisation or private lawyers if they so choose.

Having considered any response from the doctor, the GMC's screener decides whether the doctor should be formally assessed. If so, the doctor is invited to an assessment. The doctor can appeal against this decision to the Assessment Referral Committee (ARC), which usually consists of six medical and two lay members of the Council, who hear from the doctor (or doctor's lawyers), and from the complainant, and then decide whether the evidence justifies an assessment. The ARC meets in private.

Assessments take the following form. An assessment panel, consisting of two doctors chosen to reflect the doctor's specialty and circumstances of practice, together with a lay assessor, considers all of the evidence and undertakes an assessment. This will usually consists of the following:

- review of medical records at the workplace
- interviews with the doctor
- interviews with colleagues, complainants and others
- observations of the doctor's consultations
- tests of the doctor's professional knowledge and skills.

At the end of this process, the assessors report to a medical member of the GMC. There are three possible outcomes:

- no action required, on the grounds that there are no serious deficiencies
- serious deficiencies identified, in which case the doctor is invited to agree to a programme of counselling and training and, if necessary, limitations on practice. It is the doctor's responsibility to arrange a suitable programme. The doctor's performance will then be reassessed by the GMC after a specified interval
- serious deficiencies identified, and referral to the Committee on Professional Performance required because patients are at risk.

Committee on Professional Performance

A doctor may be referred to the Committee on Professional Performance (CPP) for the following reasons:

- because he or she has persistently refused to be assessed
- because the assessment has concluded that referral to the CPP is necessary
- because the doctor has refused to accept a programme of training and counselling following assessment, with voluntary restrictions on practice, or has accepted the programme but failed to co-operate or failed to improve.

Panels of the CPP are made up as follows: in hearings by the Committee on Professional Performance, cases are usually heard by five medical members and two lay members advised by independent specialist advisers and a senior lawyer (legal assessor). The GMC is legally represented and the doctor is entitled to be legally represented. Hearings currently take place in private unless the doctor requests a public hearing.

Doctors are entitled to legal representation at the CPP. The latter may hear evidence from witnesses and receive expert advice from independent specialists. At the conclusion of the hearing, if they find a doctor's performance to have been seriously deficient, they may take the following action:

- place conditions on the doctor's registration for a period of up to three years (at the end of the period the Committee will review the case, and may impose a further order)
- suspend registration for up to 12 months (this, too, is subject to review and renewal).

Doctors who comply with the CPP's requirements, and convince the Committee that they have remedied their deficiencies may be returned to unrestricted practice. In contrast, doctors whose registration has been suspended for two or more years and who have not shown signs of improvement may face indefinite suspension of registration.

The performance procedures are sometimes described as remedial, but this is really a misnomer. Although doctors are given ample opportunity under the procedures to rectify any deficiencies, the responsibility for remedial action is theirs, as the GMC does not fund remedial programmes. Furthermore, it is important to understand that the GMC's primary responsibility is to protect the public.

Rights of appeal

Doctors have rights of appeal against decisions of the Preliminary Proceedings Committee, the Professional Conduct Committee and the Committee on Professional Performance. These appeals are generally to the Judicial Committee of the Privy Council.

Discussion

There are clearly similarities between the GMC's procedures and those of the courts. Both are evidence based, as facts have to be proved and verdicts reached. Expert medical evidence may play a part in both types of proceedings.

However, there are also crucial differences. The GMC requires a higher standard of proof, but its sanctions – effectively it can end a doctor's career – are more draconian. Unlike the courts, the GMC is – in strict legal terms – concerned not with redressing the damage done to a patient, but with the risk that a doctor's behaviour might pose to patients in the future. This encompasses not just a direct physical risk, but behaviour which might undermine the public confidence in doctors without which good medical care is jeopardised.

For this reason, although there are cases of negligence which, while successful before the courts, might not justify GMC proceedings, since they do not suggest that there is any future risk to patients or evidence of misconduct, there will equally be cases in which a doctor has caused no harm to a patient but in which the GMC judges that the doctor's behaviour and practice demonstrate that patients may in future be at risk, even though the doctor has been lucky so far.

Increasing expectations among patients, the introduction of the performance procedures, Government initiatives to improve quality, and the developing proposals for revalidation mean that doctors will be under increasing pressure not only to know, but also to show, that they remain fit to practise. Robust local systems of personal and peer audit (perhaps using the new structures of Primary Care Groups and Trusts, and professional development) will enable good doctors not only to avoid 'trouble at Hallam Street' but also, more importantly, to demonstrate to their patients that they are worthy of the trust which doctors have traditionally enjoyed.

Recent developments: In 2000 the GMC launched a fundamental review of its fitness to practise procedures, which is likely to result in substantial reform. New powers of interim supervision pending hearings and to impose longer periods before an erased doctor can seek restoration to the register, have been sought. The GMC's regulatory systems can be expected to change substantially.

CHAPTER FOUR

The law of negligence

John R Griffiths

Negligence or misadventure

> It is so easy to be wise after the event and to condemn as negligence that which is only a misadventure. We ought always to be on our guard against it, especially in cases against hospitals and doctors. Medical science has conferred great benefits on mankind, but those benefits are attended by considerable risks ... we cannot take the benefits without taking the risks ... we must insist on due care for the patient at every point, but we must not condemn as negligence that which is only a misadventure.

Those were Lord Denning's words in *Roe v Minister of Health*,[1] a particularly sad case in which two men suffered severe injuries as a consequence of being given spinal anaesthetics. The anaesthetic agents were stored in glass ampoules and the ampoules themselves were kept in a solution of phenol. Unbeknown to anyone – and held to be not capable of reasonable discovery – the glass of the ampoules was flawed with invisible hairline cracks through which the phenol penetrated, adulterating the anaesthetic agent and thus causing the injuries to these two patients.

This case is an appropriate introduction because it does present succinctly the issue which makes this particular area of the law such a fraught and demanding one for the lawyers who choose to practise in it. It can, of course, very fairly be said that all personal injury cases are sad cases, but medical negligence cases derive their particular pathos because the injured party has – almost always voluntarily – placed his or her trust in the doctor or doctors whose professional help and assistance he or she has sought. When an injury occurs to the patient in the course of, or as a consequence of, diagnosis or medical treatment, then the question which arises for the lawyer is whether the injury arises from negligence (which *may* carry with it a right to compensation for the injured patient) or from misadventure, in the sense in which Lord Denning used it (which will not).

In determining whether an act or an omission by a doctor was negligent and resulted in loss, one must apply the normal analysis of duty of care/breach of that duty/and loss caused or materially contributed to by that breach. It is the interaction of these factors which makes medical cases so particularly interesting.

Duty of care

From the very nature of the doctor–patient relationship, the duty of care is almost always currently assumed to be present in any medical negligence claim, although occasionally it does become a material issue in a case. Such a Scottish case was that of *Rolland v Lothian Health Board*.[2]

Case 3: Rolland v Lothian Health Board

In this case, the irrational actions of a patient suffering from mental confusion who leapt out of a window were held by a judge not to have been reasonably foreseeable. The condition from which the patient was suffering was well recognised and documented. Violent behaviour was a well-known feature of this condition, but there was no evidence to suggest that a patient with this condition had ever tried to jump or fallen from a hospital window. The judge stated:

> what occurred could not in my opinion have been reasonably foreseeable. It was different in kind to what could have been foreseen such as a patient leaving by the door or setting herself alight with a cigarette lighter. What in fact occurred, namely the Pursuer's jumping or falling from a window, was a type of occurrence which could not in my opinion have been reasonably foreseeable. It is quite different in kind from what could have been foreseen, and the consequence must therefore be that the Defenders are not liable.

However, in medical cases a successful defence that no duty of care exists is rarely open to the defenders. Yet it is as well not to forget that that duty may not extend only to diagnosis and treatment of patients. It may also extend to examination of patients for employment purposes as well as for the purpose of quantifying personal injury claims. There have been a number of claims arising from allegedly negligent medical examinations which have led claimants to settle for, or be awarded, damages of lesser sums than their condition would have merited. A reported Scottish case in this area is that of *Johnstone v Traffic Commissioner*.[3]

Case 4: Johnstone v Traffic Commissioner

This involved a preliminary hearing before Lord Cameron of Lochbroom, in which a bus driver sued the Traffic Commissioner and the Department of Transport for damages following the revocation of his public service vehicle licence. The licence had been revoked following a diagnosis which indicated that the bus driver might have suffered a myocardial infarction. Subsequent medical examination demonstrated that this had not in fact been the case, and the licence was duly restored, but not before the bus driver had sustained losses through being unable to work. He sued the Department of Transport because it had been the Department's Senior Medical Adviser who had formed the opinion that the claimant was likely to be a source of danger to the public in continuing to drive a public service vehicle, and it had been in the light of that opinion that the licence had been revoked. At the preliminary hearing it was argued for the Department that, whatever advice had been tendered to the Traffic Commissioner, it had been of a privileged nature which precluded the Department being held liable. In addition, it was argued that the Department owed no duty of care to the claimant and that it would be contrary to the public interest to determine that such a duty existed. In repelling that argument, the judge held that it could not be said without proof that public policy required that the Senior Medical Officer should be immune from liability in negligence through tendering advice to the Traffic Commissioner or that he necessarily owed no duty of care to the claimant.

This duty was expressly affirmed by the High Court in England in the case of *Baker v Kaye*.[4]

Case 5: Baker v Kaye

Mr Baker was a television sales executive who was offered employment as Director of International Sales by a subsidiary of General Electric, subject to a satisfactory medical report obtained from the company doctor, Dr Kaye. After very careful examination and consideration, including the analysis of two separate blood tests, Dr Kaye advised the Company that Mr Baker was likely to consume excessive amounts of alcohol in a stressful work-related context. The company withdrew the offer of employment, and Mr Baker sued Dr Kaye, alleging negligence.

The High Court held that the defendant was under a duty to the claimant to take reasonable care in carrying out a medical assessment in connection with a job offer, and in making a judgement as to the claimant's suitability for employment by reference to the prospective employer's requirements. A medical practitioner retained by a company to carry out pre-employment medical assessments of its prospective employees owes a duty of care to those whom he or she assesses in carrying out his or her assessment and in reporting his or her conclusion to the Company. Such a duty of care fulfilled all of the requirements identified by the House of Lords in *Caparo Industries plc v Dickman*,[5] namely foreseeability of economic loss, the necessary degree of proximity between the parties, and the proviso that it should be just and reasonable in all of the circumstances for a duty to be imposed. It was clear that economic loss was a foreseeable consequence of a breach of duty. It was fair, just and reasonable for such a duty to be imposed. There was no conflict between the proper discharge of the defendant's contractual duty to the prospective employers and any duty to the claimant. The defendant's duty to the company was to take reasonable care in carrying out the assessment, in eliciting information from the claimant in interpreting the test results, and in arriving at a judgement as to whether or not to recommend him for employment. The duty to the claimant could be couched in identical terms. It was the defendant's duty to judge the claimant by reference to the company's requirements, but in so doing he had to exercise reasonable care. In this case, since it was clear from the evidence that a substantial body of reasonable medical opinion would have reached the same conclusion when interpreting the results, the allegation of negligence in the interpretation of the results had to fail.

However, there have been a number of more recent cases in England which expressly restrict the duty of care owed by a doctor in the non-clinical context. It may be, therefore, that *Baker v Kaye*[4] and *Johnstone v Traffic Commissioner*[3] were wrongly decided.

Case 6: R v Croydon Health Authority[6]

In this case, Mrs R, a psychiatric nurse, underwent a pre-employment medical examination which included a chest X-ray. It was common ground that Dr M, the radiologist, was negligent in that he failed to report to the Occupational Health Physician the presence of a significant abnormality which, if reported, would have led to a diagnosis of primary pulmonary hypertension (PPH). PPH is an untreatable condition of the pulmonary aorta which limits life expectancy and creates a significant risk in pregnancy.

However, because the radiologist gave her clearance, Mrs R started work with the health authority as a community nurse and became pregnant some four months later. She thereafter suffered both physical pain and discomfort and mental stress, culminating in a reactive depression that required her to leave nursing.

The health authority accepted that, had Dr M not been negligent, Mrs R would not have been given her new job and, although she and her husband wanted children, she would not have become pregnant.

The trial judge who held that the pregnancy was a foresee-able consequence of the failure to diagnose PPH found in Mrs R's favour and awarded her damages in respect of:

- the cost of bringing up her daughter and the expenses of pregnancy
- loss of earnings and the value of subsidised accommodation past and future, and
- general damages for reactive depression.

The health authority appealed on the basis that the award should not include all of the heads given by the trial judge. The health authority's position was that their 'duty was only to protect the Plaintiff from personal injury and pregnancy is not an injury and was not foreseeable so the duty does not extend to it.'

Their duty 'was to ensure that the Plaintiff was fit for work and would be protected from personal injury or harm whilst in employment by reason of an existing health condition.'

The Court of Appeal disagreed with the trial judge. The health authority's submission was that, even if in this case conception and pregnancy could be regarded as a form of damage, there was insufficient connection between that damage and the radiologist's breach of duty to enable a court to say that damage flowed from the breach. The damage was, as is sometimes said, too remote. The chain of events had too many links. The radiologist reviewing the X-ray of an applicant for employment is not to be compared with a gynaecologist performing a sterilisation operation. The radiologist's duty is to observe and report on abnormalities, but no one expects him or her to advise on aetiology, still less about what activities wholly unconnected with employment the presence of the underlying condition may contraindicate. The radiologist never actually saw the claimant, and he probably knew very little about her except her age. He would no doubt have accepted that in so far as he failed to observe an abnormality which could have affected her fitness for work as an employee of the health authority in the immediate future, this was something for which he could be held accountable, but her domestic circumstances were not his affair. The Court of Appeal found 'that the Plaintiff's domestic life fell outside the scope of the radiologist's duty' and restricted the damages to:

1 the complications of pregnancy attributable to PPH (but not the pregnancy itself)
2 any heart catheterisation which on the balance of probabilities would have been avoided if PPH had been diagnosed shortly after the X-ray
3 any complications of the hysterectomy which would probably not have occurred if the diagnosis had been made after the X-ray, and
4 exacerbation of the reactive depression.

The Court of Appeal also said:

Whatever duty of care was owed to the Plaintiff by the Health Authority as her prospective employer, the scope and extent of that duty stops short of responsibility for the consequences of the decision by the Plaintiff and her husband that she should become pregnant ... There was nothing in the evidence ... to suggest that the relationship between the

> Plaintiff and her prospective employer had anything to do with whatever plans the Plaintiff and her husband may have had for starting a family.

Another very recent case which limits the duty of care further is that of *Powell v Boladz.*[7]

Case 7: Powell v Boladz

There were six defendants to this action, the first five being the general practitioners who treated the boy, Robert Powell, who suffered from Addison's disease. The sixth defendant was the hospital authority, which had negligently failed to diagnose the disease in time. The boy died and the health authority settled their liability to the sum of around £100 000. However, the parent claimants pursued the claim against the general practitioners on the grounds that there had been a 'cover-up' over Robert's death, including the removal of original documents from the GP records and the substitution of different documents. In particular, Robert's father claimed that he had developed panic disorder after the death, as a consequence of the cover-up. Reliance was placed on the dicta in the case of *Caparo Industries plc v Dickman,*[5] and it was argued that the three elements enunciated in *Caparo*[5] were present in this case. One of those elements is that there must be 'a sufficient relationship of proximity between the parties', and it was on this matter that the parents' case foundered in the opinion of Stuart Smith LJ. He very firmly took the view that it was only to Robert, the patient, that the general practitioners owed a duty of care. After a death, a doctor may owe the relatives of a patient a duty of care, but only if he treats them as patients. 'There are many situations where a doctor will have close contact with another person without the relationship arising so as to involve the duty of care.' He considered, for example, examinations on behalf of an insurance company and stated that the only duty incumbent on the doctor was 'not to damage the employee in the course of examination'. Stuart Smith LJ went on to say that a doctor who has been treating a patient who has died and who tells the relatives what has happened *does not* undertake the doctor–patient relationship towards the relatives. The situation may call for sensitivity, tact and discretion, but the mere fact that the communicator is a doctor does not without more mean that he or she undertakes the doctor–patient relationship. There is no authority 'for a free standing duty of candour, irrespective of whether the doctor–patient relationship exists; for there to be so would be a startling extension of the law.'

Case 8: Kapfunde v Abbey National plc[8]

In this case, the claimant, who was applying for a permanent post, was requested to complete the company's standard confidential medical questionnaire. In doing so, she disclosed that she had suffered from sickle-cell anaemia which in the past had led to her being absent from work.

The completed questionnaire was then reviewed by the general practitioner who was retained by the company to provide pre-employment assessments. He considered that she was likely to have a higher than average level of absence from work, and assessed her as unsuitable. The company accepted his advice and rejected Mrs Kapfunde's application. At no time did the doctor see Mrs Kapfunde.

Mrs Kapfunde then brought negligence proceedings against the company and the doctor, alleging that he was in breach of a duty of care to her to exercise the degree of skill and care to be expected of a reasonably competent occupational health physician.

Mrs Kapfunde failed in the County Court and appealed to the Court of Appeal. She lost her appeal. Lord Justice Kennedy said: 'In my judgement there was no special relationship between Dr Daniel and the appellant such as to give rise to a duty of care.'

Lord Justice Millett said:

> The critical facts are that the applicant is required by the prospective employer or insurer to submit himself to medical examination by a doctor who is instructed by the employer or insurer to advise it and not the applicant. The advice is given to the employer or insurer and not to the applicant, who is a patient only in the sense that he is the subject of the examination and advice. The doctor is taken to assume responsibility for his advice, but only to the employer or insurer who commissioned it and not to the 'patient' who is the subject of the advice.

Case 9: Palmer v Tees Health Authority[9]

This was a particularly sad case in which a 4-year-old girl was abducted, sexually abused, murdered and mutilated by a perpetrator diagnosed as very disturbed. It was alleged that the health authority had failed to assess the perpetrator, Armstrong, properly and to identify him as a risk. They failed to provide him with appropriate treatment which would have substantially reduced if not eliminated the risk of his committing such offences, and would have ensured that he was contained during periods of risk.

The judge, in applying once again the analysis provided in *Caparo*,[5] held that there was not sufficient *proximity* between the claimant and the defendant. The claimant's daughter was not someone who fell within a special or exceptional category of risk from Armstrong's activities. She simply belonged to a wide class of individuals who might be at risk from Armstrong.

Secondly, he held that where the injury was not directly caused by the negligence of the defendant, but by the activities of a third party, to hold that a duty of care existed would considerably widen the category of potential claimants. It would lead to an increase in claims against health authorities which would significantly divert manpower and attention from the authorities' primary function of caring for patients. Thus the claimant mother failed in her action although the judge did sound a warning note that *if* the case had shown that there existed *some distinctive feature or characteristic* which demonstrated that the child was *at some special risk from Armstrong*, then he would have found that the necessary degree of proximity was present.

The Court of Appeal dismissed an appeal against the decision of the trial judge (1999) *LR Med* **351**.

Breach of duty of care

This is the essence of whether or not a doctor has been negligent. In *Scotland*, the law remains firmly based on the words of Lord President Clyde in the case of *Hunter v Hanley*.[10]

Case 10: Hunter v Hanley

Interestingly, this case involved a jury trial arising out of injury to a patient when a hypodermic needle broke. The trial judge directed the jury that 'there must be such a departure from the normal and usual practice ... as can reasonably be described as gross negligence'. However, on appeal, Lord President Clyde set out the definition for medical negligence in the following words: 'The true test for establishing negligence and diagnosis or treatment on the part of a doctor is whether he has been proved to be guilty of such failure as no doctor of ordinary skill would be guilty of if acting with ordinary care.' Later he said that:

> To establish liability by a doctor where deviation from normal practice is alleged, three facts require to be established. First of all, it must be proved that there is a normal and usual practice; secondly, it must be proved that the doctor has not adopted that practice; and thirdly (and this is of crucial importance), it must be established that the course the doctor has adopted is one which no professional man of ordinary skill would have taken if he had been acting with ordinary care. There is clearly a heavy onus on a Pursuer to establish these three facts, and without all three his case will fail. The extent of the deviation is not the test. The deviation must be of a kind which satisfies the third of the require-ments just stated.'

In *England* there followed shortly the decision of McNair J in the case of *Bolam v Friern Hospital Management Committee*.[11]

Case 11: Bolam v Friern Hospital Management Committee

The test is the standard of the ordinary skilled man exercising and professing to have that special skill. A man need not possess the highest expert skill at the risk of being found negligent. It is well-established law that it is sufficient if he exercises the ordinary skill of an ordinary competent man exercising that particular art.

Not perhaps quite as specific a test as that set out by Lord President Clyde but in any event, these two cases were regarded as compelling authorities until Lord Denning's judgement in 1980 in the Court of Appeal in the case of *Whitehouse v Jordan*.[12]

Case 12: Whitehouse v Jordan

Lord Denning, in a claim on behalf of a child allegedly brain damaged because of the negligent use of forceps during delivery, created concern by stating 'We must say, and say firmly, that in a professional man an error of judgement is not negligent. To test it I would suggest that you ask the average competent and careful practitioner "Is this the sort of mistake that you yourself might have made?" If he says "Yes, even doing the best I could it might have happened to me," then it is not negligent.'

That of course was not an accurate statement of the law in terms of Lord President Clyde's opinion, and Lord Denning was politely but firmly corrected as follows by Lord Fraser of Tullibelton when the case went to the House of Lords:

> Having regard to the context, I think that Lord Denning MR must have meant to say that an error of judgement is not *necessarily* negligent, but in my respectful opinion the statement as it stands is not an accurate statement of the law. Merely to describe something as an error of judgement tells us nothing about whether it is negligent or not. The true position is that an error of judgement may or may not be negligent, it depends on the nature of the error. If it is one that would not have been made by a reasonably competent professional man professing to have the standard and type of skill that the defendant held himself out as having and acting with ordinary care, then it is negligent. If, on the other hand, it is an error that a man acting with ordinary care might have made then it is not negligent.

Clearly this can be seen as paraphrasing Lord President Clyde's opinion in *Hunter v Hanley*,[10] but that opinion did not receive explicit approval until 1985 with the House of Lords' decision in the case of *Maynard v West Midlands Regional Health Authority*.[13]

Case 13: Maynard v West Midlands Regional Health Authority

In this case, two consultants thought that a female patient with a chest complaint might have tuberculosis, but they also considered the possibility of Hodgkin's disease. Accordingly, before obtaining the result of a test which would have determined whether the patient had tuberculosis, they performed an exploratory operation to see if she was suffering from Hodgkin's disease. The operation in fact revealed that she was suffering from tuberculosis and, as a consequence of the operation, she suffered damage to the nerve affecting her vocal cords, impairing her speech. It was alleged that the consultants had been negligent in performing the operation before the result of the test for tuberculosis was known, and expert evidence was led to support both the claimant's and the defendant's case. The trial judge preferred the claimant's experts, and gave judgement for the claimant, but this finding was reversed both in the Court of Appeal and the House of Lords. Lord Scarman, in his leading judgement, said:

> It was not enough to show that there is a body of competent professional opinion which considers that theirs was a wrong decision if there also exists a body of professional opinion equally competent which supports the decision as reasonable in the circumstances. It is not enough to show that subsequent events show that the operation need never have been performed if at the time the decision to operate was taken it was reasonable in the sense that a responsible body of medical opinion would have accepted it as proper. I do not think that the words of Lord President Clyde in *Hunter v Hanley*[10] can be bettered . . . I would only add that a doctor who professes to exercise a special skill must exercise the ordinary skill of his speciality. Differences of opinion in practice exist and will always exist in the medical as in other professions. There is seldom any one answer exclusive of all others to problems of professional judgement. A court may prefer one body of opinion to the other but that is no basis for a conclusion of negligence.

So *Hunter v Hanley*[10] finally explicitly received the *imprimatur* of the House of Lords.

In court, the issue of whether or not there has been a breach of duty of care is decided by the judge after he or she has heard evidence on the matter from independent experts instructed by both sides. However, it is worth remembering that the final view is that of a medical layman, namely the judge:

> No expert witness can provide any conclusive answer ... If therefore a witness states that had he been similarly placed, his conduct would have been no different from the conduct under review, the duty of the Court to decide whether such conduct amounted in law to negligence still remains. The opinions of medical men on this limited issue may be of great value and assistance to the Court, but the Court is not relieved of the unhappy duty of having to form its own judgement. (Morris LJ in *Chapman v Rix*)[14]

It is therefore of the greatest importance that medical experts impress the judge as being honest, reasonable and logical, and this requirement of expert witnesses was emphasised with considerable force and clarity by the House of Lords in the case of *Bolitho and others v City and Hackney Health Authority*.[15]

Case 14: Bolitho and others v City and Hackney Health Authority

In this case a doctor negligently failed to respond to nursing requests to attend a child with respiratory difficulties. The child suffered a cardiac arrest which resulted in brain damage. The issue was what would have been done to assist the child *had* the doctor attended. *Five* doctors for the claimant gave evidence that the child should have been intubated, which would have provided a supply of oxygen to him in the event of his respiratory tubes being entirely blocked. *Two* experts for the *defenders* – whose credibility and reliability was not in doubt – stated that intubation was not appropriate because it would have required the child to have been anaesthetised and, on the evidence of his condition, such a course was neither necessary nor desirable. There was also a fundamental dispute between the two camps of experts as to whether the respiratory blockage was caused slowly and gradually by a build-up of mucus, which was the claimant's position, or whether it occurred suddenly as a consequence of a 'plug' of mucus blocking the trachea. It was also of the greatest importance in this case to remember what the trial judge said of one of the defendant's experts, Dr Dinwoodie: 'I have to say of Dr Dinwoodie also that he displayed what seemed to me to be a profound knowledge of paediatric respiratory medicine, coupled with impartiality, and there is no doubt in my view of the genuineness of his opinion that intubation was not indicated.' The trial judge therefore found in favour of the defence, because of the impression Dr Dinwoodie's expert evidence made on him. Whilst he was sympathetic to the claimant's case, the trial judge said that the difficulty the case as presented by claimant's counsel for him was that in effect the claimant's counsel was inviting him 'to substitute my own views for those of the medical experts.'

The claimant appealed to the Court of Appeal, where his counsel was successful in winning over one of the three judges, Simon Brown LJ, with his argument that in effect, in a matter of causation, you do not employ the *Bolam*[11]/*Hunter v Hanley*[10]/*Maynard*[13] criteria.

The claimant appealed further to the House of Lords, which unanimously upheld the decision of the Court of Appeal. They rejected the claimant's counsel's arguments once again that the *Bolam*[11] principle had no application in deciding the question of causation, and that the trial judge had misdirected himself by treating it as relevant. Lord Browne-Wilkinson said that the question which had to be asked was, if the registrar had attended, and if she had decided not to intubate, 'would that decision have been negligent?'. His answer was in the negative, given that 'it cannot be suggested that it was illogical for Dr Dinwoodie, a most distinguished expert, to favour running what, in his view, was a small risk of total respiratory collapse rather than to submit Patrick to the invasive procedure of intubation.' However, in this judgement, and this is perhaps its most significant feature, Lord Browne-Wilkinson sounded a very clear warning to experts who may seek to defend what is *illogical* or *indefensible*. He accepted, of course, the appellant's counsel's submission that:

> Ultimately, it was for the Court and not for medical opinion to decide what was the standard of care required of a professional in the circumstances of each particular case. My Lords, I agree with these submissions, to the extent that in

my view the Court is not bound to hold that a Defendant Doctor escapes liability for negligent treatment or diagnosis just because he leads evidence from a number of medical experts who are genuinely of the opinion that the Defendant's treatment or diagnosis accorded with sound medical practice.

The use of these adjectives responsible, reasonable and respectable all show that the Court has to be satisfied that the exponents of the body of opinion relied upon can demonstrate that such opinion has a logical basis.

... if in a rare case it can be demonstrated that the professional opinion is not capable of withstanding logical analysis, the Judge is entitled to hold that the body of opinion is not reasonable or responsible.

I emphasise that in my view it will very seldom be right for a Judge to reach the conclusion that views genuinely held by competent medical experts are unreasonable. The assessment of medical risks and benefits is a matter of clinical judgment which a Judge would not normally be able to make without expert evidence. As the quotation from Lord Scarman makes clear, it would be wrong to allow such assessment to deteriorate into seeking to persuade the Judge to prefer one of two views, both of which are capable of being logically supportive. It is only where a Judge can be satisfied that the body of expert opinion cannot be logically supported at all that such opinion will not provide the benchmark by reference to which the Defendant's conduct falls to be assessed.

Whilst therefore the *Bolitho*[15] decision reaffirms the paramountcy of the criteria of *Bolam*[11]/*Hunter v Hanley*[10]/ *Maynard*[13] in determining whether or not medical treatment has been negligent, it clearly warns practitioners that in seeking to establish whether or not those criteria have been met by a defender doctor, they must ensure that their experts are of a high quality, have thoroughly and carefully considered the issues at stake in that particular case, and have arrived at their view supporting the doctor on a logical and convincing basis. *Bolitho*[15] very firmly reminds the trial judge of the great power he has in deciding what value he should place on the expert's opinion. This power was recently demonstrated in the case of *Marriott v West Midlands Health Authority and others*.[16]

Case 15: Marriott v West Midlands Health Authority and others

The patient had had a fall at home, suffering a head injury. He was rendered unconscious for 20 to 30 minutes and was thereafter admitted to hospital. Following X-rays and neurological observations, he was discharged home the following day. He remained lethargic, with no appetite, and experienced headaches. His condition did not improve, and on 11 October, eight days after the accident, his GP was called to attend him at home. The GP was informed of the claimant's symptoms and history. He examined the claimant, but neurological tests revealed no abnormality. He told the claimant's wife to contact him again if the claimant's condition deteriorated, and advised the claimant to take analgesics for his headache. On 15 October 1984 the claimant's condition suddenly deteriorated, and he became unconscious and was returned to hospital. He sustained a massive left extradural haematoma which was operated on, and in the course of the operation a linear fracture of the skull was discovered and that the claimant was bleeding from the middle meningeal artery. He was left with a hemiplegia and dysarthria, and is severely disabled. The trial judge found the health authority and the GP to have been negligent, and an appeal was taken on behalf of the GP to the Court of Appeal.

At the trial, two experts had given evidence, one on behalf of the GP and one on behalf of the claimant. The defendant's expert said that the general practitioner was entitled to make a reasoned clinical decision based on his examination of the patient and assessment of the history and complaints, given that readmission and keeping the patient at home under review would both be reasonable responses if there were no apparent signs of deterioration, even if there were also no signs of significant improvement. However, the defendant's expert did agree with the claimant's expert that where a head injury involves a significant period of unconsciousness, general practitioners must be particularly careful in their assessment and cannot afford to take risks. He agreed that the general practitioner did not have available to him in general the equipment necessary to make a definitive diagnosis that excluded intracranial lesions, and that in particular the absence of neurological signs did not mean that a positive excluding diagnosis could confidently be made. He also agreed with the claimant's expert that if anything did go wrong with a head injury, it could do so very quickly and with serious consequences.

The claimant's expert was of the view that, as the general practitioner had neither the skills nor the facilities to investigate fully and rule out the possible existence of an intracranial lesion, a patient presenting with a history such as that of the claimant ought to have been readmitted to hospital where full tests would be carried out, and that not to do so would subject the patient to an unnecessary risk of complications developing suddenly and with disastrous consequences. The trial judge preferred the evidence of the claimant's expert, stating:

> Whilst a court must plainly be reluctant to depart from the opinion of an apparently careful and prudent general practitioner, I have concluded that if there is a body of opinion which supports the course of leaving a patient who has some 7 days previously sustained a severe injury at home in circumstances where he continues to complain of headaches, drowsiness, etc., and where there continues to be a risk of the existence of an intracranial lesion which would cause a sudden and disastrous collapse, then such an approach is not reasonably prudent. It may well be that in the vast majority of cases the risk is very small. Nevertheless, the consequences if things go wrong are disastrous to the patient. In such circumstances it is my view that in any case where a general practitioner remains of the view that there is a risk of intracranial lesion such as to warrant the carrying out of neurological testing and the giving of further head injury instructions, then the only prudent course judged from the point of view of the patient is to readmit for further testing and observation.

The Court of Appeal approved the trial judge's approach to the matter, stating that she had subjected the expert's opinion to analysis to see whether it could properly be regarded as reasonable, and commenting that the trial judge was entitled to do so. Reference is then made to *Bolitho*[15] and Lord Browne-Wilkinson's opinion. The Court of Appeal went on to say that 'although the risk was described as small, the judge was correct in carrying out her assessment of risk to approach it as a function of the small likelihood that there was such a

> lesion and of the serious consequences to the plaintiff if there was.' It was open to the judge, they said 'to hold that in the circumstances as she found them to have been, it could not be a reasonable exercise for general practitioners' discretion to leave the patient at home and not refer him back to Hospital.' The Court of Appeal clearly relied very heavily on the House of Lords' decision in *Bolitho*[15] in reaching their position of support for the trial judge in this case.

In practice, it is suggested, judges do not have difficulty in assessing whether they regard the evidence of an expert as 'responsible'. In *Parry v Northwest Surrey Health Authority*,[17] Curtis J states that:

> I interpose to say that I found [the expert witness] to be more of an advocate at times – for example, his preparedness to argue that the loss of the [CTG] trace was normal and often happened. Also his evidence on the anatomical impossibility points was a firm indication that I could not treat his evidence as reliable. I do not wish nor do I need to say more.

Moreover, in the case of *Rolland*[2] referred to earlier, the Lord Ordinary had this to say of one of the experts: 'Professor [X] gave his evidence in what might not unfairly be described as a didactic manner; most judges, I imagine, dislike being lectured by witnesses, and in this respect I count myself among the majority.'

In the case of *Moyes v Lothian Health Board*,[18] Lord Caplan said of one of the claimant's experts:

> It is over 10 years since Professor S gave up practice in Edinburgh. He is aged 74 and now lives in South Africa. He is a general radiologist but has had less opportunity of studying the documents in the case in advance of the Proof than the other experts. He is a particularly eminent authority on general radiology since he referred repeatedly in his evidence to his former teaching practices. I suspected that he might not be quite as up to date in his practical experience as some of the other witnesses. In any event, his experience was less specific to some of the problems being reviewed.

Lord Caplan *refused* to certify Professor S as an expert witness at the conclusion of his judgement.

And in the case of *Hepworth v Kerr*,[19] a case involving a disputed hypotensive anaesthetic technique, the trial judge said:

> I accept the advice of ... the plaintiff's experts. I found them to be impressive and compelling witnesses. I reject the evidence of [the defendant's experts]. They valiantly sought to defend the defendant's technique and its safety, but in the end it was plain to me that none of them would have done what the defendant did ... It was clear to me that they were at times fighting a cause, sacrificing their professional objectivity in the process. Their evidence was not helpful in assisting the court to arrive at a just determination of the issues.

Where then does the Bolitho decision leave us?

Each and every case must now be subjected to close scrutiny for the following reasons:

1 The case may not, in fact, truly be a clinical case. It may be a 'system' case or a 'management' case in a medical context. Examples of this would include the breakdown in a system for ensuring that reporting of cervical smears is properly communicated to the patient. Failure of such a system will not be judged on *Hunter v Hanley*[10]/*Bolam*[11] criteria. A judge is quite capable of deciding for him- or herself, without expert evidence, whether such a failure is a negligent failure.

2 It may be a 'one-off' or 'isolated decision' case such as *Hucks v Cole*.[20]

3 It should be questioned whether there is in fact a particular and accepted practice. Is there really another school of thought? There is authority for the view that even in professional negligence cases, compliance with approved practice is not conclusive in favour of the defendant – the reader is referred to the non-medical case of *Edward Wong Finance Limited v Johnson Stokes & Master*.[21] This was a case involving conveyancing practice widely followed in Hong Kong, but the fact that it was widely followed was not held to excuse those solicitors who operated it from negligence.

4 Is it the defendant's practice which is respectable? Or is it really an indefensible practice that is supported by respectable doctors?

Case 16: Chapman v Rix (House of Lords decision from 1960, but reported in 1994 Medical Law Reports)

This was a question of communication by a doctor after his patient had received a penetrating knife wound. As a result of a failure in communication, the claimant died of peritonitis. In the Court of Appeal, Morris LJ, dissenting from the majority decision which reversed the trial judge's finding of negligence, said:

> No expert witness can provide any conclusive answer ... if therefore a witness states that had he been similarly placed, his conduct would have been no different from the conduct under review, the duty of the court to decide whether such conduct amounted in law to negligence still remains. The opinions of medical men on this limited issue may be of great value and assistance to the court, but the court is not relieved of the unhappy duty of having to form its own judgement.

In this case, two defence experts said that they would have acted as Dr Rix had done, and that if Dr Rix was negligent, they would have been negligent, too. Willmer LJ, said: 'I found it impossible to say that in the light of what he then knew, the course adopted by Dr Rix was one which no professional man of ordinary skill would have taken if he had been acting with ordinary care.'

The claimant appealed to the House of Lords but the Lords dismissed the Appeal by a majority of three to two. Lord Keith of Avonholm, one of the dissenting judges, had this to say:

> There may be different schools of thought as to the treatment of abdominal wounds where there is suspected or possible or even improbable but not impossible impenetration of the peritoneal cavity. But in my opinion a doctor who is expected to look after a patient with an abdominal wound which has already been diagnosed and treated by another doctor who decides that the injury does not require operative or observational treatment in hospital should be put in possession of information on what has been observed and done by the first doctor. Otherwise, the patient is being deprived of the full skill, knowledge and aid in diagnosis that the second doctor could otherwise apply to this case. *I hardly regard this as a medical question at all*, although it has a medical background and has to be dealt with in relation to

the risks run by the patient in the absence of proper medical or surgical treatment.

Interestingly, Lord Goddard, who was with the majority, none the less said:

My Lords, I have said enough to show that I agree with Lords Justices Romer and Willmer in holding that the Trial Judges finding of negligence against Dr Rix should be reversed. But I desire to add that if Lord Justice Romer meant that *if a doctor charged with negligence could find two other Doctors to say they would have acted as he did, that of itself entitled him to a verdict. I could not agree with him if there was evidence the other way.* But this is not to say that if some doctors think one course should be followed, while others prefer another, a judge may not say without actually deciding in favour of one view or the other that he is not prepared to find negligence.

5 Is the practice outdated? Is it irrelevant? Is it logical?
6 Does the practice conform to any relevant protocol?
7 Remember Lord Browne-Wilkinson's reference in *Bolitho*[15] to the weighing up of risks and benefits. Were there facts which the defenders overlooked? Were there facilities of which the defender should have taken advantage?
8 Remember what Sachs LJ said in *Hucks v Cole*:[20] 'Where the evidence shows that a lacuna in professional practice exists by which risks of grave danger are knowingly taken, then however small the risk the court must anxiously examine that lacuna – *particulalry if the risk can be easily and inexpensively avoided.*'

So whilst the *Hunter v Hanley*[10]/*Bolam*[11] criteria for determining whether or not a doctor's clinical act or omission is negligent are firmly the law, the process by which those criteria are established or not established by a court in a particular case has recently been vigorously examined. Very clear guidance has been given in the cases we have just discussed, emphasising the court's supremacy in assessing the relative value of evidence from competing experts, and encouraging judges to apply a risk–benefit analysis to that evidence.

After all of the effort spent on the two appeals in *Bolitho*,[15] the case quite obviously was won for the defence by Dr Dinwoodie's personal and professional quality as an expert witness which so impressed the trial judge at the original hearing.

Causation

Given the complexities and difficulties facing a claimant's lawyer in seeking to establish a case of negligence against a doctor, it is not surprising that sufficient attention is sometimes not paid to the all important matter of causation and whether the act or omission complained of, if established as negligent, caused or materially contributed to the loss and injury. There is no opportunity for awarding damages on the basis of 'loss of a chance' as was attempted by the trial judge and the Court of Appeal in the case of *Hotson*.[22]

Case 17: Damage to an epiphysis

This was a case about an injury to a boy who fell whilst playing in a tree, damaging his epiphysis, with a subsequent delay of some 5 days in diagnosing the condition in hospital. The question was whether the damage to the epiphysis caused by the interruption of the flow of blood because of damage to the blood vessels was caused by the trauma of the injury itself, or by the delay. The trial judge held that it was 75% likely to have been the trauma from the injury itself and 25% likely to have been due to the delay in diagnosis. Accordingly, he awarded damages on the basis of the 25% lost chance of a good recovery, and so awarded 25% of full damages. He was supported by the Court of Appeal, but the House of Lords overturned the decision. They took the view that the crucial question was whether the cause of the injury was the fall, or the hospital's negligence in incorrect diagnosis and delay in treatment. If the fall caused the injury, then the hospital's negligence became irrelevant. That question was one to be decided on the balance of probabilities and, given the trial judge's finding that the fall was 75% likely to be the cause of the injury, then the claimant must fail on the issue of causation because the 75% finding established that, on the balance of probabilities, it was the fall and not the incorrect diagnosis and delay where the damage sustained occurred before the duty of care arises.

That decision was quickly followed by another House of Lords decision, namely *Wilsher v Essex Area Health Authority*[23] in 1988. This decision clearly resolved confusion which had arisen in arguments on causation founded on the *McGhie*[24] case.

Case 18: Premature birth

The claimant was born prematurely with a 1 in 5 chance of survival and suffering from various deficiencies, including an oxygen deficiency. In order to remedy this, oxygen was administered to him, but the monitoring catheter was twice inserted into a vein rather than an artery. This led to incorrect readings being given, with the consequence that the baby was given excess oxygen. The child was later found to be suffering from a condition called retrolental fibroplasia (RLF), a condition of the retina resulting in his being totally blind in one eye and having severely impaired sight in the other. This condition can be caused by the administration of excess oxygen, but it could also have been caused by four other conditions that are common in premature babies, all of which afflicted the claimant. The medical evidence at the trial was inconclusive as to whether the excess oxygen caused or materially contributed to the claimant's retinal condition. None the less the trial judge found that the hospital had failed to take proper precautions to prevent the administration of excess oxygen, and since therefore the claimant had suffered injury against which precautions had been designed to be a protection, the burden was on the hospital to show that there had been no breach of duty and that damage did not result from that breach. In the judge's view, the hospital failed to discharge that burden, and he awarded damages to the claimant. The Court of Appeal agreed with the trial judge in a majority decision. However, the House of Lords held that where a claimant's injury was attributable to a number of causes, one of which was the defendant's negligence, the combination of the defendant's breach of duty and the claimant's injury did not give rise to presumption that the defendant had caused the injury. Instead, the burden remained on the claimant to prove the causative link between the defendant's negligence and his injury, although that link could legitimately be inferred from the evidence. Since the claimant's retinal condition could have been caused by any one of a number of different agents, and it had not been proved that it was caused by the failure to prevent excess oxygen being given to him, the claimant had not discharged the burden of proof as to causation. Lord Bridge, in the leading judgement, quoted with approval a passage of the opinion of the then Vice-Chancellor, Lord Browne-Wilkinson, in the Court of Appeal:

To apply the principle in *McGhie v The National Coal Board*[24] to the present case would constitute an extension of that principle. In *McGhie*[24] there was no doubt that the pursuer's dermatitis was physically caused by brick dust. The only question was whether the continued presence of such brick dust in the pursuer's skin after the time when he should have been provided with a shower caused or materially contributed to the dermatitis which he contracted. There was only one possible agent which could have caused the dermatitis, namely brick dust, and there was no doubt that the dermatitis from which he suffered was caused by that brick dust. In the present case the question is different; there are a number of different agents which could have caused the RLF. Excess oxygen is one of them. The defendants failed to take reasonable precautions to prevent one of the possible causative agents, i.e. excess oxygen, from causing RLF, but no one can tell in this case whether excess oxygen did or did not cause or contribute to the RLF suffered by the plaintiff. The plaintiff's RLF may have been caused by some completely different agent or agents, e.g. hypercarbia, intraventricular haemorrhage, apnoea or patent ductus arteriosus. In addition to oxygen, each of those conditions had been implicated as a possible cause of RLF. This baby suffered from each of those conditions at various times in the first 2 months of his life. There is no satisfactory evidence that excess oxygen is more likely than any of those other four candidates to have caused RLF in this baby. To my mind, the occurrence of RLF following a failure to take necessary precautions to prevent excess oxygen causing RLF provides no evidence and raises no presumption that it was excess of oxygen rather than one or more of the four other possible agents which caused or contributed to RLF in this case. The position to my mind is wholly different from that in *McGhie*,[24] where there was only one candidate, brick dust, which could have caused the dermatitis ... a failure to take preventative measures against one out of five possible causes is no evidence as to which of those five caused the injury.

There can be no doubt that the consequence of the decisions in *Hunter v Hanley*[10]/*Bolam*[11] and *Wilsher*[23] is such as to put severe obstacles in the path of claimants/pursuers seeking compensation for alleged medical negligence. These are likely to be the most difficult cases for claimants'/pursuers' solicitors to handle in terms of the disappointment of expectations of their clients. It is possible to have a number of situations arising, all of which are associated with injury suffered, but in none of which will the claimant/pursuer recover compensation. These include the following:

1 situations where the injury arises from 'misadventure', as in the cases of *Roe*[1] and *Rolland*,[2] where there was no reasonably foreseeable risk of injury
2 even where there is error or omission, it may be non-negligent error or omission, a useful example of this being an unreported case, *Scott v Highland Health Board*,[25] which involved the interpretation of an X-ray relating to injury to a patient's thigh

Case 19: Failure to diagnose slipped epiphysis – Scott v Highland Health Board

The purpose of the X-ray was to exclude the possibility of fracture of the femur after a skiing accident, and the epiphysis itself was not very clearly identified in the X-ray. The consultant radiologist who examined the X-ray with fracture of the femur at the foremost of his mind did not notice anything untoward about the epiphysis. The patient returned to England and after some 2 weeks of suffering pain was admitted to the local hospital where she was X-rayed and found to be suffering from a slipped left capital epiphysis caused by the trauma of the skiing injury. When the initial X-ray taken in the Scottish hospital was examined with that knowledge, unsatisfactory though the quality of the X-ray was, evidence of damage to the epiphysis could be seen. The question for Lord Maxwell to determine was whether or not the failure of the Scottish radiologist to detect that damage was negligent or not. The first important point Lord Maxwell stressed in his judgement – and it is a matter of general application which should be considered in all medical negligence cases – is whether he should prefer the evidence of a consultant radiologist to other experts, in a radiological case. He said:

Turning to the evidence of the experts considered in the light of this background, I attach importance to the fact that only one of the three, Dr Davidson, was a consultant radiologist. I think it would be unsafe to draw any inference in the defender's favour from the fact that the pursuer's advisers could not or did not see fit to call a radiologist as a witness, and I certainly would not reject as valueless the evidence of consultant orthopaedic surgeons merely because they are not of precisely the same discipline as the second defender (namely a radiologist). Nevertheless, other things being equal, I consider that a generalist consulting radiologist is better placed than a consultant orthopaedic surgeon to say what another competent and diligent generalist consultant radiologist would or would not observe ... Dr Davidson's evidence, if accepted, is in my opinion to the effect that the failure to observe the slipped epiphysis in the small radiograph did not demonstrate professional negligence. He had no doubt that, with hindsight, the slipped epiphysis was definitely discernible in the small radiograph. He referred to it as 'minimal' and 'the sort of thing that gets overlooked'. He repeatedly said that to have picked up the minimal change would have been what he called 'a good spot' and when the test in *Hunter v Hanley*[10] was put to him, he was clearly of the opinion that the second defender had not failed ... I am satisfied that he considered the mistake could well have been made by a competent consultant radiologist using due diligence at the time he was looking at the radiograph in question, but bearing in mind the nature and circumstances of the task being performed. I was particularly impressed by Dr Davidson's evidence and ... I am satisfied that professional negligence is not established in this case.

3 there are cases where the act – whether negligently performed or not – may not be judged capable of having caused or materially contributed to the injury. The 'vaccination cases', such as *Bonthrone*[26] and *Loveday*,[27] are good examples of this, where it was held as a matter of fact that the administration of pertussis vaccine could not have caused brain damage

4 there may well also be cases where a 'negligent' act may be judged to be not capable of having caused or materially contributed to the injury.

Case 20: Injury to an eye – Kenyon v Bell

Such a case is that of *Kenyon v Bell*,[28] in which a child damaged an eye while playing at home. The child was taken to hospital and the eye was negligently treated. When the child's condition did not improve and the parents sought further hospital assistance, the child was found to be permanently blind in that eye. An action was brought on behalf of the child, and the negligence of the first examining and treating casualty doctor was not in doubt. However, it was established that the initial injury to the eye at home was the cause of the eye's permanent blindness, and that no intervening treatment could have saved the sight in the eye. Thus the negligence of the first casualty officer was not a relevant factor.

Case 21: Overdose of penicillin – Kay v Ayrshire and Arran Health Board

A better known case is that of *Kay v Ayrshire and Arran Health Board*.[29] In that case, Andrew Kay was diagnosed as having pneumococcal meningitis, a deadly disease. A junior doctor was instructed to inject 10 000 units of penicillin intrathecally. By mistake, he injected 300 000 units, i.e. 30 times the appropriate dose. The immediate consequence was that the child had a series of convulsions. After a few days he settled and his condition improved. The meningitis was cured, but the boy was found to be profoundly deaf. However, he was in no way brain-damaged. The problem for the Kays was that, notwithstanding this act of immediate and demonstrable negligence, there was no medical or scientific evidence available to demonstrate that an overdose of penicillin given intrathecally would cause or had ever caused deafness in a patient. Certainly brain damage and even death were known consequences of such overdoses, but not deafness. None the less, Mr Kay conducted his own case in the Outer House before Lord Davidson and was successful. Lord Davidson's judgement was overturned on appeal. The case went to the House of Lords, where the judgement of the Inner House was upheld on the basis that there was no established causal link between an overdose, however large, of intrathecally delivered penicillin and deafness.

Case 22: Faulty operation on an artery – Joyce v Merton, Sutton and Wandsworth Health Authority

Another recent case in this category is that of *Joyce v Merton, Sutton and Wandsworth Health Authority*.[30] It was a case involving brachial cardiac catheterisation. At the conclusion of the procedure, when suturing the brachial artery, the registrar inadvertently sutured part of the posterial wall to the anterior wall of the artery. This was not observed, and the patient, Mr Joyce, was discharged home. The error subsequently gave rise to vascular complications that required two unsuccessful repair/reconstruction operations once the occlusion was discovered. Despite vascular surgery, there were no improvements. Subsequently, thrombus dislodged during an aortogram, which resulted in upper brainstem infarction. The trial judge in this case found that the medical and nursing care was not negligent, but this finding was overturned in the Court of Appeal, Hobhouse LJ finding that:

> the judge ought to have found that there was a want of reasonable care on the part of Dr S and Nurse E on March the 4th. This want of care culminated in the decision to discharge Mr Joyce and to do so without a warning or advice that was appropriate to his case. It was preceded by inadequate observations of his condition and inadequate recognition of the risk category into which he was on the evidence to be placed ... the mishap which caused Mr Joyce's problems was a known and recognised risk of the procedure ... it was a risk which was aggravated by the fact that Mr Joyce's brachial artery was a small size. The fact that he had a faint pulse showed that his artery was not totally occluded, but raised more than a possibility that his artery was partially occluded. Dr S himself explained that a faint pulse could mean occlusion of the order of 90% of the available capacity of the artery ... This observation alone put Mr Joyce into a risk category ... The risk was of ischaemia, possibly with the build-up of thrombus adjacent to the constriction.

Then the learned judge moves on to the all important question of causation:

> The next question then is whether there were relevant consequences of that breach of duty. What the plaintiff has

to prove is that it was as a result of breach of duty that no steps were taken to re-open the artery during the next 48 hours to deal with the mis-suturing and consequent obstruction.

It should be explained that all the medical evidence indicated that had re-exploration of the artery taken place within 48 hours of the catheterisation procedure, this would have re-established circulation in the arm. Later re-exploration on the balance of probabilities would not have done so.

It is accepted 'that had a vascular surgeon decided to re-open his artery within the 48-hour period, Mr Joyce's injury would probably have been avoided.' What the claimant had to seek to prove was 'that a vascular surgeon would (or should) have been and would (or should) have operated.'

In my judgment, the judge was right to find that the only deterioration of Mr Joyce's condition during the 48 hours after the procedure was the wound pain, and that it was not proved that there was probably any signs or symptoms which could have justified a cardiologist or vascular surgeon in concluding that his condition had worsened or that there was ischaemia. Under these circumstances, it would have been proper for a cardiologist not to have called in a vascular surgeon and for a vascular surgeon, *if consulted*, to decide that it was not appropriate to re-explore the artery.

It follows that even if Mr Joyce had been kept in the ward for further observation or had returned within the 48-hour period, the position would have been the same – his artery would not have been re-opened.

Case references

1   Roe v Minister of Health (1954) **2** *All ER*: 131.

2   Rolland v Lothian Health Board (1981) Court of Session Outer House (unreported).

3   Johnstone v Traffic Commissioner (1990) *Scots LT*: 409.

4   Baker v Kaye (1997) *Industr Relations LR*: 219.

5   Caparo Industries plc v Dickman (1990) **2** *AC*: 605.

6 R v Croydon Health Authority (1998) *Lloyds LR Med*: 44.

7 Powell v Boladz (1998) *Lloyds LR Med*: 117.

8 Kapfunde v Abbey National plc (1998) *Industrial Relations LR*: 583.

9 Palmer v Tees Health Authority (1998) *Lloyd's Rep Med*: 447.

10 Hunter v Hanley (1955) *Session Cases*: 200.

11 Bolam v Friern Hospital Management Committee (1957) **2** *All ER*: 118.

12 Whitehouse v Jordan

(a) Court of Appeal (1980) **1** *All ER*: 650.

(b) House of Lords (1981) **1** *All ER*: 267.

13 Maynard v West Midlands Regional Health Authority (1985) **1** *All ER*: 635.

14 Chapman v Rix (1959) reported in 1994 **5** *Med LR*: 239.

15 Bolitho and others v City and Hackney Health Authority (1998) *Lloyds LR Med*: 26.

16 Marriott v West Midlands Health Authority and others (1999) *Lloyds LR Med* (Part I, February 1999): 23.

17 Parry v Northwest Surrey Health Authority (1994) (Report Pending) May, Curtis J.

18 Moyes v Lothian Health Board (1990) *SLT*: 444.

19 Hepworth v Kerr (1995) **6** *Med LR*: 13, 130.

20 Hucks v Cole (1968) reported in 1993 **4** *Med LR*: 393.

21 Edward Wong Finance Limited v Johnson Stokes & Master (1984) *AC*: 296.

22 Hotson v East Berkshire Health Authority (1987) **2** *All ER*: 909.

23 Wilsher v Essex Health Authority

(a) Court of Appeal (1986) **3** *All ER*: 801.

(b) House of Lords (1988) **1** *All ER*: 871.

24 McGhie v National Coal Board (1972) **3** *All ER*: 1008.

25 Scott v Highland Health Board (1980) Court of Session Outer House (unreported).

26 Bonthrone v Secretary of State for Scotland and others (1987) *SLT*: 334.

27 Loveday v Renton (1990) **1** *Med LR*: 117.

28 Kenyon v Bell (1953) *Session Cases*: 125.

29 Kay v Ayrshire and Arran Health Board (1987) *SLT*: 577.

30 Joyce v Merton, Sutton and Wandsworth Health Authority (1996) **7** *Med LR*: 1.

CHAPTER FIVE

The process of the law

John Pickering

Introduction

This chapter seeks to analyse the legal process involved in pursuing a claim in negligence. In the first section there is an analysis of the legal procedures involved, with review of the new Civil Procedure Rules. The second section seeks to deal with the practical aspects of handling a case and the issues that the practitioner will embrace. The remaining sections consider other important aspects, including funding, alternative dispute resolution (including mediation) and the effect of the process on those involved. It is important to note that this chapter is confined to the litigation process and does not seek to address the complaints procedure.

The litigation process – the pre-action protocol for the resolution of clinical disputes and the new Civil Procedure Rules

On 26 April 1999, the Civil Procedure Rules 1998 (CPR) came into effect. These rules represent the most significant reform of civil litigation since 1875. The previous Rules of the Supreme Court 1965 (RSC) were an extensively revised version of rules set out in Schedule 1 to the Supreme Court of Judicature Act 1875, which had themselves been derived from pre-existing procedure. The new rules are the result of the now famous review conducted by Lord Woolf. On 28 March 1994 he was appointed by the then Lord Chancellor, Lord McKay of Clashfern, to review the rules and

procedure of the civil courts in England and Wales. The main aims
were as follows:

- to improve access to justice and reduce the cost of litigation
- to reduce the complexity of the rules in modernised terminology
- to remove unnecessary distinctions of practice and procedure.

Whilst some of the general principles of the RSC practice have been
incorporated into the CPR, nevertheless the reforms comprise not
simply new rules but an entirely new procedural code.

The code is supported by pre-litigation protocols and by practice
directions. The language used is more user-friendly and less
archaic (note that the phrase 'medical negligence' has now been
replaced by 'clinical negligence').

The rules represent a response to the defects of the old system
identified by Lord Woolf. They were summarised as follows:

- too expensive with costs in many cases exceeding the value of
  the claim
- too slow in bringing cases to a conclusion
- too unequal (i.e. there was a lack of equality between the
  powerful wealthy litigant and the under-resourced litigant)
- too uncertain, with particular concern about cost and duration,
  and
- too fragmented.

In response to these complaints, the CPR commences with a statement of the Overriding Objective. This is CPR Rule 1.1(1), which
provides that 'these rules are a new procedural code with the
overriding objective of enabling the Court to deal with cases justly'.

By CPR 1.1.(2), dealing justly with a case includes, so far as is
practicable, the following:

1 ensuring that the parties are on a equal footing
2 saving expense
3 dealing with a case in ways which are proportionate to:
   - the amount of money involved
   - the importance of the case
   - the complexity of the issues
   - the financial position of each party
4 ensuring that it is dealt with expeditiously and fairly
5 allotting to it an appropriate share of the court's resources whilst
   taking into account the need to allot resources to other cases.

Further regard should be given to Rule CPR 1.3, which states that 'the parties are required to help the Court to further the overriding objective'.

Hence it is important in understanding this new procedural scenario to appreciate that the rules will be interpreted purposefully rather than literally so as to ensure that the overriding objective is achieved. Not only is there a clear obligation imposed on the parties by Rule 1.3, but also there is a very clear role for the court in terms of case management, the idea being that the court will actively participate in the running of the case so as to ensure that the process runs smoothly and that the dispute is brought to resolution as effectively and quickly as possible.

It is worth noting that so fundamental is this reform process that in interpreting the rules no regard will be given to the previous rules and their associated case law. There is quite literally a clean sheet of paper and, as yet, no interpretative case law.

The key procedural stages

There now follows an analysis of the main procedural stages that will be followed in respect of a clinical negligence case being pursued under the CPR. The intention is to highlight the main areas of interest and to explore the various tactical considerations which will be considered along the way.

The pre-litigation position

The new dispensation recognises the need to address every part of the process from the time of the identification of the adverse outcome to the commencement of litigation and its pursuit through the courts. Fundamental to Lord Woolf's thinking was a desire to minimise, so far as was reasonably practicable, the incidence of litigation by seeking to foster a less adversarial culture.

In his Access to Justice Report in July 1996, Lord Woolf recognised the 'peculiar difficulty' of clinical negligence cases and identified one of the major sources of costs and delay as being at the pre-litigation stage. There were a number of reasons for this, involving inadequate incident-reporting and record-keeping, delays in making a claim, inadequate resources for investigation and a reluctance on behalf of the healthcare professionals to admit negligence, provide an explanation or apologise.

It was as a result of Lord Woolf's initiative that an umbrella group was formed consisting of key individuals from all interested areas involved with clinical negligence. The idea was to bring the parties together so as to address the perceived problems. From this initiative was born the Clinical Disputes Forum[5.1] which was formally established in 1997.

The first initiative of that Forum was to produce the Pre-Action Protocol for the Resolution of Clinical Disputes. That protocol (the final version of which was published in December 1998) is now embodied within the CPR and supported by a Practice Direction. It is important to note that the protocol applies to every area of clinical dispute. It encompasses the position for general practitioners just as it affects the position for NHS Trusts and for private practice.

The protocol identifies two general aims:

- to maintain/restore the patient–healthcare provider relationship, and
- to resolve as many disputes as possible without litigation.

The protocol attempts to set out a 'code of good practice', and of particular importance within this are 'good practice commitments on both sides'.

Healthcare provider commitments

The healthcare providers are required by paragraph 3.4 to:

- ensure that key staff are appropriately trained (i.e. have a working knowledge of the relevant healthcare law, complaints procedure, civil litigation practice, etc.)

[5.1] The membership of the Forum is agreed at a maximum of 30 individuals drawn from all key interested constituencies. These include patients and patients' representatives (such as Action for Victims of Medical Accidents and the National Consumer Council), the clinical professions (such as the Academy of Medical Royal Colleges and the British Dental Association), NHS management (including the NHS Confederation), the private health sector (e.g. BUPA), statutory regulators of the clinical professions (e.g. the General Medical Council), ADR groups, barristers, claims managers (e.g. ALARM), claimant and defence solicitors, funders (such as the Legal Aid Board), the judges, the Department of Health and the Lord Chancellor's Department. The Forum is chaired by Dr Alastair Scotland, who is the Director of Medical Education and Research at the Chelsea and Westminster Healthcare Trust, and its Secretary is Ms Sarah Leigh of the law firm Leigh Day & Co. Further details about the CDF may be obtained by contacting its administrator, Margaret Dangoor, of 3 Clydesdale Gardens, Richmond, Surrey TW10 5EG (e-mail address: margaret.dangoor@cableinet.co.uk) or by visiting the website on http://clinical-disputes-forum.org.uk.

- develop appropriate approaches to clinical governance consistent with good standards of practice within their specific area
- create adverse-outcome-reporting systems which will also facilitate the speedy gathering of evidence
- apply the results of adverse incidents and complaints positively (i.e. learn from poor performance and try to correct practice)
- ensure that patients receive clear and comprehensible information
- establish proper systems for recording and storing patient notes and records, and
- advise patients of serious adverse outcomes and provide an oral or written explanation upon request.

The last-listed commitment is fundamentally important, for it recognises the obligation on the healthcare provider to advise the patient pro-actively of the serious adverse outcome and to provide a suitable explanation, apology, offers of further treatment, etc., so as to ensure that the patient's concerns are properly dealt with.

This commitment mirrors, for example, the professional obligation imposed on a solicitor to act in the best interests of the client, which duty will involve an obligation to advise a client if the solicitor has been negligent in his or her conduct of the client's case.[5.2] It could be said that observance of this commitment will lead to an increase in the potential numbers of cases being pursued by way of litigation. Against this, it should be noted that patients are now much more aware of their rights and much more likely to pursue litigation, particularly if they have not been handled appropriately at the time when an adverse outcome occurs. There is a strong argument that the proper adoption of the commitments and underlying philosophy embodied in the protocol may in fact help to reduce the number of claims actually proceeding to litigation.

Patients' commitments

So far as the patients and their advisers are concerned, in paragraph 3.5 the protocol identifies the following commitments:

[5.2] See the *Guide to the Professional Conduct of Solicitors* (1996) as amended (published by The Law Society).

- to report any concerns and dissatisfaction as soon as is reasonably possible, thereby affording the provider opportunity to investigate and take appropriate action
- to consider the full range of options available. The intention is that the patient should not simply focus upon pursuing litigation but should look at the full range of options available, including requests for an explanation and meeting, use of the complaints procedure and other alternative dispute resolution methods. Of particular importance is the obligation on the adviser of the patient to have this breadth of approach when considering how best to advise the patient. In many respects litigation is an option of last resort
- to inform the healthcare provider when the patient is satisfied that the matter has been concluded. This commitment recognises the frequently heard complaint from the healthcare providers that there is inadequate communication and that the threat of litigation may still be lingering when in fact the patient has decided not to pursue a matter further.

The operation of the protocol

This is best understood by reference to the illustrative flowchart which appears at Annexe A to the protocol and which is reproduced in Figure 5.1 (with permission).

It will be noted that there are two parts to the protocol, namely the initial stages and the protocol stages.

The initial stages envisage the embracing of the above-mentioned aims and commitments, and assume that a responsible approach will be adopted. Hence on the patient's side of the equation there is communication and the identification of a problem, and on the healthcare provider's side there is identification of the adverse outcome, proper investigation and proper communication with the patient. It is essential to recognise that many clinical disputes are capable of being resolved at this stage without the need for professional advisers to become involved. Pro-active risk management and sensible patient-handling strategies should be considered. A defensive attitude is to be discouraged.

The protocol stages take effect when a satisfactory solution has not been worked out between patient and doctor. They are explained below.

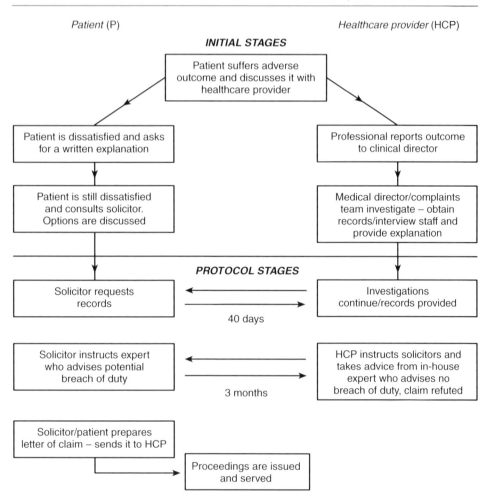

Patient (P)   *Healthcare provider* (HCP)

INITIAL STAGES

Patient suffers adverse
outcome and discusses it with
healthcare provider

Patient is dissatisfied and asks
for a written explanation

Professional reports outcome
to clinical director

Patient is still dissatisfied
and consults solicitor.
Options are discussed

Medical director/complaints
team investigate – obtain
records/interview staff and
provide explanation

PROTOCOL STAGES

Solicitor requests
records

Investigations
continue/records provided

40 days

Solicitor instructs expert
who advises potential
breach of duty

HCP instructs solicitors and
takes advice from in-house
expert who advises no
breach of duty, claim refuted

3 months

Solicitor/patient prepares
letter of claim – sends it to HCP

Proceedings are issued
and served

Figure 5.1: Illustrative flowchart. (Reproduced from the Procedure Rules
(1999) with permission from the Clinical Disputes Forum.)

Access to records

The first of the stages is for the patient's solicitor to gain access to
the clinical notes and records. This is done using a standard
request form following the model developed by the Law Society
Civil Litigation Committee and approved by the Department of
Health.[5.3] There is an obligation upon the healthcare provider to
provide the records within 40 days of request, and there are two
points to note about this.

[5.3] See Protocol Annexe B.

First, the charge for the records should be consistent with that envisaged under the Access to Health Records Act 1990,[5.4] i.e. £10.00, plus VAT plus the cost of photocopying and postage.[5.5] Secondly, it is envisaged that the patient can request records from any healthcare provider whether or not that provider is ultimately likely to be a party to proceedings. In other words, a third party healthcare provider who is not the target of any action is still required to provide records within 40 days upon request. The intention is that both the patient's advisers and ultimately the defendant's advisers will have access to the complete spectrum of records necessary to evaluate the case.

Failure to provide records within the 40-day period will be a breach of the protocol, rendering the offending party liable to sanction in accordance with the practice direction (see later). In this event, the solicitor for the claimant may under CPR 15.9 make application to court for an Order for Pre-Action disclosure of the records. However, an application to court can only be made where the recipient of the proceedings (called the 'Respondent' at this stage) is likely to become a party to the proceedings (i.e. to become the defendant). Prior to the commencement of proceedings there is no facility to seek a court order for disclosure of third-party records. However, if subsequently proceedings are commenced, and there has been non-compliance by a third party, then the fact of this breach of protocol will be relevant to the court in deciding what penalties to award against the offending party – probably in the form of an Order for Costs.

Expert opinion – and the letter of claim

Once the notes are received, then the patient's solicitor will analyse them and obtain appropriate expert opinion. There is no time limit for doing this, although the solicitor has to be mindful of the

---

[5.4] The Data Protection Act 1998 is not yet in force. When it is, it will be the primary source of the requirements regarding the holding and disclosure of records.

[5.5] Charges for the provision of records are a vexed issue. It is felt by many general practitioners that the Access to Health Records Act charge of £10.00 plus VAT is inadequate, especially when the records have to be checked so as to ensure that information which may be harmful to the patient is removed or properly handled. Thus around the country various initiatives are being undertaken to try to agree standard charging mechanisms for the provision of such records. It is hoped that overall consistency will be achieved in the near future. An example of one such system is that organised by the Devon general practitioners. This was an agreement between the Devon LMCs and two local Law Societies dated November 1998.

overall limitation period[5.6] for bringing a claim. If, after having received expert advice, it is decided to pursue the matter further, then the claimant's solicitor has to send a detailed letter of claim (*see* p. 179). This is an important point. The protocol sets out a template of matters which are to be incorporated within such a letter.[5.7] The general intention is that the letters should be sufficiently detailed to enable the recipient to understand in broad terms the nature of the case that is to be made out. The letter will incorporate the relevant dates and chronology and the main allegations of negligence and causation. It is also intended that details of the claimant's injuries should be identified and, in straightforward cases, details of financial losses. The letter of claim may also include an offer to settle. The tactics of this issue are explored in greater detail below.

The response

Upon receipt of the detailed letter of claim, the recipient healthcare provider has to (a) acknowledge receipt of the letter within 14 days and (b) within three months of the date of receipt of the letter, respond in full. There is a similar obligation imposed upon the healthcare provider to indicate the nature of their position. If the case is admitted, then that needs to be stated and it is important to note that admissions are binding.[5.8] To the extent that the claim or any part of it is denied, then the healthcare provider should make their position clear by providing specific comments on the issues and indicating the areas of challenge. If additional documentation is to be relied upon (e.g. internal protocols), then these should be disclosed. Furthermore, there should be a response to any offer to settle, ranging from acceptance to rejection or counter-proposal. Again the protocol is recognising the facility for the matter to be resolved without the commencement of proceed-

---

[5.6] The position about limitation periods is dealt with in Chapter 6.

[5.7] See Protocol Appendix C.

[5.8] At paragraph 3.25 of the protocol, reference is made to the healthcare provider's response to the letter of claim, and there is a note to the effect that the healthcare provider should indicate whether any admissions will be binding. This is a drafting point which will need correction when the next edition of the protocols is printed. As one of the co-authors of the protocol the author of this chapter can state that there was unanimity of opinion among those who drafted the protocol that any admission made by either party should be binding and not be capable of being reversed at any stage. Hence it was not intended that there should be any potential for later withdrawals of admissions.

ings. However, if the matter is not resolved, then at this point court proceedings are commenced.

The periods allowed in the protocol stages for responses were deemed to be reasonable by the Working Party that wrote the protocol. However, they are not inflexible. To the extent that any party may have difficulty in complying with a period, then there is a common-sense requirement to notify the other side and reach an accommodation. The protocol also recognises that in circumstances where the limitation date[5.9] may be very close, protocol periods may be inappropriate, but at this stage the probability is that there will have to be some flexibility in terms of the subsequent handling of the procedural steps on the case so as to accommodate the required investigation time.

It may be seen that the protocol is designed to create a greater degree of openness and exchange of information. It is suggested that if the spirit of the protocol is complied with, then many cases ought to be resolved more rapidly and before legal proceedings are commenced. The attraction of this mechanism for settlement is particularly obvious in lower-value cases.

Court procedure

The commencement of court proceedings is now a much simplified procedure. There is currently a single claim form (which replaces the old High Court Writ or County Court Summons) which can be used in all personal injury cases. The nomenclature has changed consistent with a desire for the rules to be more understandable (*see* Glossary). The standard procedure for starting proceedings is set out in Part 7 of the CPR.

High Court/County Court

Both High Court and County Court continue in existence, but the former deals with the more complex cases.

A clinical negligence case involving personal injury must not be commenced in the High Court unless the claimant expects to recover £50 000 or more. In other circumstances the claim is to be commenced in the County Court.

[5.9] See note 5.6.

The claim form itself is a standardised document which is relatively simple to fill in and which contains details about the parties, the broad allegations being made and the nature of the damages claimed. The information that is provided on the claim form is rather similar to that which was provided on the old High Court Writ form. The use of this procedure also means that it is relatively easy to issue proceedings in cases where the limitation period is about to expire.[5.10]

In the clinical negligence case the claimant will then serve detailed Particulars of Claim (this nomenclature applies whether the case is in the High Court or the County Court). The Particulars of Claim have to comply with the requirements of CPR 6.4.1 and 6.4.2, and it should be noted that in personal injury cases there is an obligation to comply further with Practice Direction PD16. In essence, the Particulars of Claim are to specify full details about the claimant, including the claimant's date of birth and details of the injury sustained, details of the nature of the case and the allegations of negligence which are being made, details of the nature of any damages claim being sought and, in particular, specific information if a provisional damages award[5.11] is to be made. Furthermore, the claimant is obliged to attach to the Particulars of Claim a schedule of any past and future expenses and losses which are to be claimed, and is required to serve a report from a medical practitioner detailing the personal injuries which are alleged to have occurred. In the context of a clinical negligence case, the claimant will have to serve a medical report detailing the injuries which, it is alleged, have resulted

---

[5.10] Where the limitation period is about to expire the position can be protected by completing the basic claim form and lodging that with the court. The previous County Court requirement to lodge detailed Particulars of Claim and supporting documentation is thereby removed.

[5.11] Provisional damages were introduced by Section 32A of the Supreme Court Act 1981 and came into operation on 1 July 1985. The intention was to allow the courts to adopt a different approach (i.e. a 'wait-and-see' approach in circumstances where the medical prognosis was particularly uncertain and where there was a chance, falling short of probability, that some serious disease or serious deterioration of a claimant's condition may accrue at a later date. For example, in the case of someone suffering head injury with an associated risk of developing epilepsy at an indeterminate future date, an award of provisional damages may be appropriate. The claimant would then receive compensation for the fact of the head injury itself and its attendant treatment and the related financial losses. However, the risk of epilepsy would not be taken into account, but the claimant would be given a facility to return to the court if at a future date epilepsy developed and could be proven to be related to the original tortious event giving rise to liability. In that event, a further award of compensation would be payable.

from the negligence complained of. The new dispensation makes the process of drafting Particulars of Claim much less formal than used to be the case. PD16 paragraph 10.3 specifically recognises that Particulars of Claim may include:

- a reference to any point of law on which the claim is based
- the name of any witness whom the claimant wishes to call
- a copy of any document which the claimant considers is necessary to the claim.

The flexibility afforded by this approach is significant, and it remains to be seen how the parties are likely to operate the tactics of this process (i.e. just how much 'new information' will be introduced at this stage).

When the defendant is served with the claim form and Particulars of Claim, then he or she has to respond. If the claim is to be admitted, then a form of admission will be completed. If the defendant wishes to contest the case, then there is a requirement to file a defence within 14 days. If the defendant wishes to contest the claim but needs more than 14 days to prepare the defence, as will usually be the case in a clinical negligence matter, then the defendant has to file an Acknowledgement of Service – CPR Rule 7.8 (1). This is part of form N9.

Assuming that an Acknowledgement of Service is filed, then the defendant gains an extension of time of 14 days to file the defence (i.e. there is a 28-day period for filing). In addition, where more time is required then the defendant and the claimant may, under CPR Rule 15.5, agree that the period for filing a defence shall be extended by up to 28 days. Where this is done, the defendant must notify the court in writing – in accordance with Rule 15.5 (2). This means that there is now a relatively strict time limit for dealing with the service of the defence, even in a clinical negligence case. If any further extension of time is required then this cannot be consented to between the parties. It has to be specifically approved by the court, and an application will have to be made under CPR Rule 3.1 (2) (a).

The defence itself is required to be a much fuller document. A simple denial of liability is unacceptable. There is a requirement to set out the extent to which any allegations are admitted or denied. To the extent that there are denials then the defendant must state the reasons for them. If there is a different version of events from that given by the claimant, then the defendant's version must be put forward. The clear intention is that the claimant should then know the nature of the case which he or she has to meet. In addition, under PD 16, paragraph 14.1, in the context of a personal injury case where the claimant has served the required medical report, then the defendant has to indicate whether that medical report is agreed or, if it is disputed, what the reasons for dispute are, and if the defendant seeks to rely upon his or her own medical evidence then it should be attached to the defence. Interestingly, the only mandatory requirement is for the defendant to attach any report intended to be replied upon *which was available at the time of drafting the defence.*

Furthermore, if the claimant has served a detailed schedule of losses and expenses then the defendant must include in or attach to his or her defence a counter-schedule indicating which items are agreed/in dispute or neither agreed nor disputed because of lack of knowledge – as set out in PD 16 paragraph 14.2 (1).

Further information

There is facility for either party to seek more information about the case. The old rules of requesting Further and Better Particulars/Interrogatories have been abolished and replaced by CPR Part 18.

The start of the process is for either party to write to the other side indicating the information or clarification which is sought and giving a reasonable period within which to respond. Ideally a date should be set by which the response should be served (PD 18 paragraph 1.1). If no response is received, or if it is inadequate, then there is facility to make application to court. The request may be made by letter or in a separate document (i.e. a much less formal process than was previously the case), but the request must comply with PD 18 paragraph 1.6 (1). The court may then make an Order detailing what information is to be provided and the appropriate timescale. The intention is that this process should help the parties to understand more clearly the nature of the case that is being brought. It should be borne in mind that the overriding objective (see above) has to be complied with, and there is also the issue of proportionality. Very detailed requests for further information which are complex and involved, requiring much time to answer, may be inappropriate in a case of relatively small value. A sensible balance has to be struck here.

Allocation

In order to ensure that contested cases are dealt with speedily and efficiently, the CPR creates three separate trial 'tracks'. The small-claims track is intended for cases worth under £5000, except for personal injury claims, where the limit is £1000. This is not likely to be applicable in the context of clinical negligence (and will not be commented on further here). The fast track is intended for cases between £5000 and £15 000, or between £1000 and £15 000 for personal injury claims. The multi-track is for more complex cases, and includes all claims which may have a potential value within one of the other two tracks but which, by reason of complexity and length of trial, are considered inappropriate for that track.

In the context of clinical negligence cases, the probability is that they should be allocated to the multi-track, bearing in mind the factors set out at CPR 26.8 and also bearing in mind the recommendations of Lord Woolf in the final report Chapter 2, paragraphs 15 and 16.[5.12] The expectation is that clinical negligence cases, regardless of value, are more likely to fall into the multi-track. However, it is possible that if the case is relatively straightforward and of low value it could still be allocated to the fast track.

Track allocation occurs when a defendant files a defence. At this time, the court will serve an Allocation Questionnaire in form N150 on each party. The allocation questionnaire requires information to be provided by both parties so that the court can then determine the appropriate track. Interestingly, the questionnaire will incorporate questions about the compliance with the pre-action protocol. If there is any uncertainty about allocation, then a hearing may be set to determine this issue – CPR Rule 26.5 (4).

Once allocation to a track has been determined, then the relevant case-management regime for the particular track will apply.

Case management

As previously indicated, one of the key features of the CPR is case management, with the aim being to ensure that a matter is brought on for trial as expeditiously as possible. The judges now

---

[5.12] It was recognised that clinical negligence cases were by definition professional negligence cases and, as such, involved more complex issues. The case management approach afforded by the multi-track was felt to be more appropriate for this type of case.

have considerable power to determine the conduct of litigation and apply sanctions, with the ultimate power being contained in CPR 3.4 to strike out a case for default.

Fast-track case management

Cases operating within the fast track will be given standardised directions – see CPR Rule 28 and see also the appendix to PD 28. Typically they will include directions for disclosure of documents (to the extent that this has not already been dealt with via the protocol), the service of factual witness statements, the exchange of expert evidence and fixing a date for trial or a period in which the trial is to take place. Note that within the fast track a 1-day trial is intended to occur within 30 weeks of directions (see below).

There is flexibility within the system. Thus at the time of dealing with the Allocation Questionnaire, the parties are encouraged to agree suitable directions to be submitted to the court, and the court will take them into account although it is not bound by them even if they are totally agreed between the parties. Furthermore, there is a facility for variation of the directions timetable, but this has to be done on application to court – CPR Rule 28.4 (1). Whilst the intention is that any time limits for compliance of directions should be adhered to, nevertheless the overriding objective (Rule 1.3) has to be borne in mind and the parties are expected to co-operate within sensible limits.

Multi-track

The multi-track approach is much more tailored to the individual case. When the case is so allocated the procedural judge will decide whether to give directions or to fix a case management conference or pre-trial review. The procedural judge will take a view as to the complexity of the case and the amount of work required to have it prepared for trial. The parties will have indicated their views about directions at the allocation questionnaire stage, and it will be open to the procedural judge to make an Order of his or her own motion giving more or less standardised directions, or to adopt the parties' suggested directions. However, in the context of clinical negligence cases, it is more likely that a case management conference will ensue where tailored directions will be given appropriate to the issues in the particular case.

Under the previous dispensation the position on medical negligence cases (as they were then called) was dealt with by Practice Direction 49, which required the parties to lodge pleadings, provide a statement of the case and then consider the appropriate directions that would be required for the matter to be brought on for trial. At the present time there is no equivalent Practice Direction supporting the CPR, although it is understood that this is being considered. It is therefore likely that a procedural judge dealing with a clinical negligence case will not only have available the relevant Particulars of Claim and Defence, but may also require the parties to provide additional information so that he or she may have a better understanding of the issues.

The case management conference is very much part of the overall system of active case management by the courts. This is not simply intended to be a directions hearing. Instead, it is intended that the parties should explore the real issues between them, and there will be considerable flexibility for the judge to make directions to deal with the disposal of the case. The solicitors actually having conduct of the case on behalf of the relevant parties should attend, and it will no longer be acceptable to send someone ill informed, such as a trainee solicitor or an inadequately briefed agent. Furthermore, it is quite likely that some procedural judges will ask for the attendance of the lay client, a point envisaged by Lord Woolf in his final report. At the case management conference the court will, as prescribed by PD 29 paragraph 5.1, conduct a thorough review of the position on the case and look at its state of preparedness, decide the directions needed to progress the case to a conclusion in accordance with the overriding objective, note any reasonable agreements between the parties as to matters in issue and as to the future conduct of the action, and record those agreements.

The court will usually issue directions dealing with any remaining issues concerning the disclosure of documents, the disclosure of witness statements and summaries of witness statements, the nature of and the terms for disclosure of expert evidence (a point that will be considered in greater detail below), whether the matter should be listed for trial, and whether any further case-management conference or pre-trial review may be required.

Split trial

There remains the facility for the courts to order a split trial and to order, for example, that trial of the issues relating to liability and causation be dealt with in advance of issues of quantum. This tactic has already been deployed with great success in clinical negligence cases, and its importance is recognised in the new rules. It is highly likely that the procedural judge will use this type of direction to ensure that the key issues are disposed of in the most expeditious way. Particularly in the more complex cases involving serious injury, the ability to have an initial trial on liability/causation may well speed up the process, involve a shorter trial length and have subsequent costs savings, both to the courts and to the funders such as the Legal Aid Board. Furthermore, in the event that the case is unsuccessful, unnecessary expense on the investigation of quantum issues will have been spared. Alternatively, if the case succeeds at split trial, then the court will have the power to make an interim payment and then to give directions for quantum trial which may involve more flexible arrangements and possibly the use of joint experts on certain issues.

Trial

Under both the fast-track and multi-track regimes there is a facility to use listing questionnaires so as to assist in fixing an appropriate trial date or trial period. The questionnaires encompass requests for information about the number of witnesses, the types of witness and their availability.

Fast-track listing

A trial date or a period in which the trial is to take place will be given in fast-track cases as part of the standard directions at the track allocation stage (see above). If a trial period is given, then it should not normally exceed 3 weeks, and furthermore the trial date of period should not be more than 30 weeks for the date of the directions. In the context of clinical negligence cases, it is recognised that this relatively short time period is likely to impose pressures upon parties, practitioners and experts alike. Although some courts may operate a block-listing type approach, it is nevertheless suggested that in the context of clinical negligence a specific direction may be required in order to actually allocate a date. There needs to be liaison with the Court Listing Officers.

Multi-track listing

The requirements for listing in the multi-track are dealt with in CPR Rule 29.2 (2), which provides that the court must fix the trial date or period in which the trial will take place as soon as is practicable. The listing questionnaire will provide source material for the Listing Office to try to achieve a sensible date and, furthermore, liaison at the case-management/pre-trial review stage will also be appropriate. It is suggested that, in the context of clinical negligence cases operating in the multi-track, application should be made to obtain a fixed trial date rather than a trial period, particularly in view of the problems relating to the availability of expert witnesses.

Not only are the issues of trial listing and length of trial determined by the court, but there is also power with a procedural judge to determine a trial timetable, and the court may determine which issues are to be dealt with, in what sequence and at what time. For example, it may be sensible to take all of the factual evidence on the first day and then to have the parties' experts give evidence on the following days, with experts of like discipline appearing one after the other. The key point is to determine the most appropriate and effective way for hearing the issue. The judge will therefore have discretion to determine the order in which witnesses should be called, and can impose time limits for the length of opening arguments, closing arguments and the like.

The trial judge will also be provided with appropriate trial bundles containing all of the necessary documentation, duly ordered and paginated. These have to be lodged not more than 7 days and not less than 3 days before trial – CPR Rule 39.5 (2).

Mode of trial

In the context of clinical negligence cases and in accordance with the general rule in CPR Rule 39.2(1), it is likely that trials will be conducted in public and will be before a single judge. The type of judge will depend upon the size and complexity of the case. Cases issued in the High Court and involving large sums of damages or complex issues will probably be tried by a High Court Judge. More moderate cases, whether in the County Court or in the High Court, are likely to be dealt with by a Circuit Judge, and there is the potential for lower-value, less complex cases to be tried by a

District Judge. Consideration as to the appropriate level of judge should be given at the case-management stage/listing.

Appeals

There is facility for either party to appeal the outcome of trial. In broad terms, appeals are limited to two areas, either the trial judge having erred in law or the trial judge having given judgement in a way which may be perceived as perverse and contrary to the evidence adduced.

The new rules are very much the same as the old ones. Permission to appeal is always required (in the context of personal injury cases). The position on procedure is governed by the practice direction (Court of Appeal: Leave to Appeal on Skeleton Arguments) 1999 1 *WLR* 2. When permission is given, then Notice of Appeal must be served not later than 4 weeks after the date on which the Judgement or Order below was sealed or otherwise perfected in the High Court, or in the case of an appeal in the County Court from the date on which the court gave its decision. Provided an application for permission is made within the 4-week period, the Notice of Appeal may alternatively be served within 7 days from the date of permission.

Once an appeal is lodged, then there is facility for the respondent party to lodge a cross-appeal. Thereafter, the Civil Appeals Office will deal with the directions necessary for the matter to be brought on for hearing.

Tactical issues – payments into court and offers to settle

This position is governed by Part 36 of CPR and complements the position envisaged under the protocol. Whereas under the old rules there was only a tactical advantage afforded to the defendant through the payment into court mechanism, now the playing field is more level as a result of the introduction of Part 36 offers to settle.

Part 36 offer

An offer to settle can be made before or after the commencement of proceedings. Whilst an offer can be made in any form, for it to be sure of having efficacy so far as the potential for sanctions is concerned, it must comply with the supporting practice direction PD 36 and should therefore appear in the prescribed form. It is open to either party to make a Part 36 offer. However, in the context of the defendant seeking to settle a monetary claim, then after the commencement of court proceedings the defendant will be required to use the payment-into-court method rather than simply to make an offer.

It is probable that the use of offers to settle will become prevalent. There is significant tactical advantage to a claimant in making a pre-litigation offer. Not only may this have the potential to bring a case to a conclusion *per se* but, noting the above comments about the protocol, a response is demanded from the defendant and if the offer is not accepted, a counter-proposal may be forthcoming. Hence it is highly likely that many smaller-value cases may be disposed of via this route.

Similarly, there are tactical advantages to the claimant in making a Part 36 offer after the commencement of proceedings. An imaginative approach can be adopted. Not only can proposals be put forward for the overall settlement of the case (i.e. a monetary proposal), but it is possible to use this mechanism to resolve areas of dispute (e.g. a formal offer to agree issues of causation, subject to particular findings on liability). In that scenario, if accepted, the offer would remove the need for investigation of the causation issue, thereby minimising costs.

In general terms, the recipient party has 21 days in which to accept an offer. If the offer is to be accepted, then this should be done on the prescribed form. If the offer is made after the commencement of proceedings, then the Notice of Acceptance will need to lodged at the court.

If a Part 36 offer is made by a claimant but is not accepted by the defendant and the matter then proceeds to trial, with the claimant recovering a sum equal to or greater than the Part 36 offer, the claimant will be entitled to ask the court for interest on the whole or part of any sum of money awarded to the claimant at a rate not exceeding 10% above base rate (CPR 36.21(2)), and in addition may recover costs on an indemnity basis and interest on those costs at a maximum of 10% above base rate. These penalties apply in any situation where a Part 36 offer has been made after the commencement of proceedings. Where a Part 36 offer was made prior to the commencement of proceedings, then this may still be effective, but the only penalty that is likely to attach relates to the facility of a court to award costs (CPR 36.10(1)).

Similarly, if the defendant makes a Part 36 offer which is not acceptable by the claimant, and is not improved upon at trial by the claimant, then the defendant will be entitled to recover the costs incurred from the date for acceptance of the offer unless it is unjust to do so (CPR 36.20). In addition, the claimant would not be able to recover his or her costs of the action incurred after the date for acceptance of the offer. The penalty is therefore very similar to that for failing to beat a Part 36 payment into court.

Part 36 payment into court

As previously indicated, the intention is that after the commencement of proceedings any party seeking to settle a money claim being made against it must effect a payment into court, and a Part 36 offer will not suffice. The new rules are virtually identical to the old rules concerning payments into court. The recipient of a Part 36 payment into court has 21 days in which to accept. If a claimant accepts the defendant's offer, then the claimant will receive that sum and costs.

If a claimant rejects a payment into court, proceeds to trial and fails to beat the payment into court, the claimant will recover whatever sum is ordered to be paid by the court but will have to meet the defendant's costs incurred after the date for acceptance, and will have to stand his or her own costs after that date.

It follows that whether in the Part 36 offer scenario or Part 36 payment-into-court scenario, either party is only likely to proceed if there is a high degree of confidence that the offer/payment can be improved upon. The overall effect should be the earlier resolution of cases, and possibly reduced incidence of trial.

General remarks

The above represents a résumé of the key features of the new civil procedure in terms of the requirements for the rules themselves and the tactical considerations that will apply. It remains to be seen how effective this reform is, but the initial impressions suggest that there will have to be a cultural change in the approach being adopted by claimant and defendants alike, with the probability being that earlier settlement will be stimulated in a significant proportion of cases.

Practical issues – case preparation and stages to trial

Preparation

This section analyses the practical considerations facing solicitors dealing with clinical negligence cases. In the same way as there has been radical reform of the civil procedure rules themselves, so the legal scene itself has undergone significant change at the close of the twentieth century. The number of solicitors handling clinical negligence claims on behalf of defendants has dramatically fallen. The main defence organisations, namely the Medical Defence Union, the Medical and Dental Defence Union of Scotland and the Medical Protection Society, have for many years operated using only very small panels of solicitors to handle their work. Similarly, with the advent of the NHSLA there has been dramatic rationalisation of the number of legal firms providing legal services for NHS Trusts, the panel now having only 18 members. The conduct of defence clinical negligence litigation is in the hands of a very small number of competent practitioners.

The claimant's scene has changed dramatically. There have been a number of initiatives. Action for Victims of Medical Accidents (AVMA) has for a number of years operated a specialist panel of solicitors whom it has judged competent to handle clinical negligence claims on behalf of claimants. To qualify for that panel an individual practitioner has to demonstrate experience and competence. This is an exacting test. Similarly, in 1995 the Law Society responded to widespread concern about the conduct of clinical negligence cases by incompetent practitioners (the case of *Blackburn v Newcastle Health Authority* being a highlighted example) by creating the medical negligence panel. Whilst not actually described as a 'specialist' panel, the test for panel membership is virtually as exacting as that demanded by AVMA, so that only those truly adjudged competent qualify. The current figures are that, as at 18 February 1999, 136 law firms had either a Law Society or AVMA panel member, the Law Society panel had 151 individual members located in 112 law firms, and AVMA had 130 individuals within 99 firms.

It is recognised that a very substantial proportion of all clinical negligence cases are supported by legal aid. The Legal Aid Board became particularly concerned that its work should be undertaken only by those judged to be wholly competent in the area, and hence introduced the concept of franchising. With effect from 1 August 1999, legal aid for clinical negligence cases will only be granted to practitioners operating within franchised firms who have demonstrated ability in the area. Membership of either or both the AVMA and Law Society panels is mandatory. As at June 1999, approximately 170 franchises had been granted by the Legal Aid Board. It should be noted that a law firm that has more than one office may thereby have more than one franchise. The author's firm, for example, has four franchises, one for each office. The total number of participant firms is of the order of 140. The Legal Aid Board's figures published in their response to the Lord Chancellor's consultation paper *Access to Justice with Conditional Fees* (May 1998) indicated that in the year 1996/1997, of 11 400 civil medical negligence legal aid cases billed to the Legal Aid Board, only 2632 (23.1%) were dealt with by a firm with at least one panel member. Hence the vast majority of legal aid cases were dealt with by seemingly less experienced practitioners. There was a very significant difference in the success rate, with panel members producing virtually double the number of successful cases, with a correspondingly higher recovery of compensation. For every £1 they cost the tax-payer in legal aid fees, the specialist won £4.10 in damages, compared to £2.50 for recognised personal injury solicitors and only £1.70 for other solicitors. There was noted to be a high failure rate, and the Legal Aid Board publicly expressed the view that one of the main reasons for this was that people were represented by lawyers who were not experts in clinical negligence law.

The effect of this change is that there should be a significant improvement in the quality of the conduct of clinical negligence litigation. Consistent with the spirit of the protocol and with Lord Woolf's ambitions, cases ought now to be properly scrutinised by those having an expert level of knowledge of the subject. In theory, the incidence of spurious or vexatious cases should be much reduced (although the evidence for this was largely anecdotal).[5.13] The incidence of early claim resolution as a result of responsible risk management and claims-handling strategies ought to be significantly heightened, and of the remaining proportion of cases where

---

[5.13] Within a recent article by Claire Dyer[1] (legal correspondent), the Medical Protection Society Director, John Hickie, is quoted as saying the following: 'all of the figures show that GPs face an ever-growing risk of having to defend themselves against lawsuits ... with both the reputation and the livelihood of our members to protect, monies spent on legal costs and expert opinion to defend doctors against claims, including many that are subsequently found to be spurious. Typically, such actions are brought on legal aid and

settlement has not proved possible, only those where there are genuine arguments ought now to appear before the courts. This may not lead to a reduction in the actual incidence of litigation claims, but at least there ought to be an improvement in the speed with which they are dealt with and resolved, with consequent costs savings.

Case-handling

The above remarks being noted, it may be worthwhile considering the appropriate approach to the handling of a clinical negligence case. This is given from the perspective of the claimant's solicitor. This section therefore analyses the practical approach to be adopted, consistent with the legal requirement set out in the first section.

Initial screening

Case screening is now a fundamental part of good legal practice. It is demanded by the Legal Aid Board under the terms of its franchising criteria. In any event, good business practice, including the obligation to give best advice to the client, demands that this type of process be performed. It is fundamentally wrong to build false hopes and expectations for a client, especially one who may be aggrieved by the performance of another profession. Furthermore, the pure financial constraints of legal practice mean only those cases which have genuine merit ought to be taken on. The remuneration now to be paid under the legal aid scheme is limited if the case fails, and of course if other funding mechanisms such as conditional fees are used, then no fee may be recoverable at all. There is no doubt that this focuses the mind.

Accordingly, the most competent claimant practitioners operate quite detailed systems for case screening. The aim is to identify the case which has genuine merit, by which is meant not only that there are viable grounds for alleging negligence and causation, but

---

then dropped by the plaintiffs when it becomes clear there is no sustainable case against the GP concerned. The Medical Protection Society have spent nearly £7 000 000 over the past 5 years on cases that were subsequently abandoned, and this money cannot be recovered from the plaintiff.'

The above point ought to go some way towards redressing this unsatisfactory position.

also that the case is economically worthwhile. It is not sensible to advise a client to pursue a claim worth only a few hundred pounds when the costs of doing so are likely to run into thousands of pounds. Furthermore, experience shows that at first interview, proper identification of the client's concerns may indicate that remedies other than compensation are appropriate – remember the commitments of the protocol. Hence it is true to say that many cases fall by the wayside at initial screening – some have no merit, some are too low in value to justify investigation, and some are more appropriate to the complaints procedure.

Assuming that the first hurdle is crossed and that there seems to be a case worthy of investigation, then the following stages will be undertaken. It is worth emphasising that at each of the ensuing stages, a review of merits is undertaken. This is therefore a constantly evolving process with appraisal and reappraisal of the position.

Access to records

Having obtained the client's account of the circumstances of the case, it is then necessary to gain access to the notes and records, and the protocol procedure described in Section 1 above is used. It is vitally important to gather together a complete medical record, including clinical notes, test results, X-rays, etc. One needs a complete understanding of the medical picture in order properly to assess the issues of liability and causation. The issues of liability may well focus on only a limited part of the clinical notes and records, but issues of causation can be highly complex, and an understanding of a patient's history is frequently necessary.

Having received the records, it is necessary to check that all are present and any omissions should be chased. The records should then be organised and paginated, analysed, and a summary of the key issues prepared, with a chronology if necessary. Most experienced practitioners will undertake this themselves, frequently supported by expert medically qualified assistants (e.g. nurses, GPs, etc.) who may have been recruited into the particular legal firm. The aim at this stage is to understand the clinical records and the issues revealed by them, and also to check how this marries with the client's testimony. It will also be necessary to research the relevant area of medicine in order to understand the prevailing clinical practice effective at the time.

It is worth noting that a proportion of cases fall by the wayside at this stage. The clinical notes may be at significant variance with the client's recollection and testimony, such that the claim is felt not to be worthwhile and/or unmeritorious.

Expert advice

Having conducted the above analysis it is then necessary to obtain expert advice. It is important to approach the correct expert (i.e. one competent to comment upon the relevant discipline). Although medico-legal experience is helpful, it is not the 'be all and end all'. It is more important to have the appropriate level of clinical exper-tise. In the case of GPs negligence, it may well be necessary to approach a GP expert to comment upon the applicable standard of care, and it may also be necessary to approach another expert to comment upon the causation aspect of the case (e.g. in a case of negligent failure to diagnose temporal arterioritis, it may be neces-sary to seek an ophthalmic opinion on outcome and whether blindness may have been avoided had prompt diagnosis and referral been undertaken). Once expert evidence has been received, then that should be analysed and any follow-up queries pursued. Again a proportion of cases may fall by the wayside at this stage.

Case conference

In the significant majority of clinical negligence cases, a case conference is the appropriate next step. At this time, the client, solicitor, barrister and relevant experts can get together to review the overall position on the case. The purpose is to test the merits of the case and to determine whether to proceed further. The confer-ence serves not only as an appropriate mechanism for testing the strengths and weaknesses of the issues, and indeed the quality of the expert evidence, but is also vitally important for the client. They need to know and understand the nature of the process with which they are involved, and to participate in the decision-making process of whether to pursue the case further. Furthermore, frequently the client has a perspective to offer which can funda-mentally affect the expert thinking with regard to circumstances of the case and hence its merits (e.g. the client may well have a clear recollection of the discussions which took place with the GP and the advice given, which may help to clarify an absence of informa-tion in the notes).

Pursuant to the conference an opinion may be written for purposes of legal aid. The solicitor will be in a position to formulate the appropriate letter of claim, and later the barrister will be better able to draft the Particulars of Claim. This is an important tactical consideration. The clearer the claimant's solicitor/barrister is about the case, the better formulated the claim will be, and the more seriously the case will be taken by the other side.

Protocol and court proceedings

As noted above, the clinical negligence pre-action protocol will have to be complied with, and the receipt of the defence response to the letter of claim will obviously be a key time for review and will prompt further enquiry of experts' review with the client and the like.

If the case does not resolve at this time, then the next appropriate review stage will be when the defence is received. Whether it is likely that a defence will reveal more than is indicated in the response to the pre-action letter remains to be seen, but nevertheless review is essential.

After the receipt of the defence and issuing of case-management directions, the next key stage is the exchange of factual evidence. This is a fundamentally important part of clinical negligence cases. From the claimant's perspective, it is at this stage that the clearest indication of the defence position is noted. Here one receives the testimony from the defendant and relevant factual witnesses. This frequently reveals a difference in factual account/recollection, and inevitably requires further review both with the client and with experts. It is pursuant to this stage that experts will be asked to finalise their opinions for the purpose of exchange.

There then follows the exchange of experts' evidence. It is probably only at this stage that the parties learn which experts have been instructed, and can then analyse the way in which the expert evidence is being argued. This inevitably leads to further review by the claimant and experts. It could lead to the obtaining of additional expert evidence to cover points not previously appreciated. It is at this time that there needs to be a reappraisal of the overall merits of the case, and this may involve the organisation of further pre-trial conference with counsel.

It is anticipated that pursuant to the exchange of experts' evidence, the case-management directions may require there to be meetings of experts. This issue is considered elsewhere in this book (*see* Chapter 10). Suffice it to say that such meetings require careful handling and clear agendas, and of themselves afford a further opportunity for clarification of the issues in the case. By way of example, in a case involving failure to visit a patient and diagnose meningitis, leading to complications and permanent deafness, a meeting of experts may determine the time by which treatment would have to have been effected in order to prevent permanent deafness, thus setting the scene so far as causation is concerned – a situation which could have arisen in the case of *Polson v De Silva* (unreported 4 March 1999).

Finally, the trial stage is reached and, as observed above, the use of a split trial tactic is extremely important in this area of practice. The ability to be able to bring relatively defined issues before the court which of themselves may be dispositive of the case is very important. The claimant's solicitor will be looking to identify the correct tactical approach with this viewpoint in mind. Frequently, one sees that the progression to split trial leads to the resolution of the whole case.

The above analysis serves to demonstrate a sensible, careful approach to the contested case. The actual incidence of contested clinical negligence trials is exceedingly low, with most experienced practitioners in the field indicating that they personally only handle one or two fully contested trials at most in any given year.

Funding

It is not proposed to go into any great detail in this section, but merely to outline the possible funding mechanisms available for clinical negligence cases, and thereby to demonstrate the very significant practical hurdles which the vast majority of people face who contemplate bringing even a perfectly valid claim. The main funding mechanisms are legal aid, conditional fee agreements, legal expense insurance policies, after-the-event insurance policies and private funding.

Legal aid

As noted above, this remains the principal area of funding for clinical negligence cases. Whilst the Lord Chancellor has announced the intention to remove legal aid from personal injury cases, and has included provision for this within the Access to

Justice Act, clinical negligence cases are, for the time being, to continue to receive legal aid support. The franchising criteria noted above apply so far as the practitioner firms are concerned.

For the individual to qualify for a Legal Aid Certificate there is a twofold test. First, the case has to be proved to be meritorious (i.e. there has to be a reasonable prospect of succeeding). Secondly, the client has to fall within the financial threshold. The current qualifications (as at June 1999) are as follows:

- income – to qualify for free legal aid, £2625 per annum – upper limit beyond which legal aid is not available, £8571
- capital – to qualify for free legal aid, £3000 – upper limit beyond which legal aid is not available, £8560.

So far as the merits test is concerned, the Legal Aid Board are themselves taking on board Lord Woolf's concerns for proportionality. The recently issued consultation document on legal aid funding[5.14] envisaged a merits test which would have as part of its criteria the potential value of the case measured against the potential cost of pursuing the litigation. A case could fail to qualify for legal aid simply because it was felt to be too expensive when judged against value and the prospects of success. It is likely that a test of this type will come into force.

It should be remembered that, whilst the vast majority of children will qualify for free legal aid (having no income or savings of their own), of the remaining population, only those who are likely to qualify for means-tested benefit are likely to obtain free legal aid. For the majority of people who continue to work or who have modest savings, legal aid will simply not be available.

Conditional fee agreements

Conditional fee agreements came into force in July 1995, pursuant to the amendment of Section 8 – Courts and Legal Services Act 1999. The intention of conditional fee agreements was to try to meet the need of the MINELAS (Middle Income – Not Eligible for Legal Aid). This is the so-called no-win, no-fee arrangement which is now seen as the desired funding option to replace legal aid for other personal injury cases (despite much protest from consumers,

---

[5.14] *Modernising Justice – The Funding Code*, issued by the Legal Aid Board, January 1999.

the Law Society and Bar Council). In simple terms, the conditional fee agreement operates on the basis that the solicitor enters into a contractual arrangement with the client whereby the case will be pursued on a no-win, no-fee arrangement. If the case is lost, the solicitor does not recover any costs from the other side and further is not able to charge the client. Any disbursements (i.e. court fees, medical report fees, etc.) are either to be met by the client or will be funded under the terms of an insurance policy. The client still has the liability to meet the defendant's costs, and again this is protected by an insurance policy. There are a number of insurance products on the market to support this conditional fee arrangement. For example, the Medical Accident Protect Scheme (offered by the same brokers as Accident Line Protect) requires a premium payable in three stages:

- stage 1 – £1250 plus insurance premium tax
- stage 2 – £2500 plus insurance premium tax
- stage 3 – £3900 plus insurance premium tax.

The total indemnity provided is £100 000. The different stages are to cover the different stages of investigation. Hence stage 1 is up to the receipt of the defence, stage 2 is up to the point just before setting down for trial, and stage 3 goes to trial or the conclusion of the case. It may be seen that these insurance premiums are very expensive, and for many clients will be prohibitively so. However, they are still significantly cheaper than private funding.

If the case is successful, then the claimant recovers the assessed compensation and the losing defendant meets the claimant's legal costs. However, the claimant also has to pay a success fee to the claimant's solicitor which in essence recognises the risk taken by that solicitor in operating on a no-win, no-fee basis. The success fee is calculated as a percentage of the claimant's solicitors costs. The success fee will not exceed 100%, and in any event will be capped so as not to exceed 25% of the client's damages. By way of example, if the claimant's solicitors costs are £10 000 and a success fee of 100% is agreed and the claimant recovers compensation of £50 000, then the success fee is £10 000 to be deducted from the compensation, leaving a net figure for the claimant of £40 000.

Whilst the advent of conditional fees in broad terms is to be welcomed as offering at least another funding mechanism, its role in the clinical negligence field is not to be over-rated. Not only are the supporting insurance premiums extremely expensive, to the point that many clients are deterred, but the insurers offering supporting policies also impose a very strict eligibility criteria in any event, such that (a) only competent firms on their nominated panels can apply for coverage (and these panels are significantly smaller than the above-mentioned Law Society and AVMA panels) and (b) insurers tend to apply high prospects of success criteria for eligibility so that their risk is essentially minimised. A case which has, say, a 60% prospect of success with modest damages potential is not likely to be accepted by an insurance underwriter for a conditional fee agreement. It is for these reasons that, even in the busiest of experienced claimants solicitor practices, only a very small number of conditional fee agreements have been taken out.

Legal expense insurance policies

This is an emerging area. Legal expense insurance policies are becoming a feature of the insurance market-place. Many are included within or bolted on to existing insurance arrangements such as household insurance, and many clients may not appreciate that they have such protection. The insurance premiums payable are currently very small indeed, typically £10–£15 per annum, and the policies can typically provide cover of up to £25 000 or £50 000. This product is useful in facilitating the bringing of clinical negligence claims. However, there are a number of drawbacks.

First, the above-mentioned policy limits quite often mean that if the case is fully contested to trial, there will not be sufficient coverage to meet the overall costs exposure. A fully contested clinical negligence case lasting for 3 or 4 days at trial may easily cost in excess of £30 000 per side.

Secondly, a number of the legal expense insurers themselves have become extremely wary about offering cover in this type of case, having had particularly poor claims experience. The market has witnessed something of a re-trenchment in this area, and it remains to be seen whether the insurers will continue to provide products, or whether they will withdraw, perceiving the risk as not financially worthwhile.

After-the-event insurance policies

There are a few policies currently on the market which allow the purchase of a certain amount of cover (e.g. £100 000) for a given premium. Traditionally, these relatively new products have been aimed at the more conventional personal injury market, and there has been a reluctance on the part of insurers to offer this type of cover to support clinical negligence cases. Thus whilst the product in theory exists, its actual accessibility is very limited.

Private funding

The above options being exhausted, private funding is the fall-back position (i.e. the client funds the case him- or herself). It is recognised that clinical negligence cases are extremely expensive, and hence privately funded cases are taken on with extreme caution, both on the part of the client and on the part of the solicitor. Generally speaking, a high threshold for prospects of success is set so as to justify the pursuit of proceedings, and the economic return in compensation has to be seen as worthwhile. This is a matter of judgement in the individual case, but it is understandable that AVMA and similar consumer organisations report a high level of deterrence amongst claimants as a result of the prohibitive cost.

By way of example, it is quite usual for a client to be quoted an initial charge of up to £5000 for the costs of carrying out an initial investigation, including the obtaining of notes and records and suitable supporting medical experts' opinion. The costs thereafter will be entirely dependent on the complexity of the case and the nature of the defence response – the more the case is contested and the more complex the issues, the higher the cost will be.

Alternative dispute resolution

Alternative dispute resolution (ADR) is a generic term covering a multitude of options for the resolution of disputes (including clinical negligence). It encompasses options such as mediation, arbitration and negotiation. Of these, mediation is the mechanism which has been most closely looked at in the context of clinical negligence. There are a number of points that deserve mention.

First, in other jurisdictions mediation is an integral part of the process of resolving clinical negligence issues. In America, for example, in many of the States mediation is a mandatory prerequisite for the commencement of proceedings (i.e. the mediation has to be performed before any court proceedings can be commenced). Whilst it is reported (cynically) that as a result of this stipulation the mediation process is used merely as a mechanism for testing the merits of the ultimate litigation and frequently as a fishing expedition, nevertheless the reported success rate of the process is astonishingly high. For example, there is anecdotal evidence that in Dallas, Texas, 80% of cases referred to mediation resolve successfully. If that level of success may be achieved in the particularly adversarial culture of the USA, what could be done in England and Wales if the process were properly supported?

Second, it is clear that there is considerable judicial support for the usage of mediation, even though there is no ability to require its use. Historically, the above-mentioned PD 49 included an enquiry as to whether the parties had been prepared to consider mediation. Whilst the approach of the parties was generally to try to avoid this question, the very fact that it was there indicated its perceived relevance.

Third, there have been two attempts at mediation pilots. The NHS Mediation Scheme commenced operation in April 1995. It has now finished and its outcome and report are awaited. Sadly, it seems that few cases were submitted through the scheme, although there were a number of reported successes. Unfortunately, owing to the confidential terms of the pilot, no case reports are yet available.

The other scheme was the Central London County Court Pilot Mediation Scheme. The evaluation report on the scheme by Professor Hazel Gen was issued in July 1998. This, too, indicated a poor response from the personal injury area. Only seven cases involving personal injury were mediated and, of these, only one was a medical negligence case. That case did not settle through the mediation process. The case was ultimately contested, went to trial and the claimant was awarded £12 000. It is therefore extremely difficult to draw any conclusions from this poor response, although the broad view of the pilot was that mediation was capable of promoting early settlement in a wide range of cases 'when parties are volunteered to attend mediation sessions'.

Notwithstanding the disappointment of the foregoing attempts, it is highly likely that mediation will become a feature of the conduct of clinical negligence cases. The Protocol at Section 5 recognises its importance, and remember that the 'good practice commitments' require the patients and their advisers to consider other appropriate dispute resolution methods, including mediation.

Furthermore, the Civil Procedure Rules themselves facilitate a stay of proceedings for 1 month to allow for settlement, and within this consideration is the use of ADR, including mediation. If a new practice direction emerges to replace PD49, then it is quite likely to include mediation provision. (In terms of the use of mediation, in the absence of the report of the NHS mediation pilot, there are no reported mediation cases. At this stage, the anecdotal experience indicates a reluctance to explore this approach such that progress is only likely to be made if court compulsion arrives. The author's personal attempts to mediate have all met with either no response or refusal from the defendants.)

There is an issue as to whether, given the disappointing take-up of mediation at this stage, it may be necessary to make its usage compulsory. There is much debate about this. However, the anecdotal experience indicates a reluctance on the part of claimants and defendants alike to explore this approach, and it may therefore be that court compulsion will be necessary if this mechanism is to have any impact.

The effects on the participants of the process

It would not be appropriate to leave the analysis of the process without at least considering the effects of the process upon both claimant and defendant. On both sides the litigation process is highly stressful, sometimes debilitatingly so. It is a process not to be entered into lightly, and is not an option of last resort.

The claimants' perspective

The fact that this subject has spawned organisations such as AVMA, and that AVMA at the time deliberately chose to include the word 'victim' in its title denotes the importance of this subject to the claimant. The very nature of the patient–healthcare provider relationship is such that immense trust is reposed and is by definition undermined. This can be devastating. Hence when the protocol refers to one of its principal aims as being to have helped to restore the healthcare provider–patient relationship, this is no trite sentiment. On both sides of the equation a responsible, mature, professional approach needs to be adopted, and promptly.

The claimant's solicitor has the responsibility to identify at the outset the claimant's real objectives and concerns. As is frequently stated, many claimants pursue the litigation option as a result of failure to obtain an adequate explanation or apology.

Noting the above-mentioned concern, it is important for any defendant and his or her adviser to consider a prompt response. An apology is not an admission of legal liability, but it is an extremely important matter for the patient. Consider the following case, which demonstrates the appropriate response to a clinical negligence scenario, and which is illustrative of the true spirit of the protocol.

Case 23: A failed anaesthetic

Mandy King was diagnosed with chronic arthritis at the age of 15 years. She underwent a number of major orthopaedic operations, and on 30 October 1997 was admitted to Northwick Park Hospital in Harrow for an elbow replacement operation. She was duly taken to the operating-theatre, but regained consciousness approximately 20 minutes into the operation owing to the anaesthetic gas not being turned on. Theatre staff were alerted when irregularities showed on the blood-pressure machine.

Mandy stated: 'The operation went ahead and when I woke up I thought I was in the recovery room. I could hear noises, talking and clanking sounds and suddenly realised something was wrong. I was in pain and absolutely terrified. I heard someone ask the surgeon how old I was and remark that I looked young for my age. I felt so helpless and scared. I was awake and couldn't do anything about it. I tried to move something to show the nursing staff that I was awake, but I had been given a drug to paralyse my muscles. I tried to hold my breath so that something would register on one of the machines, but this didn't work because my breathing was being controlled. Someone must have noticed that my blood pressure had increased. I heard someone saying I wasn't getting enough anaesthetic. Then I blacked out. The next thing I knew I was coming round in recovery and screaming.'

Pursuant to this terrifying event the hospital launched an investigation. The hospital's Claim Manager promptly visited Mandy and her husband, accompanied by a Consultant Anaesthetist. It was important to ascertain Mandy's account of what had happened. Having done this, the Trust launched an immediate internal investigation which revealed the above circumstances. Mandy then received a full report, an immediate admission of liability and apology. She was reassured that the relevant procedures had been changed so that the same kind of mistake could not happen again, and indeed was actually taken to be shown the equipment used in theatre so that she could understand the nature of the changes effected. The hospital also paid compensation, having afforded Mandy the opportunity for independent legal advice. Those legal costs were also met.

The case clearly demonstrates the most responsible and effective approach to be adopted in this circumstance. Mandy King, whilst obviously unhappy about the event itself, is extremely positive about the responsible attitude shown by the hospital management. The healthcare provider–patient relationship has been restored.

If the case is not resolved and the litigation continues, then the claimant continues to be in a stressful position. He or she will be quizzed frequently by his or her solicitor/barrister/medical experts, and will feel threatened if there are conflicts of evidence between their recollection (genuinely held) and the clinical record for defence testimony. This is very undermining. Claimants do not enjoy the legal process, and the vast majority are completely unfamiliar with it and regard it as threatening. It is not usually a cathartic process. However, if properly handled and speedily dealt with, the litigation process can help to ameliorate some of the damage done, especially if a constructive approach is adopted.

The defendant

No one would pretend that the process is not equally stressful for the recipient defendant. By definition, their professional judgement is being challenged and possibly found wanting. That can be very undermining of self-confidence to the point that, in extreme cases, there are reports of doctors being unable to continue in practice. There is a hanging sword of Damocles for as long as the case is ongoing, and with the added concern that their professional integrity may be undermined and, worse still, that the matter may be exposed to media attention with all that that connotes.

A recent article[2] considered the impact of litigation on consultants and senior registrars within the North Thames (West) Regional Health Authority. A total 769 doctors responded, of whom 288 (37%) had been involved in litigation at some point during their career. Anger, distress and feeling personally attacked were common responses to litigation. The article concluded that there was a need for support at several levels, from the personal to the managerial.

In a separate study[3] conducted by the Department of Psychiatry at the University of Kentucky, Lexington, it was stated that:

> factor analysis showed clusters of symptoms including psychological trauma, job strain, shame/doubt and active coping ... Stress was increased amongst those with cases pending or multiple suits ... malpractice litigation is a major life trauma that should be dealt with as any other trauma, including use of positive coping strategies such as knowledge of the psychological sequelae, cognitive re-framing and collegial and personal support systems.

The vast majority of practitioners have similar fears to those of the claimant. They, too, need to be guided through the litigation and be reminded of its purpose. They should be encouraged not to stand on unreasonable points of principle and not to lose sight of the fact that whatever their perspective, the claimant's perspective is of having been caused actual injury. Where appropriate, the principles of the above example involving Mandy King should be adopted and regarded as good professional practice.

Conclusion

This is a time of enormous reform in the process of the law. For the first time in this sphere of clinical negligence, there has been multidisciplinary analysis of the issues which has led to major changes resulting in improved handling from the stages prior to litigation all the way through to the conduct of the trial itself. We are only at the beginning of this new era, but if the underlying philosophy is embraced, as it should be, then there is a genuine prospect that these cases will be dealt with much more expeditiously, sensibly and cheaply. That can only be beneficial for GP and patient alike.

References

1   Dyer C (1999) GPs face escalating litigation. *BMJ.* **318**: 830.

2   Bark P, Vincent C, Olivieri L and Jones A (1997) Impact of litigation on senior clinicians: implications for risk management. *Qual Health Care.* **6**: 7–13.

3   Martin CA, Wilson JF, Fiebelman ND, Gurley DN and Miller TW (1991) Physicians' psychologic reactions to malpractice litigation. *South Med J.* **84**: 1300–4.

CHAPTER SIX

The law of limitation

John R Griffiths and John Pickering

Limitation in the UK

All claims for damages are subject to the law of limitation. There are strict time limits imposed within which court proceedings must be commenced. Failure to commence court proceedings within the specified time limit will result in the case being out of time and thus statute barred. The law relating to this matter in Scotland differs from that in the rest of the UK, and we have therefore dealt with this topic in two different sections in this chapter.

Limitation in the UK, except in Scotland

The primary limitation period

The current law is governed by the Limitation Act 1980, and in the context of claims for damages for personal injury, the starting point is Section 11. This prescribes that there is a 3-year time limit in which to bring a claim. That time limit runs from the date of the negligent act or the date of the knowledge (if later) of the injured person. Thus, by way of example, in the case of negligent mis-prescribing, the 3-year period would in the first place be taken to run from the date of the issue of the first negligent prescription.

Limitation based on knowledge

However, the reference to the date of knowledge is important because it was recognised that the strict application of a 3-year time limit could cause undue hardship, particularly in cases where it was not immediately apparent that there had been negligence resulting in injury. Thus, in Section 11, reference to knowledge is specifically defined in Section 14 of the Limitation Act. This provides that the 3-year period will only start to run from the date when a person has knowledge of the following facts:

- that the injury in question was significant, and
- that the injury was attributable in whole or in part to the act or omission which is alleged to constitute negligence, nuisance or breach of duty, and
- the identity of the defendant, and
- if it is alleged that the act or omission was that of a person other than the defendant, the identity of that person and the additional facts supporting the bringing of an action against the defendant.

Unsurprisingly, this definition has given rise to a plethora of case law, and it is not the purpose of the present discussion to analyse this in detail. However, a few examples are set out below to illustrate the main points.

Case 24: Khan v Ainslie and others (20 February 1992; Queen's Bench Division (Waterhouse J))

This was a GP negligence case decided before Mr Justice Waterhouse in 1992. In May 1983 the claimant complained to the defendant, his general practitioner, of eye trouble. He was referred to an ophthalmic medical practitioner who gave him eyedrops. The claimant saw his doctor again complaining of further eye trouble, and was given painkillers. In June 1983 he underwent an iridectomy which was unsuccessful, and he was left blind in one eye. He sought legal advice and legal aid was granted for an expert report in an anticipated action against the ophthalmologist. This report concluded in January 1985 that the treatment had been correct, and consequently the legal aid certificate was discharged. Thus between March 1985 and the end of 1987, the claimant had no medical or legal aid support for his case. He then saw a television programme about medical accidents and contacted new solicitors who persuaded the legal aid authority to fund a new medical report. This was obtained in February 1989, and it concluded that there was delay in treating the eye caused by the defendant, and that this fell below an accepted standard and that it was this delay that had caused the loss of the eye. Proceedings were issued but the defendant contended that the case was out of time and thus statute barred. The question of limitation was therefore tried as a preliminary issue.

Mr Justice Waterhouse held, giving judgement in favour of the claimant, that he had established on the evidence that until the second medical report in 1989 he had no knowledge of the attributability of his disability to the defendant's delay, and also that he had acted reasonably within the constraints of the limitations on legal aid, especially bearing in mind the understandable reluctance of the legal aid authorities to fund the matter and the initial report. There was nothing in the first report to put the claimant on notice that his injury was the result of the defendant's delay.

Case 25: Kenneth Corbett Briggs v (1) Dr J Pitt-Payne (2) Dr M Lias (Court of Appeal, 20 November 1998)

This was a rather involved case in which the claimant, who was a retired solicitor, sought to pursue a negligence case against his general practitioners relating to the prescribing of Valium. The claimant had a long history of physical and mental health problems. Prior to consulting the defendant general practitioners, he had been prescribed a number of drugs, including Librium and Valium. In the 1960s he stopped taking Librium and then suffered withdrawal symptoms. In 1972 he had started taking Valium. He actually consulted the defendant general practitioners in the early and mid-1980s and they continued to prescribe Valium for him. In September 1991, the claimant abruptly ceased taking Valium, aware that it could have been having injurious effects and that his ill health might have been attributable to it. He commenced court proceedings in September 1994, alleging that he had suffered from a number of symptoms due to the prescription of Valium. These symptoms included 'zombification', drowsiness, lack of concentration, irritability, impaired judgement and night-time incontinence. The allegations against the defendants were that they had been negligent in having continued to prescribe Valium or in having failed to stop prescribing it when it was causing harm. The defendants raised a limitation defence, arguing that the claimant had had actual knowledge in February 1991, and that his claim was therefore out of time. The judge in the first instance accepted the defendants' arguments and ruled that the case was out of time. The case then went on appeal to the Court of Appeal, who upheld the judge's decision, contending that the judge had been entitled to uphold that the claimant had actual knowledge in February 1991. This was consistent with evidence which he had given in a separate case, namely the group action against the manufacturers (the so-called 'benzodiazapine' litigation). The court also upheld that the claimant's injuries were significant and that he had known the injuries were significant and might have been attributable to the taking of Valium. Accordingly, the claimant had the requisite knowledge that those injuries might have been attributable to the doctors who had prescribed the Valium. Any issue of negligence or fault was irrelevant at that stage and had no bearing on the issue of attributability. Accordingly, the action failed because the claimant had brought his claim outside the 3-year knowledge period.

There was also a separate argument under Section 33 of the Limitation Act (see below), but the court refused to exercise its discretion under that section as well.

The court's discretion

In addition to the analysis under Sections 11 and 14, as described above, there is a further facility for the court to allow a claim to proceed even though the primary limitation period has passed. This is provided by Section 33, and gives the court an overriding discretion to dis-apply the time limit if it would be equitable to do so. The court has to balance the prejudice to the claimant of being denied the ability to pursue the claim against the prejudice to the defendant of having to deal with a late claim.

The terms of Section 33 are involved, but they do clearly lay out the matters to which the court has to have regard. The position is as follows:

Section 33 (3) – Discretionary exclusion of time limit for actions in respect of personal injuries or death

(3) In acting under this Section, the Court shall have regard to all the circumstances of the case and in particular to:

(a) the length of, and the reasons for, the delay on the part of the claimant
(b) the extent to which, having regard to the delay, the evidence adduced or likely to be adduced by the claimant or the defendant is or is likely to be less cogent than if the action had been brought within the time allowed by Section 11 [by Section 11A] or (as the case may be) by Section 12
(c) the conduct of the defendant after the cause of action arose, including the extent (if any) to which he responded to requests reasonably made by the claimant for information or inspection for the purpose of ascertaining facts which were or might be relevant to the claimant's cause of action against the defendant
(d) the duration of any disability of the claimant arising after the date of the accrual of the cause of action
(e) the extent to which the claimant acted promptly and reasonably once he knew whether or not the act or omission of the defendant, to which the injury was attributable, might be capable at that time of giving rise to an action for damages
(f) the steps, if any, taken by the claimant to obtain medical, legal or other expert advice and the nature of any such advice he may have received.

Again, this is fertile ground for the lawyers, and there are many cases which pass before the courts analysing the circumstances of the delay, the conduct of the parties and the equity of the position. Put simply, the court is required to have regard, in broad terms, to the overall merits of the case. Thus an obviously strong claimant's case which, if denied, is likely to amount to a windfall for the defendant's insurers, is more likely to succeed than one which appears weak or less obvious.

In the context of negligence by general practitioners, some examples are given below.

Case 26: Michelle Eileen Barr v Dr S R Matthews (31 March 1999, Queen's Bench Division (Alliott J))

In this case the claimant had presented herself to the defendant general practitioner in December 1988 seeking an abortion. She was an entirely proper candidate under the abortion laws, but unknown to her the defendant was philosophically opposed to abortion. Without disclosing this, the defendant allegedly represented things in such a way as to prevent the claimant having an abortion. The claimant contended that the defendant made remarks to the effect that she was too far advanced in her pregnancy for an abortion to be carried out. It was argued that this was wrong, improper and in breach of the defendant's duty of care to a young and vulnerable patient. The defendant general practitioner absolutely refuted such conduct or remarks. The claimant alleged that the consequence of the advice as she recalled it was an unwanted pregnancy which ought to have been terminated, a disastrous ante-partum haemorrhage and the birth of a catastrophically brain-damaged child.

The claimant's claim was not commenced until a writ was issued in April 1996. It was common ground that the claimant was fixed with the requisite knowledge (Sections 11 and 14 of the Limitation Act 1980) from mid-January 1989, and that the primary 3-year period had therefore expired by mid-January 1992. The case was therefore well out of time. The claimant argued that the court should exercise its discretion to disapply the Limitation Act under the terms of Section 33. In support of her argument, she maintained that the crucial facts in the case were either agreed or firmly refuted by the defendant, and the defendant had been alerted to the facts in contention in 1991 before the primary limitation period expired. The defendant, on the other hand, argued that there was no reason why the case should not have been brought in time and that, as a result of the delay, the cogency of the evidence had been reduced. The defendant further argued that the claimant had been dilatory, and that if she had really believed that the defendant was seeking to dissuade her from having an abortion, then it would have been easy to obtain a second opinion.

The judge decided that he would exercise discretion to allow the action to proceed. It was equitable to do so having regard to the seriousness of the case, and in particular it was noted that the crucial facts were either agreed or absolutely refuted. Thus it was possible to try the matter without injustice. Having dealt with this, however, the judge found against the claimant, preferring the defence evidence and particularly the evidence contained in the contemporaneous notes.

Case 27: Pratima Rani Das v Dr Durga Ganju (Court of Appeal, 31 March 1999)

This case concerned a claimant who sought to bring a claim against the defendant general practitioner relating to the birth of a child which was subsequently diagnosed as having congenital rubella syndrome. The child was born on 24 October 1978. The claimant had visited the general practitioner at the time of her pregnancy. On 28 February 1978 she had visited complaining of a rash on her face, and had informed the defendant that she might be pregnant. No action was taken by the defendant, and the claimant later gave birth to a baby daughter. It was subsequently discovered that the daughter was deaf, blind and severely handicapped. The claimant did not realise that she might have a claim in negligence against the defendant until June 1987. She sought advice and was given legal aid, but was then advised by her barrister that she could not bring a claim for personal injury on the grounds of wrongful birth. The barrister also gave her inconsistent advice about the issue of limitation under Section 11 of the Limitation Act, and indicated that he thought that this point would be overcome. The claimant also received advice from her solicitors indicating that the claimant's daughter would be entitled to legal aid on reaching the age of 16 years, and that the claim could then be pursued in the child's name. Taking into account these factors and the fact that the claimant had been asked to pay a contribution to legal aid, she decided not to pursue the case any further at that time. Then, in July 1993, she instructed new solicitors and a legal aid certificate was acquired in order to pursue a claim against the defendant for the personal injury caused by the defendant's negligence. A writ was issued in September 1996, some 18 years after the cause of action arose. The defendants sought to contest the case, arguing that it was statute barred by virtue of Section 11. The judge at first held that Section 11 did apply, but he exercised his discretion under Section 33 to allow the case to be brought in any event.

The defendant then appealed to the Court of Appeal. The Court of Appeal dismissed the defendant's appeal. They accepted that there were no grounds for criticising the claimant personally. She had relied upon the advice being given by her legal representatives. The Court of Appeal felt that it would be wrong for the claimant to have to bear the

burden of her lawyer's incorrect advice. She would undoubtedly suffer considerable prejudice if her claim was struck out,
and so she would then have to consider a speculative claim
against her former legal advisers. Furthermore, the Court of
Appeal looked at the question of cogency of the evidence
under Section 33(3)(b) and noted that the court must concen-
trate on what had happened after the 'date of knowledge'
arose. In this case, the date of knowledge was 10 years after
the alleged negligence. The defendant's prejudice was therefore
small, given the likely failure of recollection by 10 years in any
event.

Persons under disability

In addition to the discretion provided under Section 33, the law
also recognises that the imposition of limitation dates can work
very unfairly on those who are disadvantaged. In the case of
children or adults under disability, the law provides (Section 28A)
that the Section 11 and Section 14 time limit shall not start to run
until, in the case of a child, he or she attains majority or, in the
case of a patient, until the disability ceases.

Hence, a child has until his or her twenty-first birthday to
commence proceedings.

In the case of someone under disability – such as an individual
who may have suffered permanent brain damage – the time limit
may never run. The result is that cases may be brought years after
the negligent act that caused injury, and the case will not be
dismissed purely because of the passage of time. However, it should
be noted that anyone seeking to bring such a claim still has to
achieve the evidential standard of proving the case.

By way of example, consider the following:

1 A child aged 6 years develops meningitis which – negligently – is
  not diagnosed by the general practitioner. The child suffers a
  severe physical injury (e.g. amputation of the feet) as a consequence, but does not have brain damage, and their mental
  capacity is unimpaired. In this case the child has until the age of
  21 years to bring a claim.
2 Assume the same scenario as the above example, except this
  time assume that the child suffers brain damage such that its
  mental capacity is permanently impaired. The child is to be

regarded as under disability (i.e. a patient within the meaning of the Mental Health Act). In this case, no time limit will operate because of the child's permanent disability. Hence in theory a claim could be brought at the age of 30 years or even later.

It is important to note that the above analysis represents only a cursory discussion of what is a highly involved subject. It is intended to provide no more than an initial guide to the workings of limitation.

Limitation and actions for medical negligence in Scotland

Medical negligence actions, as with all cases of personal injury, are subject to the provision of the Prescription and Limitation (Scotland) Act 1973 (as amended). It should be noted in passing perhaps that prescription does not apply to actions relating to personal injury and death by virtue of the Prescription and Limitations (Scotland) Act 1984, but limitation of medical negligence actions is subject to the requirement that they be brought within 3 years, a period known as 'the triennium'. Sections 17(1) and (2) of the 1973 Act provide that the period of 3 years in a personal injuries claim begins to run from:

1 the date on which the injuries were sustained, or
2 where the act or omission was of a continuing nature, the date on which the injuries were sustained or the act or omission ceased, whichever is the later.

It should be noted that for the purposes of determining the date from which the triennium begins to run, any time during which the injured party is under a legal disability by reason of non-age or unsoundness of mind falls to be disregarded in terms of Section 17(3) of the 1973 Act. It should be noted that the Age of Legal Capacity (Scotland) Act 1991, which came into force on 25 September 1991, made important changes with regard to the position of children who are entitled to pursue claims for personal injuries. The position now is that an action will require to be raised within 3 years of the child reaching the age of 16 years.

Limitation does not apply to an injured party who suffers continuing unsoundness of mind. However, it is well recognised that in cases of alleged medical negligence, the pursuer may initially and indeed for an appreciable time be unaware that he has been injured, and the provisions of Section 17(2)(b) of the Act make allowance for such situations. In such cases, the 3-year period will run from the date on which the pursuer became aware or the date on which the court deems that it would have been reasonably practicable for him or her to become aware of each of the following:

1 that the injuries were sufficiently serious to justify an action of damages on the assumption that the defender did not dispute liability and was able to satisfy decree
2 that the injuries were attributable in whole or in part to an act of omission, and
3 that the defender (or his employer or principal) was a person to whose act or omission the injuries were attributable.

In a case where death has resulted within three years of the date of injury, the three-year limitation period runs from the date of death unless one of the statutory exemptions outlined above applies, and if a person dies after the expiry of the triennium, no action can be brought by a relative or executor in terms of Section 18(4) of the 1973 Act.

The aspect of limitation which is probably most reported and of greatest interest to lawyers is that related to the discretion which a court has to allow an action to proceed 'late' – outwith the triennium if it deems it equitable to do so. This very important discretionary power is found in Section 19(A) of the 1973 Act. The test has been succinctly summed up as follows:

> The essence of the matter is that the court has to have regard for all relevant considerations in determining how to exercise its discretion in relation to determining what is equitable in the particular case. (*Wilson v Telling (Northern) Limited*[1])

It should be noted that the onus is on the pursuer to persuade the court that it is equitable to proceed with the action. The defender will almost always argue that the extension should not be allowed on the grounds that investigation of the matter becomes more difficult with the passage of time and that the defender will be prejudiced by the delay. This is particularly relevant in medical cases, where tracing staff (both nursing and medical) who may have been involved in an incident obviously becomes more difficult with the passage of time. Although there are judicial dicta to the effect that this discretionary power should be employed with restraint because the purpose of the Act was to protect individuals against stale claims (*Carson v Howard Doris Limited*[2]), practising lawyers recognise that on balance the courts are often likely to exercise this discretion in favour of the 'late' pursuer. The case of *Carson*[2] set out criteria which the courts should consider before exercising discretion. These are as follows:

1 the conduct of the pursuer since the occurrence of the accident, including the reason why the action was not brought timeously
2 any prejudice which might be caused to the pursuer if the extension were not granted, and
3 any prejudice which might be caused to the other party by granting of the extension.

Two cases conveniently highlight the issues which may arise in an application for the discretion under Section 19(A).

Case 28: Comber v Greater Glasgow Health Board[3]

In this case an action was raised 14 years after the event and 6 years after the expiry of the triennium. The pursuer raised an action against the Greater Glasgow Health Board for reparation following operative treatment in hospital. The operation had been carried out in 1973 and the 3-year limitation period in respect of injuries then suffered expired on her twenty-first birthday in 1981.

The action was raised in January 1987 and came to a preliminary hearing on limitation in 1989 as she founded on Section 19(A) of the Prescription and Limitation (Scotland) Act 1973 (as amended). After hearing evidence, the judge *allowed* the action to proceed, and the summary of his judgement on the facts is of interest:

The pursuer gave evidence that when she was at Alder Hay Children's Hospital in Liverpool in 1973 for treatment for a squint, her mother had asked if anything could be done about a dent in her forehead. A doctor had referred her to a plastic surgeon at another hospital in the Liverpool area, who had referred her to the second defender at Canniesburn Hospital. The pursuer was seen both at the Southern

General Hospital and at Canniesburn, and her first visit was for assessment. She attended with her parents and it was agreed to have the operation, which was carried out in September 1973. The operation was a disaster which made her appearance much worse. Thereafter she continued to attend the Glasgow hospitals and over the years had many operations. She wrote frequently to the second defender (the named consultant plastic surgeon who had operated on her), asking what had gone wrong and that he should correct her disfigurement. After 1980, the second defender left Glasgow and the pursuer was treated by another consultant plastic surgeon. She stated that she had asked 'until she was blue in the face' what had gone wrong, but that the attitude of the doctors was that 'the past did not matter, it was the future which counted.' From the time of the operation her desire was to get the doctors to do something to correct the position, and to obtain a second opinion from other doctors, but it did not occur to her to consult a solicitor. She at various times complained to or sought advice from her general practitioner, the Local Community Health Council in Liverpool and the Secretary of State for Health and Social Security, as well as the plastic surgeons. None of these had suggested she could or should get legal advice. In about 1983 she read a notice in a woman's magazine about the existence of the organisation Action for the Victims of Medical Accidents, and wrote to them. Her letter is produced. She stated that she thought they would give her advice on what she could do either by acting as a mediator or by suggesting some way of approaching her doctors to get them to answer her questions. She had no idea that compensation might be available until she received a letter from them.

The pursuer was questioned at length about her knowledge relating to the law and what lawyers did. She said that she had no idea that she might be able to take legal action, she had not heard or read of anyone suing doctors. She only occasionally read a newspaper, the *Daily Mirror*, and then only about television programmes and the horoscopes. She had read of MPs obtaining damages for libel and of film stars obtaining money on divorce. She knew solicitors existed, but considered that they were provided for people accused of crime. She had never heard of legal aid. She discussed her position with her parents, who had never suggested that she should see a solicitor. She lived with her parents in a council-housing scheme in Liverpool. She had few relatives who were not living close to her. She did not discuss matters with neighbours, and after the first operation if anyone came to the house she went to her bedroom to avoid seeing them. At school, which after the operation was seriously disrupted, and at the job creation work she obtained after she left school, she avoided discussing her position. If anyone asked about what had happened to her face, she said she had had an accident and resented being asked about her appearance. It is clear that after the first operation she became something of a recluse.

The judge continued:

From observing and hearing the pursuer giving evidence, I agree with her solicitor's assessment that she is both naive and determined. I considered also that she was an honest witness giving evidence as accurately as she could. It is no doubt strange and unfortunate that anyone should be as ill informed about modern society as the pursuer and her parents appear to be, and difficult for lawyers to appreciate that there can exist people who have no appreciation of what lawyers do and what remedies the law provides. Further having heard and seen the pursuer and her parents, I have no doubt that the pursuer did not know until 1983 that there was any possible right to claim compensation for her condition.

There then follows a discussion by the judge of the evidence in relation to legal advice that the pursuer received in 1983 and the delays which occurred before an action was raised in June 1987.

The judge then continued:

The pursuer's counsel contended that to refuse the remedy would result in injustice. The pursuer had sustained a most serious injury and the situation was exactly what Section 19(A) was designed to meet. The pursuer had no further remedy such as a good or cast-iron case against any solicitor, and she should not be penalised by a lack of knowledge of the law. Any delay after she consulted solicitors was explained and in any event was after the expiry of the limitation period and was not on the evidence shown to cause any material prejudice to the defenders.

In the present case, the pursuer if she were to establish negligence and that the disfigurement was caused by the negligence would clearly be entitled to receive a very substantial award or damages. The disfigurement is great and she has undergone protracted operative treatment. The treatment has affected her education and future employment prospects. I cannot judge how strong her case is or what the prospects of success are, but I consider that I cannot say that she has no reasonable chance of success. She did not raise an action before the expiry of the limitation period because she did not know she could do so. She would be prejudiced if the action were not allowed to proceed. The defenders have been prejudiced by the expiry of the limitation period, but apart from that there is no evidence or averment that they would be in any different position than they would have been if the action had been raised in August 1981 before the limitation period expired. There is no averment, for example, that any witness has been lost or that any particular witness cannot remember any crucial matter or that the hospital records are in any sense incomplete. The operation clearly was an almost unique one, and one would therefore expect that those involved would have a clearer recollection of the circumstances than, for example, if the case related to a simple routine operation such as the removal of the appendix.

I consider on the whole facts and circumstances that it would be equitable to allow this action to proceed.

Case 29: Kaye v Argyll and Clyde Health Board[4]

This is a case in which the contrary view was taken, in a recent decision of the Inner House of the Court of Session. The facts were that in 1977 Kaye had both her breasts removed as a treatment for cystic mastopathy. In 1995 she raised an action of damages against the relevant Health Board, alleging that the removal of both her breasts for a non-malignant condition without her consent amounted to negligence. A preliminary hearing before a judge in the first instance was held to determine whether the court's discretion under Section 19(A) should be exercised. Evidence was lead on behalf of the pursuer that she had attempted unsuccessfully to obtain her medical records in 1977, that she tried again in 1993, having heard of the passing of the Access to Health Records Act 1990, and was again unsuccessful, and that she consulted solicitors in 1993, which then resulted in her records being recovered and an action of damages being raised on her behalf. She argued that it was equitable to allow the action to proceed as *inter alia* she had no knowledge prior to 1993 of lawyers' legal remedies, or the availability of legal aid. She and her husband had suffered from ill health, and the defenders would not be prejudiced as a result of the time lapse. The judge at first instance rejected the pursuer's case and she appealed. The Inner House upheld the decision of the judge at first instance against her. In doing so, they made two points of particular interest. The first related to the pursuer's explanation for not seeking advice timeously. It was partly that she was not out to make a complaint against anyone, and that she just wanted to get on with her life. The Appeal Court said:

> That explanation may be entirely credible and entirely honourable. But it will not necessarily be regarded as sufficient basis for allowing an action to proceed many years later, long after the expiry of the normal time limit upon some change of mind or re-assessment of the overall position.

The second interesting point was the pursuer's case based on her alleged ignorance of the law, lawyers and legal aid. The trial judge stated: 'I find that I cannot hold that any ignorance of the law or of lawyers or of the availability of legal aid on the part of the pursuer was such as to provide a reasonable explanation of her failure to seek advice.'

The trial judge had found that the pursuer read newspapers and books and watched television, that she had sons in managerial positions and a daughter employed as a legal secretary, and that the family was not one that was in any way isolated from society. The pursuer herself had a full-time job until 1984, and the Appeal Court held that these were not 'insignificant matters when comparisons were even being made between her and the pursuer in *Comber v Greater Glasgow Health Board*.'[3]

The trial judge came to see the pursuer as a woman 'who is sufficiently worldly to take decisive action when she feels dissatisfaction with a firm of solicitors she has consulted, and who is familiar with doctors, having worked as a nursing auxiliary for many years.'

The appeal court judges considered that the trial judge could 'quite legitimately' see the pursuer as having a degree of worldliness and self-confidence and thus being unable to provide a 'reasonable explanation for failing to seek advice – which we would observe might not initially be advice from a lawyer but could be advice which would lead to contact being made with a lawyer.'

Thus in *Kaye*[4] the pursuer failed in her application to the court to apply the discretion in Section 19(A).

Case references

1   Wilson v Telling (Northern) Limited (1996) *Scots LT*: 380.

2   Carson v Howard Doris Limited (1981) *Session Cases*: 278.

3   Comber v Greater Glasgow Health Board (1989) *Scots LT*: 639.

4   Kaye v Argyll and Clyde Health Board (1999) *Scots LT*: 823.

CHAPTER SEVEN

Risk management in general practice

Nigel Ineson

The last decade has seen an increase in potential litigation against general practitioners, although the incidence of successful claims is not increasing at anything like the rate of initial approaches indicating that an action is contemplated. It is now the case that all general practitioners will from time to time receive correspondence from solicitors about a potential clinical negligence action, and the concept of risk management, already taken up by health authorities to reduce potential claims against them, can usefully be applied in general practice.

The accusation of clinical negligence is always a traumatic event for any doctor. In general practice the support received from the medical indemnity organisations is invaluable. They should always be consulted immediately a letter before action is received, and they will then communicate with the solicitor acting for the claimant. Other than acknowledging the letter and identifying which indemnity organisation will be acting, it is best not to enter into correspondence with the claimant's solicitor where a claim is to be brought. The new rules for civil litigation put a tight timetable on all involved, and it is very important that the doctor deals with correspondence promptly, as severe penalties may be imposed if defendants do not respond in a timely manner. Delay in communicating with the defendant's legal advisors can potentially seriously harm the defence by prohibiting evidence being introduced if it is 'out of time'.

The doctor will often have no direct memory of events – actions are often started months or years after events, and the details of one out of hundreds of consultations in a general practitioner's week will rarely be vivid in memory (except perhaps when the circumstances were unusual and tragic).

The doctor will have to rely on two sources for his or her defence:

- the contemporaneous records that were made
- his or her common practice in such situations.

There can be no substitute for a decent contemporaneous record of events. Such records are persuasive to the court and to the lawyers on both sides. They are also all that the experts acting for the claimant will have, initially, to see the other side of the story – and if the records are good then this may help to defuse litigation at a very early stage.

The notes must be dated when they are made – ideally contemporaneous records should be written at or shortly after the consultation. However, the notes may be expanded as long as the new entry is dated at the time it is made. Under no circumstances should contemporaneous records ever be altered later, other than by a dated additional entry.

The reality of general practice means that it is just not possible to make full contemporaneous notes of every event, particularly as often the significance of the consultation will not be apparent at the time – retrospective vision is always illuminating. It is then reasonable for a doctor to state what his or her invariable practice would be in the situation that applied. In the absence of evidence to the contrary this is often compelling.

The advent of protocols and guidelines for the management of conditions can assist the doctor in demonstrating what would be his or her normal practice – for example, in the management of diabetes, hypertension or asthma. Thus practice guidelines can be important documents, although it is important to be aware that non-adherence to a practice guideline will be difficult to defend given that the doctor has thereby defined his or her standard of care (*see* Chapter 1).

I prefer the word 'guideline' to 'protocol', as the latter implies more rigid adherence whilst the former allows some variation to reflect individual patients – doctors often realise to a greater extent than lawyers how idiosyncratic the management of an individual patient needs to be. I also prefer practice-evolved guidelines to imposed suggestions (often written by 'experts' who do not fully understand the workings of general practice).

However, recent case law has indicated that the courts are likely to give great leeway to doctors in applying guidelines and protocols, as is illustrated by the case of *Kent v Griffiths, Roberts and the London Ambulance Service.*

Case 30: Kent v Griffiths, Roberts and the London Ambulance Service [1999] MLC0112 (QBD: Turner J, 16 July 1999)

Tracey Kent developed brain damage as a result of a respiratory arrest whilst on the way to hospital with a severe asthma attack. She was pregnant and had refused inhaled and oral steroids, and her asthma deteriorated progressively until she was seen on the day in question with a peak flow of only 60 litres/min. Her doctors had not followed the British Thoracic Society guidelines on the management of her asthma either before her emergency admission or when they visited her prior to it.

Mr Justice Turner dismissed the case against them, saying:

> to hold that, if it could be shown that the general practitioner defendants had failed to follow guidelines, the claimant succeeded, would involve the rejection of clinical judgement on the part of the treating general practitioner as having relevance in respect of decisions in regard to treatment and advice.

However, he did find that the London Ambulance Service had unreasonably delayed their attendance, and an inappropriate crew had attended, unable to offer a proper standard of resuscitation, so the claimant was awarded damages of £100 000. Interestingly, the case went to the House of Lords on the matter of whether the London Ambulance Service had a duty of care at all before they arrived at the house, the finding being that they did.

The introduction of clinical governance as a responsibility of primary care groups and with a national department with a remit to enforce it means that general practitioners will have to review their work critically and demonstrate, through clinical audit, that they do so and maintain standards. Clinical audit has long been a useful development tool, and has been widely used in education and training, but participation will now not only be regarded as good practice but will be a requirement by both the National

Health Service and indeed by the General Medical Council when performance review is introduced.

Much of the work of general practice is properly delegated to members of the primary health care team, but the general practitioner retains responsibility for the actions of his or her employees (particularly practice nurses and receptionists). This responsibility may mean that the doctor is cited as a defendant when he or she had no personal contact with the patient at all!

It is important that delegation of responsibilities is appropriate to the skills and training of the individual, and that where tasks are delegated staff are supported with adequate training. For example, if a practice nurse is to take smears, a Certificate of Competence from an outside body such as the Marie Curie organisation will be persuasive evidence of competence, although of course in-house training is valuable, too.

Guidelines can be invaluable in defining the degree of delegation and the responsibilities of each party. In our practice we have guidelines for patients attending the diabetic and asthma clinics, for vaccinations, for cervical smears and even for preparation of instruments for minor surgery, each defining the respective roles of the various professionals involved.

Training is also important for doctors, and attendance at courses, as well as postgraduate certificates and diplomas, is helpful in establishing competence. For example, the possession of the Diploma of the Faculty of Family Planning and Reproductive Health is supportive of competence in family planning, and attendance at a updating course in minor surgery or paediatic surveillance can be helpful for establishing that the defendant doctor is not only competent in the area under scrutiny, but also up to date as well.

Risk management

Perhaps half of all claims against general practitioners are the result of system failure rather than clinical error, so the maintenance of safe and effective administrative systems is vital both for maintaining patient well-being and for avoiding the traumas of litigation.

An area of increasing importance in the avoidance of claims in general practice is that of risk management. Indeed the protection societies have risk management units which can advise on the identification and rectification of areas where patients may be put at risk, and it is hoped to avoid incidents which may give rise to a claim.

A stepwise approach is recommended for identifying and resolving areas of vulnerability, as follows:

- identification of the risk areas
- consideration of potential consequences
- assessment of the likelihood of a clinical adverse event
- prioritisation of introduction of controls
- review of controls currently in place
- action plan to reduce risk areas.

Areas of risk may centre around administrative systems as well as clinical areas. Some illustrations of types of potential incidents are described below. Where an area is considered vulnerable, the potential risks of injury or harm to patients and staff, and also to reputation, should be considered with some weighting as to the seriousness of the risk so that resources can be prioritised. It is then necessary to review such controls and systems as are in place and to consider the introduction of new controls, an action plan being designed to implement the necessary changes.

Main causes of complaint

Claimants choose to consult a solicitor for a number of reasons, but the main themes underlying such a consultation are a wish to understand what happened (which has not been met by the doctors involved), a need for compensation, anger at what has occurred, and a desire to prevent it happening again, or to seek an apology for what has happened.

Of the cases that I see, which number something of the order of 1500 now for both claimants and defendants, over half proceed no further than the initial gathering of records and initial reports. In many of these cases the legal process supplies an explanation of what did happen, which has either been lacking from those involved or not heard by aggrieved and angry patients and their relatives. Of the remainder, some fail the later stages – cases strong on liability (fault) may actually not have caused much damage and so fail on causation. Of the remainder, the vast majority are negotiated settlements and only 1 to 2% of cases reach court.

The necessity to offer a consultation or visit

Patients in the UK have an expectation of home visits in excess of their doctors, and also in excess of other western societies. This situation is only slowly changing. The doctor's terms and conditions of service only require a visit when medically necessary. It is technically correct to meet a request for a visit with an invitation to attend the surgery. However, this does need negotiation to avoid anger (and recrimination if things go wrong). It is of course very difficult to defend a case when a patient asked to be seen and was not seen either at home or at the surgery.

> **Case 31: Failure to diagnose appendicitis**
>
> A 9-year-old girl became unwell with stomach-ache, lethargy and anorexia. This persisted, so her parents telephoned the emergency GP who visited and advised Calpol and fluids. The next day she was worse and her parents telephoned for a visit, and were told by the receptionist to carry on, but if she was not better after 7p.m. the emergency doctor should be called. This they did at 8.24p.m. The doctor arrived at 11.00p.m. and admitted her to hospital, where she underwent appendicectomy for a ruptured gangrenous appendix. The general practitioner was found in breach of his terms and conditions of service in not visiting her when deterioration was reported, but as the resulting delay was short, it was not considered that significant damage had resulted and civil claim was discontinued.

The need to perform an adequate examination

When the patient is seen, the two basic elements of taking an adequate history and performing a proper examination appropriate to the symptoms are essential for reaching a diagnosis and deciding on a management plan. Where either step has been inadequate, it is difficult to defend a diagnosis which in retrospect was incorrect, although an incorrect diagnosis reached after an appropriate assessment can be defended as there is not an expectation that doctors always get things right. Indeed it is often very difficult without the benefit of time to diagnose an evolving condition.

Case 32: Performing an appropriate examination

A 23-year-old woman developed a throat infection. She was seen by her general practitioner and penicillin prescribed, and by another GP 4 days later who prescribed another antibiotic, flucloxacillin. On both occasions brief but good notes were made recording appropriate examinations. Later on the same day she collapsed after experiencing difficulty in breathing, and despite being taken promptly to hospital and resuscitated, she remains severely brain damaged in a vegetative state and quite unable to do anything for herself. A diagnosis of severe hypoxic encephalopathy following an acute upper respiratory tract infection was made. However, it was not thought that her general practitioners had been substandard as they had seen, examined and appropriately prescribed for her on both occasions and could not have foreseen the very rare condition that she had.

Case 33: An inadequate examination

A healthy 35-year-old police officer consulted his general practitioner with a very severe throat infection, such that he was only able to walk supported, and could hardly speak. The note that was made read 'off colour and fever, cervical nodes, no treatment'. A week later, after seeing his general practitioner once more, again without treatment, he was admitted to hospital moribund and died of streptococcal septicaemia. It was alleged that there was insufficient examination on either occasion, and that inadequate follow-up advice was given. The case went to court and the judge found for the claimant with damages of £270 000.

Case 34: Failure to examine

The patient suffered a history of sudden and very severe headache and neck stiffness associated with dizziness, blackouts, nausea, vomiting, photophobia and diarrhoea, which progressed to paralysis and collapse over the course of 48 hours. Despite being seen by her general practitioner three times, no examination was performed or investigations arranged, and the condition was dismissed as viral. Finally, at the end of the month, she collapsed and was taken to hospital, where a large subarachnoid haemorrhage was confirmed. She has been left severely handicapped.

The absence of any examination by the general practitioner and failure to act on such clear symptoms was felt to be indefensible, and the case was settled for £700 000, 6 weeks before trial.

Communication problems

Possibly one of the major grievances that patients have concerns communication. This encompasses rudeness and manner as well as clear communication of the doctor's opinion, treatment, expectations for progress and a concept of Neighbour's 'safety net' – that is, when and how to communicate if matters do not resolve or if they deteriorate. This last is often defended on the basis that 'it is my invariable practice to advise...' rather than a specific note of when to return.

It is said, with some truth, that patients are far more willing to bring a complaint against doctors who are perceived as being rude or arrogant than against those with good communication skills, regardless of the standard of medical care offered.

Case 35: Providing adequate advice on vasectomy operation

A couple had had five children and therefore decided to undergo vasectomy. This was performed at the local hospital. Although they had been warned that the procedure was irreversible, the possibility of failure was not discussed, nor was the need for consecutive negative sperm counts before relying on the operation. Sperm counts were submitted as follows: the first one was unlabelled, the second was unlabelled, the third showed one motile sperm, the fourth showed scanty motile sperm, the fifth showed several motile sperm, and the sixth showed numerous motile sperm. Each time the couple were advised by the receptionist that the sperm count showed motile sperm and should be repeated. They resumed unprotected intercourse and the wife fell pregnant, subsequently delivering their sixth child. She has subsequently undergone sterilisation. The case was successfully defended on the basis that the correct advice was given at all times, and that it was the hospital's duty to warn of the possibility of failure – which was in any case self-evident in view of the need for repeated sperm counts.

Case 36: Failure to advise about adverse reactions to Depo-Provera

The patient sought contraceptive advice from her general practitioner, and a Depo-Provera injection was suggested and administered a week later on the basis that it had no side-effects. No leaflet was issued or warnings of any side-effects made or noted. Following this, the patient became depressed, tired and miserable, and suffered headaches, stomach pains, weight loss and vomiting, but the doctor convinced her that these were not due to the drug and administered a second injection.

It was considered that the general practitioner's standard of care fell below the minimum standard of reasonable professional competence, as he failed to counsel the patient adequately with regard to the potential side-effects of Depo-Provera, in particular weight gain and menstrual irregularities, but as the claimant's advisers felt that the symptoms she complained of might not be causally related to the Depo-Provera, nor that had she been told of the potential side-effects she would have declined the injection, the case was abandoned. Warnings would not usually be given about the effects she suffered.

The investigation of symptoms

It is, of course, important that the patient is heard and his or her symptoms considered even when they do not fit the medical framework that doctors try to apply. If patients feel that their problems have not been considered, then if matters progress they are likely to feel aggrieved, and this may lead to a complaint.

Referral

A common cause of complaint is the failure to refer appropriately for a specialist opinion, and also the failure to refer with an appropriate urgency. This can apply to emergency situations, but also to the timing of non-emergency situations when a degree of urgency is appropriate (e.g. if a possible diagnosis is a malignancy, or if time can be of the essence in avoiding deterioration). A proper letter containing adequate clinical detail will pass much of this responsibility on to the hospital, who should afford reasonable priority (letters are usually screened by a senior doctor before appointments are sent).

Case 37: Failure to refer for specialist advice about impotence

The patient, a 38-year-old diabetic, saw a consultant urologist because of impotence, and a papaveretum injection was recommended, and was performed the following week by his senior registrar. The injection produced an erection, and the patient was allowed home but not warned to seek help if the erection persisted. The erection did not subside, and the next day he saw his general practitioner who advised him to wait and see. A week later, his wife discussed matters with his diabetic consultant, who advised waiting further until his appointment three days later. He was seen at the diabetic clinic and immediately referred to the urology team who attempted aspiration. He underwent three operations, but is now permanently impotent.

The general practitioner and diabetic consultant were both considered substandard in that when the patient presented with priaprism resulting from a papaveretum injection they should have referred him immediately and as an emergency to the urology team, and not reassured him and advised him to wait. A considerable settlement was obtained, with a contribution from the hospital on behalf of the diabetic consultant.

Wrong advice

It is of course important not only that the correct treatment is offered, but also that the advice given is correct. This can be more difficult to defend as, whilst it is usual to note any treatment given, advice is often not recorded and will depend on 'invariable practice in such circumstances'.

Case 38: Failure to advise about emergency contraception

The patient was taking the combined triphasic pill Trinordiol and finished a packet on 2 March. She was on holiday when she ran out of pills, and did not start any more as she broke up with her boyfriend. She had intercourse on 17 and 19 March using a condom, but on the second occasion the condom split, so she attended her general practitioner on 20 March and was advised that emergency contraception was not needed, and that she should recommence the Trinordiol. She was shown to be pregnant by a pregnancy test performed on 18 April, and after counselling she underwent a termination of pregnancy later that month. The failure to prescribe or offer emergency contraception was clearly indefensible, and the case was settled at an early stage for a modest sum (as NHS termination of pregnancy had been available).

Case 39: Providing an informed choice

In 1982 a baby had a 'funny turn' at 6 weeks of age and was admitted to hospital, where a diagnosis of a breath-holding attack was made. EEG was normal. The GP subsequently advised against measles vaccination and against pertussis, although diptheria, tetanus and polio were taken. In July 1987, the child got measles complicated by encephalitis, and has been left globally retarded. The matter went to trial on the question of how reasonable the advice was – the claimant contending that it was contrary to DHSS advice and *British National Formulary* and Data Sheet Advice, and the defence relying on public concerns about vaccination. The trial judge found for the claimant in the sum of £825 000, but on appeal this was overturned on the basis that the parents had consulted a number of doctors and had made an informed choice.

Clinical competence

Underlying the defence of any complaint there must of course be clinical competence, and in the absence of proper clinical competence, however well-mannered and helpful the doctor may have been, it will be difficult to defend an action. Proper and up-to-date clinical competence is vital in any consultation. If the medical actions were basically wrong, the action will be difficult to defend – although the Bolam test (*see* Chapter 1) does acknowledge that treatments supported by a reasonable body of practitioners are quite acceptable even if the claimant contends that an alternative treatment would in retrospect have been preferable.

Common pitfalls in practice

Administrative errors

General practitioners are responsible for the actions of their staff, and due care is always essential when setting up systems and protocols. Particular areas of concern include the availability of appointments, the triage of patients who need to be seen on the same day, and the transmission of results to patients.

Case 40: Errors of information given by staff after vasectomy

The patient underwent vasectomy at the local hospital, the arrangement being that he should produce two sperm counts before relying on the procedure, the results of which he would obtain from his general practitioner. No clinical information was provided on the forms. The second sperm count showed many active sperm and the general practitioner marked it as 'normal'. The receptionist, when asked about the result, said that it was OK, and the patient assumed that this meant that he could abandon contraception. He did so and his wife soon conceived. The claim was indefensible, and was settled for a considerable amount of money. However, the lesson was learned by both general practitioner and health authority, and it was agreed to print clinical details on result forms in future, ensuring correct interpretation of the results.

Prescribing errors

Much of a general practitioner's work involves prescribing, and care always needs to be taken in this sphere. Many doctors now use computers in the consultation and for prescribing. This does have the potential advantage of sophisticated drug-interaction modules, but it must be remembered that such safeguards are limited and the doctor must always assume clinical responsibility for what he or she prescribes. One advantage of computers is that few doctors now use receptionists to write out repeat prescriptions, as most use the computer to do this task – but the doctor who signs must still take responsibility and check the prescription.

Case 41: Faulty prescribing of contraceptive pills

A new patient saw her doctor and requested contraception with the combined pill, telling him that she had previously been prescribed Trinordiol. He issued a prescription for Trisequens, and she soon fell pregnant and underwent termination of pregnancy. After this procedure she returned to the doctor and obtained still more Trisequens, with another pregnancy soon following. At this point the error in her contraception was discovered and a claim was brought which was settled with agreed damages.

Foolishly, the doctor tried to change the records to disguise the error, and this led to him being brought before the General Medical Council and censored.

Case 42: Faulty prescribing of unopposed oestrogen tablets

A postmenopausal woman was prescribed the oestrogen estropipate (Harmogen) from 1980 by her general practitioner for relief of menopausal symptoms. She had not had a hysterectomy, but despite this no progesterones were prescribed for her. After 12 years she developed endometrial carcinoma and was admitted for total abdominal hysterectomy. She has also developed two benign breast lumps. The case was indefensible and was settled for a considerable amount.

Minor surgery

Minor surgery (small procedures that can be undertaken with the use of local anaesthesia) is increasingly being undertaken by general practitioners in their surgery. Since the 1990 contract there has been an increase in the number of general practitioners doing minor operations in the surgery. Whilst it is necessary for health authority approval to be given if payment is to be claimed, there is no restriction on what procedures general practitioners can choose to perform.

In order to perform minor operations safely, there need to be adequate facilities at the surgery, the minimum standard including the following:

- a theatre or treatment room
- adequate lighting
- adequate washing facilities
- adequate sterile supplies (i.e. an autoclave)
- proper arrangements for disposal of clinical waste
- a good adjustable couch
- a range of instruments and equipment
- resuscitation equipment.

It is very often a condition of continuing approval that such facilities are available. Indeed that they are inspected on surgery approval visits by the health authority.

Each Family Health Services Authority operates criteria for admission to the minor surgery list. For example, the admission criteria for Hertfordshire Health Authority at inception were as follows:

- currently carrying out regular minor surgery (at least 20 procedures each year)
- held a post at SHO level or above in surgery
- obtained minor surgery experience during vocational training
- attended an approved course in minor surgery.

If something goes wrong, then it would be expected that facilities to the standard required by the health authority, and personal training and experience at least to the standard of admission to the health authority approved list, can be demonstrated. A general practitioner will be vulnerable if his or her experience and/or facilities are not up to this standard.

Case 43: Substandard skills in minor surgery

The patient, a 63-year-old retired man, underwent excision of a sebaceous cyst on the occiput of the skull performed by his general practitioner, and a further excision a year later and six

months and nine months after that, so there were four procedures in total. During the last procedure there was uncontrol-
lable bleeding, so the patient was sent to the Accident and
Emergency Department where he was bandaged and sent
home with a follow-up appointment to see the general
surgeons. The wound still did not heal, and he required skin
grafting performed by a plastic surgeon. Histology showed that
the cyst was in fact a rare malignant eccrine hidradenoma
which has now been completely excised. Although it was
considered substandard to operate four times on the same
lesion, and at no time to send tissue for histology, the ultimate
result was excellent and it was not thought that earlier
diagnosis could have lessened the procedure or significantly
improved the prognosis, although there would have been
fewer procedures. The case was therefore settled for a modest
sum.

Chest pain

Chest pain is a common diagnostic problem in general practice,
and whilst many cases are not cardiac in origin, the consequences
of missing a cardiac cause may be very serious, as the condition
can proceed to arrhythmias and sudden death. Litigation may
follow if the chest pain has been dismissed in the period leading up
to death.

Diagnosis is by consideration of the triad of history, electrocar-
diogram and cardiac enzymes. The general practitioner may not
have available to him or her the last two of these, and so will have
to decide on the basis of history whether referral is necessary. Of
course the risk for the patient must be evaluated, and age, sex,
smoking history and any relevant past medical history will help to
decide whether the patient is at high risk. A careful evaluation of
the particular symptoms is then essential to assessment.

A loose diagnosis of 'non-cardiac pain' is not impressive in the
courts, and in a high-risk patient a positive diagnosis of the cause
of pain should be made before investigations are discounted.

Recent case law entitles the judge to evaluate the cost-benefit of
actions previously defended by a Bolam defence, and where there
is a risk of sudden death the judge will need convincing that low-
cost investigations were not indicated where a claim is brought.

Case 44: Failure to investigate chest pain adequately

The patient, who was aged 53 years and was very overweight, smoked 30 cigarettes daily, but other than hayfever was in good health. He was advised to lose weight and stop smoking three years before when he was seen with sleep apnoea. He attended his general practitioner one Friday evening with pain in his chest radiating to the right shoulder, and an antacid was prescribed. Later that evening he collapsed and was certified dead, the cause of death being a coronary thrombosis.

It was clearly unacceptable to fail to investigate possible cardiac causes of pain in such a high-risk patient, and the claim was settled.

Ectopic pregnancy

Ectopic pregnancy is an important cause of maternal and foetal mortality, being the sixth commonest cause of maternal mortality in 1982–84, with 10 deaths. At present there is an increasing incidence, which has doubled in the last 20 years. Missed ectopic pregnancies are common causes of medical negligence claims, especially if a Fallopian tube has been lost and fertility compromised.

Pain usually precedes the bleeding, and may radiate to the shoulder tip. There is classically a history of a missed period (in 80% of cases), and slight, brown vaginal blood loss is common (75% of cases) – so-called 'prune juice'. In 75% of cases there has been amenorrhoea. Initially temperature and pulse are normal. Palpation of the abdomen reveals tenderness and pelvic examination may produce acute pain on moving the cervix (cervical excitation) – often an enlarged uterus. In 70% of cases a mass may be felt.

Any patient with vaginal bleeding, the possibility of an early pregnancy and abdominal pain should be considered to have a possible ectopic pregnancy in view of the seriousness of rupture if this is missed, and the fact that it is common for the presentation not to be clear-cut. For this reason, any suspicion of an ectopic should be referred to hospital, where a positive pregnancy test (a blood beta-HCG test rather than the urine test) and ultrasound scan are helpful in diagnosis. If there is a uterine pregnancy on ultrasound scanning, this virtually excludes an ectopic pregnancy, the incidence of the coexistence of uterine and ectopic pregnancies being as low as 1 in 30 000, but if there is not, and the pregnancy test is positive, laparoscopy is indicated.

All women who present with pain and bleeding, a positive pregnancy test and no intrauterine pregnancy on ultrasound examination should be referred for investigations including laparoscopy.

Case 45: Failure to diagnose a ruptured ectopic pregnancy

The patient, who was an actress working away from home, was a few weeks pregnant when she developed severe abdominal pain and was twice seen during that evening by a local general practitioner (who had performed an antenatal check 1 week previously). Although she was faint, unable to sit up and in severe pain, a diagnosis of gastroenteritis was made, and no blood pressure or pulse measurements were recorded in the notes. She collapsed in the early hours of the next morning and an ambulance was called. She was taken to hospital, where she was found to have hypovolaemic shock and disseminated intravascular coagulopathy due to a ruptured ectopic pregnancy. Resuscitation was unsuccessful, and she died later that morning.

The family decided against litigation, although they were advised that there was a strong case, and have instead devoted their energies to setting up a trust to increase awareness of this tragic and potentially fatal condition.

Case 46: Failure to diagnose a ruptured ectopic pregnancy

The patient was diagnosed as being five weeks pregnant and referred to hospital for antenatal care. The next day she developed severe lower abdominal pain and was seen by a locum who diagnosed pelvic inflammatory disease. Her pain became worse, and she began to produce a red discharge. She was seen again that evening by a locum, and the next day by his general practitioner, who diagnosed a bowel problem. Three days later she was admitted to hospital where a ruptured ectopic pregnancy was diagnosed and she underwent urgent right salpingectomy.

The clinical features of a possible ectopic pregnancy were clear and classical in this case, and it was further considered that earlier admission might have saved her tube. Substantial damages were agreed.

Meningitis

There are differing perspectives regarding meningitis between the public and doctors as a consequence of the publicity that tragic cases have generated, and the work of the Meningitis Trust in heightening public awareness of this tragic but rare disease. Thus parents will fear the condition in any febrile child or teenager, even though the vast majority of such illnesses are self-limiting viral illnesses. In retrospect, when things go wrong the rarity of the condition will not absolve the doctor accused when the patient has typical symptoms.

The condition is responsible for 1% of all claims against general practitioners, but 24% of damages, particulary when the diagnosis is missed or delayed and the patient is left with a handicap.

All patients with suspected meningitis should be admitted urgently to hospital for lumbar puncture. Immediate treatment with penicillin should be commenced before the diagnosis is proven.

Case 47: Meningitis – a reasonable diagnosis

The patient, a teenager, was taken to his general practitioner on 7 May with flu-like symptoms and was prescribed penicillin and paracetamol. His condition deteriorated and his mother took him back to the general practitioner on 10 May, who referred him on to the hospital where *Haemophilus influenzae* meningitis was diagnosed after a lumbar puncture. He was in hospital for 2 weeks and has been left with permanent damage to his hearing as a result of his illness, and could initially no longer walk, talk or feed himself. The general practitioner was exonerated on the basis of clear clinical notes and an agreed careful examination on the first occasion, it being felt that at that stage there would not be signs of meningitis and the diagnosis made was reasonable.

Case 48: Meningitis – an unreasonable diagnosis

A teenage boy was taken ill on a Sunday and he was visited at home by a deputising doctor at around 11.50 a.m. He was suffering with flu-like symptoms associated with sickness and diarrhoea, and he had a flat rash which was reddish to purple in colour. The doctor diagnosed chicken-pox and advised that he should be given plenty of fluids and paracetamol. He was admitted to hospital by ambulance two hours later, but died the following day of meningococcal septicaemia.

Liability was clearly established as flu-like symptoms associated with such a rash were clearly indicative of meningococcal disease and required immediate admission. The case was settled by the defendants with damages agreed.

Appendicitis

Appendicitis is a common condition, but is only one cause of abdominal pain that affects young people. Acute appendicitis may progress rapidly to perforation and peritonitis in under 12 hours, or it may settle spontaneously. In cases where there is doubt, if it is decided not to admit the patient to hospital for observation there does need to be close clinical review.

Case 49: Acute appendicitis – undiagnosed but reasonable care

A 25-year-old man suffered with sickness on 6, 7 and 8 September and was seen by his general practitioner on Saturday 9 September, who advised that he could eat and drink as he liked, and should be brought to the surgery on Monday 11 September if he was not better. That day he was again examined and it was arranged to review him later that day at home, when he was admitted to hospital, as there had been no improvement. It was discovered that he had appendicitis, and he underwent appendicectomy, although this diagnosis was not made for several days after his admission to hospital. Although a case was brought against the general practitioner, his repeated and careful reviews were thought to be in line with good practice, diagnosis being difficult in the early stages of appendicitis, and the case was dropped after receipt of expert evidence.

Breast lumps

Carcinoma of the breast is a common condition in this country, and it is the commonest cancer in women. Each year 21 000 women develop the condition and 12 000 die of it in the UK, reflecting a one in 14 chance that a woman will develop this condition during her lifetime. Thus any patient presenting with a breast lump requires careful assessment.

Breast cancer usually presents as a painless lump in the breast. The lump is typically solitary, unilateral, solid, hard, irregular, non-mobile and non-tender. About 75% of cases are in those over 50 years of age.

All discrete lumps need histological or cytological assessment. It is thus universally accepted that any lump in the breast should be taken very seriously. Unless the lump disappears, referral for investigation up to and including excision biopsy is essential. Close observation and follow-up of any lump are mandatory until a definite diagnosis has been made.

Case 50: Breast cancer – failure to examine adequately

The patient, a shy Asian lady, attended her general practitioner with pain in her left breast. He performed no examination either then or when she subsequently returned to see him on several occasions, and made a dismissive comment that the pain was caused by her husband, which caused her embarrassment. Some months later she returned to see a different doctor who again performed no examination and dismissed the complaint. Eighteen months later she returned, and on that occasion the doctor examined her and referred her to hospital where a large malignant breast tumour was discovered in her left breast. She pursued a variety of treatments, both conventional and alternative, but sadly died 6 years after diagnosis. There was considered to be a strong case on both liability and causation, but the case went to trial on limitation and it was held that the delay in bringing the case meant that it could not proceed, particularly as the doctor concerned had retired and had advanced dementia and so would be unable to defend himself.

Cancer of the colon

Carcinoma of the colon, usually adenocarcinoma, is the second commonest cause of death from cancer in the UK and causes 16 000 deaths per year. Around 4% of the population will develop cancer of the colon. There are 21 000 new cases each year in the

UK and a general practitioner with an average list will see one or two new cases each year.

If blood or mucus is being passed in the motion, lower-bowel studies – including sigmoidoscopy, colonoscopy and barium enemas – are essential. Failure to take a full history from a patient of cancer age with constipation can lead to a disastrous missed diagnosis. In particular, the diagnosis of irritable bowel syndrome, which is in many ways similar to cancer of the colon, should only be made after a negative barium enema and sigmoidoscopy have been obtained.

Case 51: Cancer of the colon – inadequate examination and investigation

The patient, a 62-year-old man, attended his general practitioner on frequent occasions after April 1993 complaining of severe abdominal pains, change in bowel habit, and persistent constipation. His symptoms were considered psychosomatic and no investigations were arranged. He developed weight loss and occasional blackouts in November 1995, but his condition was still thought to be psychosomatic. Only in August 1996 was he investigated after he collapsed, and an obstructing carcinoma of the colon was discovered. Perforation had taken place and this led to faecal peritonitis from which he sadly died. No expert evidence was produced to support the actions of the general practitioner and an offer of £80 000 was made which settled the case.

Case 52: Failure to investigate rectal bleeding

The patient, a 55-year-old man, attended his general practitioner from the 1980s with recurrent gastric symptoms and a duodenal ulcer. In September 1993 he attended with a swollen stomach, blood in his stools, and abdominal pains and was variously prescribed De-Noltab, Zantac, nizatidine and bisacodyl before finally being admitted to hospital in July 1994. There it was discovered that he had a Dukes C adenocarcinoma of the sigmoid colon and he underwent sigmoidcolectomy. His prognosis is uncertain.

The general practitioners were considered to have been substandard in failing to investigate his new symptoms, especially rectal bleeding, thereby delaying his diagnosis. Substantial damages were paid.

Failed contraception

Any form of contraception can be associated with a failure rate. The fact that the method has failed does not imply that there was negligence in advice or prescription. There are pitfalls – particularly drug interactions leading to inactivation of the oral contraceptive – and these can lead to expensive claims. In particular, antibiotics and anticonvulsants can inactivate the pill. Advice on the necessary measures that should be taken when such drugs are prescribed should not only be given to the patient but also recorded in the notes.

Case 53: Intrauterine contraceptive devices – adequate advice

The patient was fitted with a Nova-T intrauterine contraceptive device by her general practitioner in March, and she fell pregnant in April. The doctor did issue a warning of the small failure rate associated with this method of contraception, and recorded this in the notes. Based on her expected date of delivery of 4–6 January she would have conceived on or around 10–12 April 1993, 1 month after the coil was fitted.

All methods of contraception have a failure rate associated with them, and it was considered that the failure of a coil in this manner does not imply substandard treatment or incorrect fitting of the device. However, this failure rate should always be discussed with the patient, as it was in this case by the general practitioner, and the case was abandoned.

Case 54: Oral contraception and antibiotics – inadequate advice

The patient, a pupil barrister, was using the combined oral contraceptive pill Microgynon and developed sinusitis for which a broad-spectrum penicillin was prescribed without any warning about the need to take extra precautions. She fell pregnant and decided against termination on moral grounds. She delivered a healthy daughter but lost her pupillage, and retrained as a teacher with considerable loss of income. Very substantial damages were agreed in what was regarded as an indefensible claim.

Case 55: Failed intrauterine contraception but reasonable care

After three pregnancies in succession, the patient had an intrauterine contraceptive device fitted by her general practitioner in September and checked in December, when no threads could be detected. She was sent for an ultrasound scan, but lost to follow-up, in fact being pregnant. She delivered her son the following August and the coil remained. She fell pregnant again and underwent termination of pregnancy and removal of the intrauterine contraceptive device in February two years later.

It was advised that the general practitioner's standard of care did not fall below the minimum standard of reasonable professional competence in that there is a failure rate associated with any contraceptive method, and the patient suffered such a failure which was due to the method used, and not to any act or omission by her general practitioners. The case was accordingly abandoned.

Brain tumours

Headache is a very common symptom in general practice. The annual consulting rate for headache (excluding migraine) is 13 per 1000 patients, whereas the annual incidence of all tumours of the brain is 0.1 per 1000, or 5 per 100 000 members of the population. Thus a general practitioner is likely to see one case of cerebral tumour every eight years, and the majority of these are secondary tumours. Primary tumours generally affect children rather than adults.

An initial silent stage is typical when the diagnosis is impossible, followed by a localising stage of definite neurological symptoms and signs, including epileptic fits, muscle inco-ordination, visual disturbance, sensory loss and reflex loss. A third stage of raised intracranial pressure is followed by a terminal stage if intervention is not successful.

The dilemma is that if the doctor refers every headache to a specialist, an excessive burden may fall upon the hospital, and the suggestible patient may be worse off. Many other causes of headaches need to be considered, including psychogenic headaches, migraine, vascular headaches, meningitis, post head injury, sinusitis, cervical spine abnormalities, subarachnoid haemorrhage, encephalitis, hypertension, temporal arteritis, neuralgia and glaucoma.

Case 56: Appropriate examination for headache

The patient, a 12-year-old girl, presented with visual problems and recurrent headache to her general practitioner in November and the following January, and to an optometrist on 9 and 23 January and 13 February. No abnormality was discovered, although glasses were prescribed. It transpired that she did in fact have obstructive hydrocephalus secondary to a benign brain tumour, an astrocytoma and also *café-au-lait* spots due to neurofibromatosis type one. The records indicated that when the general practitioner saw her with headaches he performed a full examination, advising her to return if the headaches persisted. When she did so, he referred her to a consultant paediatrician for further investigations. He then did not see her again, although he did receive two letters from the optometrist. Expert evidence was supportive of his management and the proceedings were discontinued against him.

Case 57: Failure to examine adequately for headache

A teenage girl developed headache and neck pain through the later part of the summer and saw her general practitioner in September 1992. The cause was thought to be infective. Her headaches continued and in addition she underwent a behavioural change, became tired and listless, and experienced nausea and vomiting. She saw her general practitioner twice in December and a blood test was arranged. Just before Christmas she was admitted to a specialist children's hospital via the local hospital with papilloedema and raised intracranial pressure due to a benign cerebellar astrocytoma, which was removed surgically. There was no evidence in the records of any examination by the general practitioner on the two occasions she was seen, when it is likely that she had had papilloedema and raised intracranial pressure. Her admission to hospital was delayed, but only by 24 hours, and given her good result from surgery this delay fortunately did not adversely effect her condition or prognosis, so the claim was settled for a modest amount.

Case 58: Failure to examine adequately for headache, resulting in GMC erasure

The patient, a 9-year-old girl, was born prematurely but developed normally. In April 1989 she suffered headaches and vomiting following glandular fever in January 1989, and blood tests at that time were normal. The headaches returned in October 1989 and this time were associated with an unsteady gait and blurred vision. She was treated homoeopathically by her general practitioner.

In April 1990 she moved to Liverpool and was taken to a new general practitioner who immediately diagnosed hydrocephalus and referred her to Alder Hey Children's Hospital. There a malignant brain tumour was diagnosed and she underwent emergency decompression and surgery. She has been left hemiplegic, almost blind, and with poor speech and memory.

The general practitioner in Yorkshire was not insured and had no assets, so it was not possible to pursue a civil case against him despite the strength of the case. Following a complaint to the General Medical Council he was found guilty of serious professional misconduct and his name was removed from the register of doctors.

Subarachnoid haemorrhage

Subarachnoid haemorrhage is caused by the rupture of an intracranial saccular aneurysm. Around 5% of the population have cerebral aneurysms greater than 3 mm in diameter. Subarachnoid haemorrhage is uncommon in general practice, with an incidence of 0.3 per cases per year for the average general practitioner or 10.3 per 100 000 (there being 6000 cases per annum). There is a familial tendency. There is an association with hypertension, polycystic kidneys and coarctation of the aorta, and subarachnoid haemorrhage is the cause of about 10% of all strokes. It is a frequent cause of medical negligence claims when the diagnosis is missed or delayed.

Early diagnosis of a subarachnoid haemorrhage is important, as treatment is often operative and can avert severe handicap. The condition often presents in adolescents, young adults, or especially in the 55–65 years age group with a very sudden, very severe headache, 'the worst headache ever, as if hit on the head', and can be associated with faintness and vomiting. It is this history which is the main clue. Such a history always requires referral. Transient loss of consciousness occurs in 45% of cases and then there is severe prostrating headache, often with vomiting. In some there are neurological signs affecting the third cranial nerve (lid or eyelid palsy, dilated pupil) or the sixth cranial nerve (diplopia).

Early recognition of warning leaks is a major priority for general practitioners. The warning leaks present as acute severe headache with vomiting, neck and shoulder pain, and patients with sudden-onset severe headaches and vomiting, without a history of migraine, should be referred for diagnosis by CT scanning and early surgical clipping of the aneurysm.

Case 59: Failing to consider the possibility of subarachnoid haemorrhage

The patient, a student at university, collapsed and was taken to the University Medical Centre with a severe headache, neck stiffness and sickness, and was diagnosed as having migraine. She remained in the sick bay and 2 days later suffered two convulsions, and was transferred to hospital, where it was discovered that she had suffered a subarachnoid haemorrhage. She was critically ill for some time, but is now making a recovery, although she remains confined to a wheelchair, and has problems with short-term memory.

The general practitioners were found to have been substandard in failing to consider the possibility of a subarachnoid haemorrhage given the absence of previous history of migraine and the sudden and severe onset of the pain.

Case 60: Failing to consider the possibility of subarachnoid haemorrhage

At midnight the patient, a 40-year-old taxi-driver, suffered a sudden very severe pain in his head that caused him to vomit and crash his taxi. He attended the Accident and Emergency Department on two occasions over the ensuing days, and was seen by his general practitioner and by a locum. Minor concussion and osteoarthritis of the cervical spine were diagnosed. A week later, after pressure from the family, a CT scan was undertaken which showed that he had in fact suffered from a subarachnoid haemorrhage. Despite treatment, his condition deteriorated and he sadly died a month later.

The hospital and general practitioners were considered to have been substandard in failing to arrange a CT scan sooner to exclude a subarachnoid haemorrhage, given the classical presentation, but the case did not proceed as it was not possible to show that earlier diagnosis would have affected the outcome.

Hip pain in children

Hip pain in children should always be taken seriously, as it can indicate serious pathology which, if left untreated, can lead to permanent disability. It is a not uncommon cause of litigation. The differential diagnosis includes Perthe's osteochondritis, slipped upper femoral epiphysis and septic arthritis.

A slipped upper femoral epiphysis is three times more common in males and affects those in the 10–16 years age group. About 20% of cases are bilateral, and 30% are obese and hypogonadal. There is displacement through the growth plate and the epiphysis slips down and back. In 70% of cases the slip is gradual and in 30% of cases it is acute after trauma. A slipped femoral epiphysis resembles a pathological fracture in that even if trauma precipitates it, there is underlying abnormality predisposing to the slipping. This abnormality is not understood, but it may be related to growth hormone and the sex hormones produced at puberty.

The patient presents with limb pain around the hip and knee, and hip movement is limited and painful, especially in flexion, adduction and medial rotation. There is usually a limp. Pain in the knee in children should always indicate the need for the hip to be examined. An X-ray will confirm the diagnosis (especially a lateral view), and the patient should be referred for a specialist opinion. If left untreated, the condition may lead to avascular necrosis of the femoral head or malunion leading to later osteoarthritis.

Perthe's disease is an osteochondritis involving the hip joint. Osteochondritis only affects bones in the growing phase, and it therefore affects children and adolescents. The incidence of osteochondritis is 0.2–1.2 per 1000 per year.

Early diagnosis of Perthe's disease is essential as, if untreated, the condition will lead over the course of months to bone deformity and spontaneous healing, resulting in residual disability and later osteoarthritis of the hip.

Perthe's disease occurs more commonly where there is a family history – it predominantly affects the 3–11 years age group. The ratio of boys to girls is 4:1, and 80% are in the 4–9 years age group. Around 10–15% of cases are bilateral. The condition may be associated with trauma, and involves a vascular disturbance to the bone which leads to softening and necrosis of the femoral head. If the patient continues to weight bear, the femoral head becomes flattened and as revascularisation occurs the bone hardens, with resulting deformity.

Septic arthritis can be very destructive to the joint, but is now rare. It affects children in the 2–5 years age group, and presents with pain and a limp. Tuberculosis was formerly a common cause.

Case 61: Failure to diagnose a slipped upper femoral epiphysis

A 12-year-old boy injured his hip playing rugby and had pain in his hip over the next year. He saw his general practitioner and two school doctors during this time and was told he had growing pains. Finally, he was referred for an orthopaedic opinion and found to have a left slipped upper femoral epiphysis, and was operated on the hip to pin the epiphysis. He has fortunately been left with little disability, but a modest settlement was achieved for his one year of unnecessary pain and suffering.

Case 62: Failure to diagnose bilateral slipped epiphyses

A 14-year-old boy fell awkwardly after a triple jump and sustained an injury to his hips. He saw his general practitioner, who said that the hip was just bruised. He was eventually taken to the Accident and Emergency Department a week later and discharged home with a presumed groin strain. Three months later it was discovered that he had sustained bilateral slipped upper femoral epiphyses and he had to undergo surgery. A settlement was agreed with contributions mostly from the hospital, given that the general practitioner had seen and appropriately examined him soon after the injury.

CHAPTER EIGHT

Defending allegations of negligence – the role of the Medical Defence Organisations

Simon Dinnick

Introduction

The role of the Medical Defence Organisations (MDOs) in UK medical negligence has been a pivotal one. Very few if any professions can boast the fierce and wide-ranging support that these organisations have provided to doctors, and in many ways their story and evolution mirror the change in attitudes and social mores of this country from the outraged 'never criticise a professional' attitude through the paternalistic 'doctor knows best' phase to the current 'if something goes wrong it must be someone's fault' era. The MDOs have so far weathered all storms, and in their current role as predominantly GP organisations at the approach of the new millennium, the greater threat seems to come from the challenge to the role of independent general practitioners, and indeed their very survival.

Historically there have been three Medical Defence Organisations, namely the Medical Defence Union (MDU), the Medical Protection Society (MPS) and the Medical and Dental Defence Union of Scotland (MDDUS). They were all founded approximately 100 years ago as medical support organisations to help members in times of trouble, to maintain high standards in medicine, and to co-operate in ousting quackery and bad practice. They were always, and still are, companies limited by guarantee, owned by the members without a share capital, and non-profit-making. In the early days, the indemnity of doctors against negligence claims was a very small part of the work.

However, the growth of claims for negligence throughout the 1980s changed all that, and the defence of negligence became the central activity of all these organisations, in terms of both cash and effort.

The factors which brought about this explosion (for such it was) are now well documented and can be found in social factors to do with consumerism and the raising of expectation in a compensation culture, together with the demand for guaranteed success in the application of medical science. Similarly, the widespread availability of legal aid for any medical mishap to be investigated permitted an industry to develop where there had previously been none, and this development was well exploited by highly expert solicitors specialising in medical accidents. Having been an occasional misfortune for the professional, a medical negligence suit now became a normal industrial risk.

Similar growth in claims expenditure and reserve funding can be found in each of the defence organisations. In 1999, the MPS had an annual income of £83 million and an annual expenditure of £69 million on claims and associated costs. In 1979, the equivalent figures were £3.3 million on income and £1.3 million on costs and damages. The MDU in its annual accounts for 1999 revealed an income of £105 million and expenditure of £114 million. In 1985, the MDU's income was £23 million and its expenditure was £11 million (data from Annual Reports of the MDU and MPS).

The defence organisations had historically held a position at the heart of the medical community. They were a friend to all doctors and dentists, and a decision to join a defence union, usually at the outset of a medical practitioner's career, almost invariably led to a loyal membership being maintained until retirement or death. The defence unions were very much the professional society to which every responsible practitioner wanted to belong (even without any legal requirement), although in the hospital sector membership of an MDO became contractually required.

Life remained relatively stable for the MDOs until the mid-1980s, when the signs of major financial crisis became evident due to historical underfunding and a failure to anticipate the growth in claims. Rising subscription rates were required to deal with the increase in the cost and number of claims, particularly for brain-damaged infants, and the underlying principle for MDO membership throughout the decades – that of a uniform subscription for all doctors regardless of risk – could not be sustained. General practitioners started to complain that their subscription bore no relationship to their risk, and that they were in effect subsidising hospital doctors, who were experiencing the main burden of the litigation explosion.

This led to a decision to introduce differential subscriptions for hospital doctors, particularly those specialising in obstetrics and anaesthetics, and the consequence of this demonstrated to the medical public at large, and to the Government of the day, that hospital doctors had indeed been subsidised by general practice. The differential subscriptions asked of hospital doctors, particularly those on captive NHS salaries in training grades, were clearly untenable and therefore in 1989 the Government introduced Crown Indemnity for all hospital doctors and dentists. Traumatic though this was, the MDOs passed over a substantial proportion of their accrued assets to the Government in return for being relieved of the burden of hospital claims, and from 1990 onwards the defence unions in the UK became effectively general practitioner societies and indemnifiers for private practitioners. This was a watershed in the role of MDOs in UK medical life.

Although the membership mix of the defence unions changed radically by virtue of these reforms, the essential philosophy did not. It was to support an individual practitioner in time of trouble, and it is in that role that GPs have found them invaluable. GPs are now facing the litigation explosion in their own right, and the MDOs have successfully managed to remain pre-eminent in that market.

It is important to understand that part of the reason for this successful maintenance of role lies in the constitutional nature of the MDOs themselves. First, as 'not for profit' mutual organisations they have no duty to shareholders but merely an obligation to provide and invest safely and prudently for the needs of the medical profession itself. Thus traditionally they have been able to maintain an acceptable market advantage over commercial intrusion.

Secondly, because of the discretionary powers vested in the governing bodies, the organisations have not been regulated under the Insurance Companies Acts and have not had to have provide the statutory levels of reserve funding or financial guarantees required under that legislation.

Thirdly, the defence organisations have traditionally relied on a date-of-incident basis for cover. Thus provided that a clinician was in benefit with a particular MDO at the time of a medical incident, then that MDO would protect the member (subject to constitutional compliance) in respect of that incident regardless of when a claim was notified. Commercial insurance competitors have *per contra* normally offered a date-of-claim basis for cover, thus only protecting the clinician in the event that he or she was in benefit at the time when the claim was made. The MDO system when coupled with the discretionary powers vested in the Councils means that all members can be reassured of protection against a negligence claim, even if that claim arises, say, 21 years or more after the incident (as might well be the case with a missed diagnosis of meningitis leading to brain damage) or if that claim was notified to the MDO after the retirement of the practitioner or even after his or her death. The practitioner's estate or personal assets would be protected. This basis of indemnity provides the ultimate reassurance to clinicians that their problems will not fall on their nearest and dearest after their retirement or death.

However, the cumulative changes of the late 1980s led to inevitable reform, and without the major washthrough of funds that hospital indemnity claims had provided, the defence unions embarked on a period of intense navel contemplation and re-evaluation in order to cut costs and provide a service that was more tailored to their majority general practice membership. This had its most dramatic effect in the approach to claims management.

Claims management within the MDOs

Philosophically, the MDOs had developed on the back of a culture that 'doctor knows best'. Although clear negligence would always be promptly and fairly compensated, the MDOs had always reflected an innate feeling that a poor medical result did not equate to negligence, and that rigorous defence of claims was the best way of demonstrating this. Equally, the stigma of a finding, or concession of negligence, was substantially greater in former days.

The effect of this closed and supportive culture was that cases nearly always commenced with a denial of liability, and were often only settled when it was clear that a trial was in sight. Whilst this was not the intention, the consequent delay in facing up to legal suit and the philosophy that defensive and attritional methods would deter claims became increasingly unacceptable as consumer and social attitudes developed towards a culture of accountability and openness. The MDOs, prompted by actuarial advice and professional internal and external analysis, began to realise that in many cases legal costs represented a disproportionate element of the total expense on a given claim, particularly in general practice when claims values were obviously in the majority of cases much smaller. This has led to a major cultural shift in the attitude to defensibility. Commercial reality, as well as an awareness that both patient and increasingly doctor alike did not wish to be troubled by the process of litigation, has meant that indefensible claims are now settled with speed and that evenly balanced complaints of negligence are subjected more and more rigorously to a 'balance of benefit' test which leads to settlements at a much earlier stage.

Equally, the development of in-house legal and management resources, scepticism about the cost of external advisers and frustration with the heavy charging of some claimants' solicitors out of medical negligence continue to accelerate a trend towards 'no-fault' compensation by stealth. The truly defensible medical negligence claim is, if not a rarity, certainly a far less frequent event.

However, it is noteworthy that after such analysis and investigation, cases on breach of duty which are litigated by the MDOs are increasingly professionally assessed and, more often than not, result in a successful defence for the practitioner. It has often been said from analysis that 98% of medical negligence cases are either settled or abandoned by the claimant and only 2% go through to trial. Those that do so are more often than not resolved in favour of the practitioner.

Management of a claim by the MDOs

The underlying principle of an MDO's approach to medical negligence claims remains unaltered. 'Doctors for doctors' is not only a byword but still a principle on which MDOs operate. All cases will be assessed and managed by a medically if not medico-legally qualified Claims Manager and will, except in the most obvious cases, be subjected to independent expert opinion. In cases of value, complexity or uncertainty, they will be subjected to detailed legal analysis by specialist solicitors and barristers. Only after that process will a decision about the defensibility of a case be taken. The core values of the organisations have therefore survived all changes so far.

However, what is different is the process within the organisations and the nature of the scrutiny to which medical claims are subject.

Historically (and this, of course, was easier in earlier, more leisurely and academic days), all cases would be subject to analysis and discussion by a committee of eminent medical men. Each MDO had a Council or a Cases Committee drawn from the most senior members of all medical branches. These committees, sometimes consisting of 30 practitioners, would meet perhaps monthly and review large numbers of cases in great detail before opining on their defensibility. The tablets of wisdom that were handed down from the committee were expected of themselves frequently to bring about the collapse of the claimant's case. Members of the MDOs could be sure that impartial and senior men had considered their conduct and their medical practice. Apart from the confidence that this induced and the marketing benefit that resulted when dealing with intrusion from commercial insurers, the courts themselves were aware that a medical negligence case would only find its way to trial following scrutiny of the most senior medical and legal experts, and these cases would find themselves in trial before a judge who had, if not innate sympathy for the doctors, then certainly a keen understanding of professional difficulties and a knowledge of the checks and balances undergone before trial.

However, this process has been forced to evolve dramatically by virtue of the number of claims and the speed with which decisions are required. Committee decision-making has been curtailed, and many decisions are now delegated to managers or small audit committees.

Finally, major changes in the rules of court covering Civil Litigation Procedure in England and Wales will mean that litigation, except in the most substantial and complex cases, will no longer be the route by which most medical negligence disputes are resolved. The practices and attitudes of claims managers in MDOs will have to change to reflect this.

The court's procedural rules no longer permit the timetable to be dictated by the parties, nor do they allow an unlimited number of experts to mass behind the defendant. Indeed, the importance of the change in the early 1980s which led to the compulsory exchange of expert evidence was a major evolutionary factor, as has been the timetable for the exchange of those reports, which has become markedly faster in recent years.

Not only does this process force earlier assessment of the outcome, but now the courts themselves in all medical negligence cases have become managers of the process and its timetable. Judges have been given real powers to compel earlier evidence from the parties by imposing penal rates of interest for delay, and they can throw out cases which they believe have no prospect of success prior to trial. Litigation is stated by the reforms to be the last resort, not the first port of call, and this will in time change the landscape of medical negligence for ever.

However unrealistic this may be, a defendant doctor is now given only three months' opportunity after a detailed letter of claim to obtain advice, and with his indemnifier to assess the likely outcome of the complaint against him. The doctor is required to give a detailed response by the end of this period. If he resolves to fight thereafter and subsequently loses, he may be penalised in costs or by punitive rates of interest for his deemed failure to appreciate his failing at an early opportunity.

Draconian, unrealistic and unfair though these measures may seem, when the claimant may have had three years to prepare their own case, it is, however, the consequence of Government's view that the process of litigation had taken over the purpose of litigation. Hopefully in time the pendulum will swing back to a more balanced view, but for the moment doctors are having to pay the price.

A claim from the doctor's perspective

The first thing all doctors are advised to do is to contact an MDO quickly. Death, serious injury or an act of obvious negligence should be reported directly and without delay. A medico-legal adviser for the MDO is very often the most practical and probably the most friendly face in such a situation. Doctors should also always consider reporting untoward incidents even if they are less obvious medico-legally. The time spent in doing so is seldom wasted.

All of the MDOs appreciate being given a legible set of copy case notes and detailed factual comments on the incident as soon as possible. Recollections that have been put down and reported soon after the incident are often the best evidence. Doctors should also identify other clinicians involved and give their comments in a professional way on the issues as they appear. This will help MDOs to identify which, if any, others should also be held accountable, and whether issues of relevance to causation need to be pursued. Increasingly, the only true medico-legal issue is whether the loss claimed by the patient is, on the balance of probabilities, caused by the breach of duty of the doctors or is for some unconnected and possibly inevitable medical reason.

All relevant documents need to be identified (in addition to the notes) – for example, non-clinical correspondence, complaint file and details, and statements taken from others in the surgery.

Under rules adopted in England and Wales from April 1999, a defendant doctor is asked to sign a statement of truth that he has both searched for and provided all of the relevant documents, even those that are not helpful to his case.

The lawyer appointed will prepare a defence which must at least attempt to set out the practitioner's version of events and their probable case on the issues. This document must, too, be attested by a statement of truth by the doctor who is drawn much more into the process of litigation by the new rules than previously. This is on the basis that involved defendants are likely to face the issues more acutely if they have to be confronted by the litigation process at an earlier stage.

Before any suggestion of trial, the doctor will certainly be asked to attend a meeting or a barrister's conference at which any experts appointed by the MDO will also attend. These meetings, although sometimes intimidating and certainly inconvenient for the doctor, are a vital part of defence evaluation.

The ability and willingness of a GP to undertake the trial process is as much a part of the assessment as the support of an experienced independent expert. It is therefore important that the doctor is as open as possible with his or her advisers. It is better to identify at an early stage that the doctor's own angina or some longstanding family illness will undermine the defence than to invest major cost and substantial time only to discover this shortly before trial.

It is also important to bear in mind that it is the intent of Civil Justice Reforms in England and Wales (*see* Chapter 5) to encourage the parties to address issues early and explore them well before trial. Trial is now firmly regarded by the courts as a last resort and not an inevitability. Cost and interest sanctions, together with active judicial management, will further reinforce that view. Doctors may be forced to consider formal admissions of liability more frequently and much earlier than has hitherto been the case. All of this provides further support for the proposition that negligence is gradually being both destigmatised and, arguably, devalued.

At trial, the role of a defendant general practitioner may often seem bewildering and certainly stressful. It is important to understand that a doctor attending a trial expecting to give his or her evidence and preparing himself solely for that purpose, often over many months, may well spend much of the time of trial listening to other people's evidence, attending conferences where his or her own performance is picked over relentlessly in the light of adverse criticism, and watching while lawyers act in what may seem mysterious and ineffective ways to try to achieve a disposition of the case. At this stage a doctor's role is to preserve his or her equilibrium and to understand, as in any alien process, that there is a point – however hidden it may seem – to everything that is going on. What is not in doubt is that time spent in court is wasteful, stressful and to be avoided except where preparatory assessment proves conclusively that the case should be contested. Once there, a doctor should trust in his or her advisers and have confidence that the outcome will be in his or her best interests. One has to acknowledge as a legal practitioner in this field that this is an act of faith on the part of the defendant doctor.

The following four case summaries illustrate some of the problems presented in the defence of negligence claims.

Case 63: Renal failure – a doctor's actions weaken his defence

A young woman consulted her GP because of a missed menstrual period. The GP found no indication of pregnancy and her blood pressure was normal. Over the next few months the patient made repeated visits to the GP complaining of amenorrhoea, and the GP referred her to a gynaecologist. The patient was noted to be oedematous and anaemic with raised blood urea, creatinine and potassium levels. There was a delay in diagnosis and eventually, 10 months after the patient had first presented to her GP, renal failure was diagnosed. She claimed against both the hospital and the GP. Although on expert advice the GP's failure to diagnose the patient's condition was theoretically defensible, he had made subsequent amendments in his notes following the receipt of the complaint which severely compromised the strength of his defence. The hospital in fact negotiated an out-of-court settlement. The Medical Defence Organisation concerned had to contribute on behalf of the GP because of the effect of the alteration of notes on the viability of his defence.

Case 64: Inadequate notes

A patient experienced surprisingly intense and prolonged pain following a straightforward inguinal hernia repair. Although his condition improved and he was eventually discharged, he was subsequently diagnosed with testicular atrophy, and three years later claimed against the surgeon who carried out the original repair. The rare though recognised complication was felt to be caused by damage to the testicular artery and therefore not negligent. However, more detailed investigation of the claim led to difficulties because of the inadequacy of the surgeon's pre-operative notes and the impossibility of reconstruction of the details of the procedure. The passage of time meant that the surgeon had no real memory of the operation or the consultations and, given these factors, it was decided to seek an out-of-court settlement rather than take their case to trial.

Case 65: Bronchopneumonia – appropriate assessment

A 44-year-old woman visited her GP complaining of cough and wheeze. The GP diagnosed bronchitis and treated her with antibiotics and bronchodilators. A more serious episode occurred some four months later and the patient was followed up in surgery with salbutamol and tetracycline. Chest radiographs showed a shadowing at the bases of both lungs consistent with chronic bronchial damage. An emergency call in the middle of the night two weeks later found the patient to be wheezy again, and the GP prescribed further treatment and arranged further investigations, including a repeat chest radiograph. The patient died six hours later. It was alleged that the GP had failed to diagnose bronchopneumonia and arrange for the patient to be admitted to hospital. Experts instructed on behalf of the practitioner felt that he had acted appropriately at all times and the case was dependent on the strength of that advice throughout. Shortly before trial the widower claimant abandoned the claim. It was possible to mount a rigorous defence in this case because of the GP's thorough assessment and appropriate treatment on each occasion, with clear and unambiguous records of what had taken place.

Case 66: Evidence given in court by defendant loses case

A 28-year-old man was seen by his GP who noted 'sepsis of the right toe. Advised re nails. Erythromycin prescribed'. Nearly three weeks later he attended the Accident & Emergency department of his local hospital complaining of abdominal pain and heartburn associated with nausea and anorexia. He was discharged home. He subsequently attended GPs complaining of feeling sickly with a slight tachycardia and persistent gastritis. Six days after his last GP consultation he was taken moribund to the local Accident & Emergency hospital having collapsed in the early hours of the morning. He was diagnosed on post-mortem as having suffered staphylococcal septicaemia of the kidney, heart and big toe. Against the GPs it was alleged that they failed to take a proper history or examination and to heed the continued sepsis in the great toe. Expert advice suggested that this course of management by the GPs could be defended.

The case was taken to trial, and after the GP had given evidence in court, Leading Counsel advised that he had damaged himself beyond repair and a settlement was therefore agreed at court.

The difference between success and failure in this case was dependent entirely on the GP's ability to cope with fierce cross-examination. He conceded under cross-examination that he could and should have done more to help the patient, and those concessions went well beyond that which he had made in earlier pre-trial preparation. Whilst no criticism can attach to a GP for such a situation, it shows how litigation is a risky and uncertain business.[8.1]

The MDO as practitioner's friend

The role of MDOs as indemnifiers is of course almost taken for granted. However, their unique constitution and mutual role is the key to other activities without which many practitioners would have been bereft. The discretionary powers vested in the governing

---

[8.1]Reproduced from the Medical Protection Society Casebooks by kind permission of the MPS.

bodies of each organisation as to whether and, if so, to what extent they support members in professional difficulty allow them not only to indemnify members against negligence but also to look after them in times of professional difficulty. Thus a major disciplinary or public inquiry involvement for a member can be supported by an MDO providing specialist legal and medico-legal support. The Cleveland Child Abuse inquiry, the Public Inquiry into the workings of Rampton Hospital and, most notably, the Bristol Paediatric Cardiac Surgery investigations are prime examples of the unique way in which the MDO discretionary powers can be exercised to provide support for a clinician who would otherwise struggle to find any form of appropriate help in these most demanding and high-risk professional situations.

Equally, the MDOs have been at the heart of professional defence when it is required within the criminal courts. Leonard Arthur, the eminent paediatrician charged with the murder of a Down's baby in his care, and the case of Dr Cox, a consultant geriatrician who was charged with the murder of his terminally ill elderly patient, are just two high-profile examples of the most serious capital charge that can be laid against a medical practitioner. Over the years countless clinicians charged with the manslaughter or reckless treatment of their patients have found robust specialist and experienced support in the criminal courts from the MDOs and their lawyers. Without such support, in all of these cases the doctors concerned would have been dependent on public legal aid for their defence, and those professionally involved in these cases can attest to the much more limited expertise and investigation that would have been permitted at the expense of the public purse alone.

These major cases highlight the very flexible and positive way in which the MDOs' discretionary powers can be exercised for the benefit of the profession at large. The discretion vested in the governing bodies is from time to time the subject of attack by commercial insurance-based competitors as being uncertain and capable of abuse. Occasionally, a disgruntled member who has not been supported may seek to attack the good faith and to him whimsical nature of MDO support. Overwhelmingly, however, it is accepted as a genuine and professionally unique support system to the medical body politic. The nature of medico-legal difficulties means that such a system is essential if the profession is to be properly protected.

However, two important points of principle arise in this respect which underpin the role of the MDO in this area.

First, it highlights the need for the MDOs to continue to demonstrate both wisdom and transparent fairness in their decision-making. Only because the profession sees these decisions being made properly and in the interests of the profession with the involvement of senior and respected clinicians can such a discretionary system remain credible.

Secondly, the MDOs' role can only realistically continue to be discharged against a continuing critical mass of clinical negligence funding remaining with the MDOs themselves. Governmental change or successful commercial intrusion could both effectively undermine the MDOs' ability to discharge this function, which can really only be perpetuated if the body of excellence maintained by critical mass and the respect in the eyes of the profession that currently exist can be perpetuated.

Where now?

There is no doubt that medical negligence as an industry is at a crossroads for a number of reasons:

1 Negligence itself is being destigmatised. Subliminally, doctors are being encouraged by commercial pressures, by the change in court rules, by complaints procedures and by a society keen to see all damaged patients properly compensated, to accept findings of fault as both normal and inevitable. The balm of 'make it all go away' is therefore a powerful one.
2 The true accountability for poor medical results or performance is being shifted to the professional regulatory arena. Patients, managers and courts alike clearly do not regard the payment of money by an indemnifier as punishment for fault or protection of the public. The removal of a doctor's ability to practise or obtain work is a much more potent threat, and negligence is consequently downgraded.
3 The change in process, other demands on time and the aggravation of compliance are already diluting the willingness of the profession to become involved as experts in the defence of claims, and will continue to do so. The willingness of senior medical practitioners to give their time against an unrealistic timetable of court administration will certainly decline. Without the support of impartial and senior experts, the concept of negligence may well suffer.
4 Society would rather patients were automatically compensated

without proof of fault. However, successive Governments have baulked at the cost and so subtle pressures emerge to allow compensation through legal suit 'on the nod'; the attitude of the judiciary (often themselves now former claimants' Counsel with many years' experience) has unquestionably changed. The change in court rules that are now more interested in administrative competence than in outcome may well downgrade justice founded on the legal principles so clearly expounded elsewhere in this book.

Historically, patients have had to prove a case against a doctor on the balance of probabilities. Now a defendant doctor may well have to show exemplary conduct whilst the patient in effect says 'I am injured – why should I not be paid money?' The burden sits squarely on the shoulders of the professional to demonstrate his competence, rather than on a patient to demonstrate through expert advice that there has been a lapse.

Coupled with the changes in practices and culture discussed above, society, MDO and patient have come together in a curious alliance of approach which, whether inadvertent or not, is resulting in an administered medical compensation system. The emphasis is almost entirely on control of time and cost, and if care is not taken, the concept of professional negligence will dissipate insidiously but inevitably.

For the MDOs and the medical profession, therefore, the challenge in this field is the same. Without the funding brought by the medical negligence claims business, the MDOs may struggle to a point where viability would become an issue. Deprived of the need for an insurance safety-net felt by most practitioners, the desire to belong to the organisations may diminish and a real battle for survival must begin.

For the GP, the challenge is: 'Can you and do you want to retain control of your indemnity needs?' The development of primary care Trusts and the widely discussed possible demise of the truly independent general practitioner do pose a threat to the MDOs. Experience has shown that State Indemnity does inevitably dilute the influence of the practitioner on medical negligence. As professionals, GPs may soon have to decide. The cosy chat with a doctor colleague at your mutual club about the possible risk of being sued is already an anecdotal museum piece. However, images of babies and bathwater need to be addressed for the new millennium.

CHAPTER NINE

When it all goes wrong

Stuart Carne

It is sometimes difficult for doctors to realise the extent to which the attitudes of ordinary members of the public have altered over the past quarter of a century. In the past, doctors often gave the impression that they were doing their patients a favour by seeing them. Although patients may not be paying doctors for medical services at the time they receive them, they are nevertheless paying for them indirectly via their taxes. In addition, the Government, which in this respect is the paymaster, has the right to lay down the terms and conditions of service for which they are paying. Equally, the medical profession is governed by certain 'rules'. Doctors are not obliged to provide every treatment the patient demands, but the patient is still entitled to make the request. If the demand appears unreasonable – and possibly unsafe – it behoves the doctor to explain carefully why it cannot be met. Indeed, a common feature in many allegations of negligence is the failure of the doctor to explain how and why he or she came to the decisions that were made.

The letter before action

There can be very few doctors who have never made a mistake – and that applies as much to specialists as it does to general practitioners. Nevertheless, few letters in the morning post can be more distressing to the recipient general practitioner than one containing a notice of intent that the doctor may be sued for negligence. When a patient is contemplating suing their general practitioner, they will usually have consulted a solicitor first. It will then be the solicitor who sends the doctor a 'letter before action', and this may be the first intimation of trouble. This letter is couched –

as it has to be – in formal legal language. This can make it sound even more threatening than it really is. However, a 'letter before action' is no more than a notice that the solicitor has been asked to prepare a case for a dissatisfied patient. Very often, after the solicitor has had his or her experts (*see* Chapter 10) peruse the papers, the case will eventually be dropped, although that process can at present sometimes take as long as two or three years.

The 'letter before action' does warrant a reply. However, it cannot be over-emphasised that a hasty reply from the practitioner, dismissive of the allegations and critical of the complainant, is just about the worst action that can be taken. Before sending even a formal acknowledgement, the doctor should always seek the advice of his or her 'defence' society. After discussing the issues involved with the GP, they will draft the reply, and indeed will normally take over the management of the doctor's defence.

The 'letter before action' will almost always include a request for sight of *all* the general practice records, including the doctor's own notes – both handwritten and computer stored – as well as his or her telephone message and appointment books. The general practitioner can initially refuse to release these to the solicitor, but the solicitor will almost certainly have no difficulty in getting a court order compelling the doctor to submit them. The usual advice of the defence society is that the general practitioner should release his or her records, although preferably via the defence society. Photocopies of all of these should be kept by the doctor.

Sometimes the general practitioner will have received an earlier warning that action was being contemplated. The patient may have said something, or even sent a threatening letter to the doctor. Again, it cannot be over-emphasised that the general practitioner should never reply without seeking expert advice from his or her defence society.

Sometimes, too, when the records are requested, it is not the general practitioner against whom the complaint is being made. The solicitor may ask for sight of the records because action against a hospital is being contemplated. This may be stated in the letter, but that situation can change. As the claimant's case against the hospital develops, his or her legal advisers may decide that there is also a case against the general practitioner or, indeed the solicitors acting for the hospital may consider that all or part of the blame lies with the general practitioner. The same advice still applies – never deal with solicitors without seeking advice from a defence society, as after all, that is what they are there for.

On the other hand, the general practitioner who receives a 'letter before action' should also avoid over-reacting and thinking 'My God, how could I have been so careless? Let me admit my guilt straight away'. Although it can rarely be wrong to apologise, or at least to express regret for any discomfort which may have been caused, a total admission of liability is not usually a wise response until the case has been gone into in detail by the general practitioner's defence society. Indeed, an early apology by the doctor can often abort a potential complaint, especially if the apology is accompanied by an explanation from the general practitioner about what had happened (*see* Chapter 2).

Adverse publicity

Not least among the worries of a general practitioner when they learn that they may be sued for negligence is the possibility of adverse publicity in the local press and on television. This may reflect upon their private and social life as well as their professional standing. The media sometimes appear to take the view that the doctor must be guilty. Should that happen, the doctor is well advised not to respond to the criticism without first obtaining expert advice. Even if the defence is watertight, it will not always prevent the critics from repeating the allegations. They protect themselves from a libel suit by commencing their new articles: 'Doctor X, who was accused by the parents of one of his patients of refusing to visit their child who was dying of meningitis, now says...'. This is one of those catch-22 situations in which the doctor cannot win. The advice is best summed up in the old adage that 'the best answer to a bad argument is to let it ride'.

Few general practitioners who have been the recipient of a suit for negligence come out of the process totally unscathed. To the lawyers and the medical experts that case will usually be only one of many they have to deal with. Their reputation is not on the line, and they can get on with the rest of their work, rather as a general practitioner does after he or she has had to give a patient bad news. The practitioner who is in the firing line cannot abandon their practice for the 3 or 4 years it may take before the case gets to trial. Nevertheless, during that time they must spend hours going over their evidence, and days in conference with their defence society and their legal advisers. In addition, there will of course be the days – and sometimes weeks – in court at the trial (if the case gets that far). To add to their worries, the general practitioner will not be reimbursed for either their lost time or for their travel and other expenses.

Perhaps one of the hardest tasks facing the practitioner is how to approach the patient, should he or she opt to stay on the doctor's list, and the patient's neighbours who have no special reason to change doctors. Practitioners may find it tempting to remove from their list the patient who has sued for negligence. Hopefully, the patient will take that action without being asked. However, if they do not do so, it is usually wise for the general practitioner to continue treating the patient – having first taken advice from his or her defence organisation.

Prevention

Any complaint – whether a formal notification of a suit for negligence or a criticism dropped into the practice suggestion box (assuming they have one) – is an expression of a dissatisfied patient, and that *might* mean that something in the practice organisation needs to be reviewed. Within the practice, the doctor should expect support from his or her partners. Support in that situation is akin to counselling – it should be non-judgemental.

It is always appropriate for the practice to consider any rearrangements that they might need to make in order to prevent similar mistakes occurring again. Nevertheless, they should allow the dust to settle before rushing in to make changes which may not always be appropriate. For example, 15-minute appointment slots sound fine in theory, but can be counter-productive if they result in a patient having to wait 2 weeks for an appointment. Similarly, going immediately to *every* emergency call during surgery hours can be unfair to those patients who have made an appointment – and who may be more ill than the emergency caller.

Efforts within the practice to improve the efficiency of management are always worthwhile. The current phrase is 'risk management' (*see* Chapter 7). Simple audit of ordinary everyday matters such as the control of repeat prescriptions and the efficiency of the appointment system are not difficult, and will usually repay the time and effort spent several times over – and not just in reducing the number of complaints. There are some general practitioners who boast that their appointments are always running late – 'but my patients know this and it doesn't worry them'. However, these doctors are deceiving themselves, and are more likely to 'come a cropper' than their colleagues who plan their surgery appointment slots more carefully.

There has been a considerable increase in the number of daytime 'emergency' requests to be seen. General practice co-operatives, who now undertake much of the night work, use a triage system to allocate the degree of urgency of each call and decide whether or not it can be dealt with over the telephone. Adopting a triage system to cope with daytime emergency calls may well help to increase patient satisfaction and reduce the number of complaints. However, the person responsible for the triage must be adequately trained to do that job – it almost certainly cannot be left to an ordinary receptionist. Remember that an inappropriate delay in arranging to see the patient can well lead to a negligence suit. A preliminary audit of the problem may reveal a regular pattern to the number of emergency calls, in which case there may be a simpler solution to the problem.

It is important for general practitioners to differentiate in their minds between plans for reorganising the practice in the light of an informal complaint, and the planning of the legal defence against a complaint of negligence. The latter will often be settled on a legal technicality. For example, the case may fail on the grounds of causation (*see* Chapter 4) even though, at least in their own minds, general practitioners realise they were at fault. Alternatively, they may feel that what they did was more than satisfactory in the light of what they understood to be the practice of their colleagues – and yet the court may rule against them.

Case 67: Cervical cytology – a breakdown in communication

In 1985, Miss C had a cervical smear taken by the nurse at the surgery where she was registered at the time. The report – recommending that the smear be repeated 6 months later – arrived after she had married and moved home. The general practitioner therefore had no opportunity to recall the patient. The Family Health Services Authority (FHSA) had already requested the return of the medical record envelope. The general practitioner therefore included the smear report in the next bundle of medical record envelopes he returned to his FHSA. For reasons which have never been satisfactorily explained, the smear report was not forwarded to the new FHSA. When Miss C, now Mrs C, consulted at the new practice a few months later because her periods were irregular, the general practitioner suggested she ought to have a cervical smear. Mrs C said that she had had one just before she moved. The new general practitioner therefore asked his receptionist to phone the previous practice. The receptionist there told the receptionist at the new practice that the smear was all right. What she had done was check with the practice smear follow-up register which listed the patients whose previous smears had been abnormal. As Miss C had left the practice when the report arrived, they had not – logically as it might have seemed at the time – included her name in their follow-up register. The new general practitioner treated Mrs C's irregular periods symptomatically for the next 12 months, at which stage new symptoms appeared. Further tests identified an inoperable carcinoma of the cervix and she died 6 months later.

Both practices believed that they acted correctly. They had both asked themselves 'What else could we have done?' The two doctors involved were members of different defence societies. Each society consulted their own general practice expert. The first expressed the opinion that what had been done was what many other general practitioners would have done. The second expert felt that competent practitioners would have taken more careful steps to ensure that they were properly appraised of the correct information to pass on both to other practices and to the patient. At the trial, the judge decided in favour of the claimant, taking into account the Bolitho judgement (*see* Chapter 4). Damages were shared between the two general practitioners. The FHSAs were also criticised by the judge.

Case 68: Cancer of the breast – a failure to read the records

In November 1980, when she was 18 years old, Miss X consulted her general practitioner. Her mother's two sisters had died at an early age of breast cancer, and now her mother, who was only 39, was going to have a mastectomy. The general practitioner recorded all this in his notes and discussed a possible connection between the contraceptive pill and breast cancer. The treatment Miss X's mother received was apparently initially successful but, unfortunately, five years later, in 1985, she was killed in a road traffic accident.

The previous general practitioner had retired, so when Mrs X – now married and with a young child – sought advice about bereavement counselling, it was one of the other doctors she saw. That consultation, too, was recorded in the general practice records.

A year later, in 1986, when she was 24 years old, Mrs X consulted her general practitioner about a small lump she had found in her right breast. The practitioner thought he knew the family history – that Mrs X's mother had been killed in a road traffic accident the previous year. He examined Mrs X clinically and said he thought it was a cyst but that she should come back in about a month's time for a second examination shortly after a period. This Mrs X did. This time she saw a locum who felt the small lump. He noted what the general practitioner had written in the notes at the previous consultation, and concurred with that finding. Reassured by the opinion of two doctors, Mrs X took no action over the next 12 months, even though she noticed that the lump was steadily getting larger. When she did see her general practitioner again, in early 1987, it was about a cough she had had since Christmas. The doctor asked her about the breast lump and examined her. He found the lump to be very much larger and, disturbingly, he felt some nodes in the axilla. He referred her as an emergency to the breast unit at the teaching hospital in a nearby town. Mrs X was treated with radical surgery, radiotherapy and chemotherapy, but to no avail, and she died later in the same year.

Her family consulted a solicitor about the possibility of suing the general practitioner for negligence. The solicitor sent the general practitioner a standard 'letter before action' (*see* above) together with a request to see all of his records about Mrs X. Acting on the advice of his defence society, the doctor sent the medical record envelope to the solicitor. The solicitor then sent the notes to a general practice expert for comment on the standard of care provided for Mrs X. The expert identified the reference in 1980 to the history of breast cancer in Mrs X's mother and both of her aunts. In the opinion of that expert, the failure of the practitioner to identify the reference *in his own notes* to such a strong family history when Mrs X first consulted him about a lump in her breast fell below the minimum standard of care expected of a reasonably competent general practitioner.

A legal action was then commenced. The defence society

now sought an opinion from an expert of their choosing. The expert said that general practitioners could not be expected to read the notes of every patient who consulted them and, furthermore, it was not obligatory at the relevant time for general practitioners in a non-teaching practice to summarise their records. When the case came to court, this was one of the main issues which had to be resolved. The judge decided in favour of the claimant, quoting the Bolitho case (*see* Chapter 4). A strong family history of breast cancer at an early age was highly relevant when a young girl consulted about a breast lump. It cannot be reasonable, the judge argued, for a practice to hold highly relevant data in its records and not seek to identify that data when the occasion warrants it.

As general practitioners we need to look carefully at all aspects of the organisation of our practice. We are being remunerated as professionals, and we therefore have a duty to provide a professional service. Every time we sign our name to a document, be it a sick absence certificate, a prescription or a report for an insurance company, we are in effect saying that we have come to that conclusion after checking *all* the data.

Case 69: Failure to check a prescription

A patient had been complaining of intermittent sharp pains in his right cheek for 2 months. It did not respond to analgesics and his dentist could find nothing amiss with the teeth. His general practitioner suspected that Mr C had trigeminal neuralgia, and referred him to a neurologist. The neurologist confirmed the diagnosis and intended to advise the general practitioner to prescribe carbamazepine, starting with a low dose and increasing by one tablet a day every 3 weeks until the symptoms were under control. The specialist added that he would see the patient again in 6 months' time. Unfortunately, the neurologist's secretary typed 'carbimazole' instead of 'carbamazepine', and the neurologist signed the letter without reading it. The general practitioner glanced at the neurologist's letter and felt rather pleased at his own diagnostic acumen. He telephoned the patient to tell him what the neurologist had said, and told him to collect a prescription from the reception desk for some tablets which he was to take at a dose of one a day. If he was still no better, he should then increase the dose by one tablet every three weeks until the pain was under control, and then continue with that dose until he saw the neurologist for review in six months' time. The general practitioner instructed his receptionist to prepare the prescription which he would later sign with that day's repeat prescriptions. Over the next 6 months five further repeat prescriptions of carbimazole were issued by the practice without Mr C having been seen by a doctor.

By the time Mr C was seen again by the neurologist he was very hypothyroid. Discontinuation of that medication led to a slow recovery but, not unnaturally, Mr C sued the neurologist for recommending carbimazole instead of carbamazepine, and the general practitioner for issuing the prescriptions for carbimazole – which he should have realised was not appropriate for trigeminal neuralgia. The neurologist's expert argued that the general practitioner should have identified the typing error in the letter and that, had he seen Mr C when repeat prescriptions were issued, he would soon have realised the mistake. The general practitioner told his defence society that he was only doing what he was sure many other practices did. The defence society (tactfully) pointed out to him that the responsibility for the content of a prescription rested with the doctor who signed the prescription form. After much argument, the solicitors for the Hospital Trust (on behalf of the neurologist) and the general practitioner's defence society agreed to share the responsibility.

Patients have every right to reject all or any part of the advice their doctor offers them. If they do so, the physician should try to explain the likely outcomes. A controversial issue is whether, when offering that explanation, the doctor should point out some of the serious possible consequences that might ensue if the patient rejects the advice proffered.

Case 70: A non-compliant patient

Mr D was an insulin-dependant diabetic who lived with his unmarried daughter. His three sons and their families visited him fairly frequently. He gave himself his injections regularly, but was almost totally non-compliant with regard to his diet. His general practitioner tried on many occasions to explain the need to balance the amount and timing of insulin to be injected against the food (calories) consumed. He referred to this – albeit briefly – eight times in his notes. Mr D's glycosylated haemoglobin was generally around 10%, and was never below 8%. Increasing the dose of insulin exposed him to several bouts of hypoglycaemia which Mr D seemed unable to identify in the early, treatable stage, and which necessitated his going to hospital on several occasions. A diabetologist to whom the general practitioner had referred Mr D agreed that it was difficult to maintain the blood glucose at a satisfactory level. He added that hypoglycaemia might be a greater risk. Mr D developed a neuropathy and arteriosclerosis in his legs. An ulcer developed and failed to heal. When he asked what he should do to improve the condition of his legs, the general practitioner said he could probably prevent further deterioration if he took more care to regulate his diet. Mr D said he could not do any more in that respect, as he felt he needed to eat to keep up his strength and he could not take his meals at regular times. That conversation had taken place several times and it, too, was recorded on four occasions in his general practice notes.

The condition in the leg deteriorated and amputation was recommended. Unfortunately Mr D died from a pulmonary embolus 48 hours after the operation. The family alleged negligence by the practitioner for failing to control the diabetes adequately. The general practice expert, whose opinion was sought by the claimants' solicitor, identified the 12 references to non-compliance in the general practice records and reported this to the solicitor. When the family were told what the expert had discovered, the daughter with whom Mr D had been living admitted that she was aware that her father rarely followed his diet. She had not told her brothers about this because she did not want them to argue with their father. The case was withdrawn.

There was a happy outcome. The family asked the general practitioner to meet them to discuss what had happened. At that meeting one of the sons said: 'Perhaps it was better that Dad didn't lead too restricted a life because of his diabetes. I think he chose it that way, and he certainly would not have been happy to have an artificial leg'. The son then produced a packet from his briefcase and handed it to the doctor, saying 'Dad often told us how you and he were keen stamp collectors. We know he would like you to have his collection of penny blacks!'

As we said at the start of this chapter, the arrival of a letter of claim can send a chill down the spine of any doctor. Below is a copy of such a letter addressed to one of the medical defence organisations.

Case 71: A letter of claim submitted to a defence organisation[9.1]

To the Medical Defence Union Limited

18 August 1999

Dear Sirs

RE   Our Clients   Mrs X (D.O.B: 1.1.70) and
                             Master Y (D.O.B: 2.9.95)
  Address   1 Home Road, Hometown Drz
  MDU Member:

We now submit a detailed letter of claim in respect of the above-named action in compliance with the Clinical Negligence Pre-Action Protocol.

CLAIMANT'S DETAILS AND GENERAL BACKGROUND
We represent Mrs X (D.O.B: 1.1.70), who is now 29 years of age, and her son, Master Y, who will soon be 4 years old.
   Their address is 1 Home Road, Hometown. Master Y was born at Hometown Hospital, on 2 September 1995. He suffers from congenital rubella syndrome. Mrs X suffered from a widespread rash in the first trimester of her pregnancy. There was a complete failure by her GP, Dr Z, to even consider the diagnosis of rubella. In consequence, Mrs X had no opportunity to terminate the pregnancy. Master Y has significant developmental delay and Mrs X will have an ongoing responsibility for his care.

EVENTS GIVING RISE TO THE CLAIM AND CHRONOLOGY
This was Mrs X's first pregnancy. It was unplanned and she was on the oral contraceptive pill at the time she became pregnant. She performed a home pregnancy test which was positive, and therefore stopped the contraceptive pill immediately. On 9 January 1995, she visited Dr Z to arrange antenatal care for her and check her dates. At this visit, her

---

[9.1]Case prepared by Mr John Pickering.

last menstrual period was noted as being 28 November 1994. Her estimated date of confinement was 3 September 1995. In her records, Dr Z states 'for ante-natal clinic in 6 weeks'.

On 12 January 1995, Mrs X developed a widespread rash all over her body. She describes it as being red and from head to toe. It was flat in nature. Mrs X did not feel ill at the time. She was sent home from work (as a sewing machinist) by her supervisor. The reason for this was concern at the effect on other people of the appearance of the rash.

Dr Z visited Mrs X at home. She recorded the following:

'Covered in rash from head to foot
– sore throat with follicles – Coxsackie B virus –
caps – Amoxil 15'

Dr Z diagnosed tonsillitis, although Mrs X stated that she did not have a sore throat. Dr Z informed her that the body rash was a reaction to being pregnant. In particular, no blood tests were arranged at this time. There was no discussion about how the rash might affect Mrs X's pregnancy. She completed the course of amoxycillin.

On 16 January 1995, Mrs X was booked at home by the midwife. It is stated that she would have routine blood tests at the next visit. Her rubella status was noted as being unknown. On 14 February 1995, two antenatal blood tests, including rubella, were taken from Mrs X.

As the pregnancy progressed, the baby's fundal height remained compatible with Mrs X's dates. In July 1995, her blood pressure rose to 140/90 mmHg, and this was followed by an admission to hospital on 27 July 1995 for raised blood pressure. She then returned home briefly.

On 2 September 1995, Mrs X was admitted in labour. Following a vaginal examination, an ultrasound scan was performed which confirmed the presence of a breech presentation. Mrs X proceeded to an emergency lower Caesarean section and delivered an infant weighing 2.11 kilograms. The Apgar scores were 3 at 1 minute and 9 at 5 minutes. The condition of the baby was described as poor. Thick meconium and oligohydramnios were noted at the operation.

The baby, Master Y, had a widespread red rash over his body. He was transferred to the neonatal unit.

It was immediately suspected that Master Y had congenital rubella infection, and this was confirmed by blood tests. Mrs X's blood was tested. In the microbiology report dated 11 September 1995, it is apparent that the blood sample taken on

14 February 1995 was also re-tested. The result from this test showed that rubella IgM was detected, confirming that Mrs X had suffered from an acute rubella infection in the first trimester of her pregnancy.

On 18 September 1995, Master Y was discharged from hospital. The neo-natal discharge summary describes Master Y's ongoing problems as follows:

'Congenital rubella syndrome
right eye cataract
left undescended testis
query hearing problem
patent ductus arteriosus.'

Since his discharge, Master Y has had ongoing multiple problems. His heart defect has been treated at Anypiace Hospital by non-invasive surgery. He has one undescended and one non-functioning testis for which he has been seen at Hometown Hospital. He has required treatment at the St Robert's Hospital for these problems, and he has had two operations. He has had cataracts and amblyopia treated at Anypiace Hospital. He has damage to his hearing and wears hearing-aids.

Master Y's development is delayed, he is unable to walk, and he has little speech or comprehension.

On 25 November 1995, Mrs X wrote to Anytown Health Authority to make a complaint about the treatment provided to her by Dr Z. She requested an independent review and the matter was considered by the Authority's convenor.

The failure of Dr Z to consider the possibility of rubella infection in Mrs X's case and the consequential events were considered. The panel were of the opinion that Mrs X had grounds for complaint in this instance because they believe that if a blood test had been taken on or shortly after the visit by Dr Z on 12 January 1995, rubella would have been diagnosed and Mrs X could therefore have terminated the pregnancy. The panel concluded that Dr Z did not give sufficiently serious consideration to the possible diagnosis of rubella. They recommended that Dr Z should undertake 'as a matter of urgency' further training.

THE CLAIMANT'S INJURIES, CONDITION AND FUTURE PROGNOSIS

The claimant's condition and prognosis as at 1998 are as set out in the reports of Dr R, NB, FRCT, DCH Consultant and

Paediatric Neurologist, Royal Liverpool Children's NHS Trust, Alder Hey Children's Hospital, Eaton Road, Liverpool L12 2AP, dated 5 May 1998. A copy of this report is attached.

QUANTUM

We identify the following heads of damage:

1 General damages: Mrs X had to continue her pregnancy and go into labour. She then underwent a Caesarean section. This would have been avoided had the pregnancy been terminated. After discharge home, Mrs X was effectively house-bound with Master Y since he was still excreting the virus and Mrs X had to comply with public health advice. She required gynaecological monitoring because of the presence of the rubella virus; this was an extremely unpleasant and upsetting experience.

2 Care: Master Y spent approximately 3 weeks on the neonatal unit, at which time Mrs X was providing care and support for him. Following his discharge, Master Y has delayed development, is unable to walk and is much more difficult to look after than a healthy child. It is not at present clear what his ultimate level of function will be and further evidence will be required as he grows older to assess the long-term outlook for him. At present, it seems likely that he will require care support throughout his life.

3 Travel: Master Y has received care from Hometown Hospital, the St Robert's Hospital, Anypiace Hospital and Children's Clinic. This has entailed considerable travelling for regular follow-up visits. The costs of these visits are claimed.

4 Education: Master Y has been through the assessment process of special education needs. It is clear that he will need support throughout his education.

5 Loss of earnings: Mrs X's responsibilities have meant that she has been unable to consider other forms of work. In addition, Master Y will most probably be unable to support himself and will be dependent upon Mrs X.

6 Occupational therapy: Master Y will be reliant upon employed carers if he is to achieve any level of independence. This will require advice, support and management of his care needs. There will be long-term occupational therapy input, and in due course this will be quantified and costs claimed.

7 Aids and equipment: Master Y requires hearing-aids. He is registered partially sighted and will require visual aids for

his education and also to give him a reasonable quality of life. He also requires special shoes with insoles. It is not clear what his level of mobility will be, and it is likely that he will need special equipment to be made available.

8 Transport: Master Y will be reliant upon transport by Mrs X or employed carers.

9 Accommodation: Since it is likely that Master Y will not achieve independence, then long-term decisions will be necessary over how he may be accommodated and cared for.

CONCLUSION

Please acknowledge receipt of this letter within the stipulated 14-day period and let us have your full response within 3 months.

We take the view that there is a very strong case against Dr Z and invite you immediately to admit liability and causation and thus confirm your willingness to negotiate a full settlement. Consistent with the spirit of the protocol, we also indicate that we are prepared to consider dealing with this by way of mediation. Please note that this case has been explored in detail with Counsel and experts, and if it is that the matter is not resolved, it will be our intention to promptly commence Court proceedings.

We await your response

Yours faithfully

IRWIN MITCHELL

CHAPTER TEN

The duties and responsibilities of medical experts

Nigel Ineson and Stuart Carne

The need for a medical expert

We have shown earlier in this book (*see* Chapter 4) that for a medical negligence claim to succeed, three basic elements have to be established:

- that there was a duty of care on the part of the doctor to that patient
- that the doctor failed to meet the expected standard of care – known as *liability*
- that as a consequence damage has occurred to the patient – known as *causation*.

Duty of care

In many non-medical civil law suits it may be difficult to prove that the defendant owed a duty of care to the claimant. In medical cases this issue is usually crystal clear. When a doctor is consulted by a patient, the doctor automatically assumes a duty of care. That duty encompasses a need for the doctor to provide competent and appropriate advice.

It goes without saying that general practitioners owe a duty of care to everyone on their NHS list, but that duty also extends to any other person to whom they offer professional advice.

Case 72: Informal consultation – the duty of care

A doctor's golf partner told him that his wife had a fungal infection of one of her toenails and asked him what would be a good treatment for this. The doctor wrote out a prescription for a course of an antifungal treatment. Six weeks later the golf partner told the doctor that his wife's toenail was no better. The doctor issued a second prescription for the wife to continue the treatment for another three months. At that stage she consulted her own general practitioner who diagnosed a subungual malignant melanoma. Having opted to offer professional advice, the first doctor assumed a duty of competent care for someone who had now become his patient, even though he may not have seen her.

Case 73: Hospital advice – the general practitioner's duty of care

A general practitioner referred a patient of his to hospital for tiredness and loss of weight for which he could find no explanation. After investigation, a diagnosis of Addison's disease was made. After a number of hospital attendances the general practitioner was advised of a dose of steroid, and she was put on to long-term follow up at out-patients. The role of the general practitioner appeared to be confined to issuing repeat prescriptions of corticosteroids, and he did not see the patient. The patient developed obesity, hirsutism and skin striae. When she was told at the hospital that this was due to too large a dose, she sued. Even though the general practitioner had only followed the hospital's advice, he was held responsible, as the doctor who issued the prescription had the duty of care.

Most of what follows in this chapter involves a breach of that duty of care.

As a side issue and contrary to popular opinion, it has not yet been established whether or not a 'Good Samaritan' act (e.g. offering medical assistance at the site of a road accident or in an aircraft) is covered by the usual criteria for 'duty of care' owed by a physician. In practice, physicians in the UK – and even in the USA – have rarely, if ever, been sued in this situation.

Establishing liability

In deciding if the actions of a doctor were negligent, the courts apply a number of precedents. Once again the 'Bolam test' (*see* Chapters 1 and 4) is applied when determining the standard of care required. That test is the standard of the ordinary skilled person exercising and professing to have that special skill. He or she need not possess the highest expert skill. It has been established that all that is necessary is that the doctor exercises the skills of an ordinary common professional practising that particular art. A doctor who acts in accordance with the practice accepted as proper by a responsible body of medical practitioners skilled in that art is not negligent, nor is he or she negligent if he or she is acting in accordance with such a practice, merely because there is a body of opinion which would take a contrary view.

In order to assess an individual case it is necessary for the legal advisers, and ultimately the courts, to rely on the advice of medical experts as to what was an acceptable standard of care in the particular circumstances.

The test is not the 'gold standard' of exemplary care or even necessarily 'best practice', but it is what could reasonably be expected from a competent general practitioner at the time when the incident occurred. The expertise needed will be that of the speciality involved. Therefore it is not relevant for a consultant surgeon to say that the standard of care provided by a general practitioner fell below an acceptable standard, as he cannot be an expert on the standards in general practice – that advice can only be provided by another general practitioner.

Case 74: Causative damage but no liability

The patient had *Helicobacter pylori* infection and so was prescribed triple therapy, including omeprazole. Whilst on treatment he suffered severe alopecia, which is an unusual effect of the drug, and which was thought in his case to be due to the drug (i.e. establishing causation). However, this side-effect is rare, and not one which would generally be warned about, and thus liability was not established.

Establishing causation

Once it is established that there has been care below a competent standard, the next link is to establish what effect this has had on the patient – this is known as causation. Here the experts may be (and usually are) from other specialities because what is needed is an opinion as to what would have been the probable outcome if the doctor had got it right. Often this is a difficult area to establish, particularly for example in cancer cases, where there may have been a potentially fatal disease, but at various stages of the illness the effects of delay will have different outcomes. Delay at the beginning may deny the patient a chance of cure, whereas delay later may only lessen the time of survival. In many forms of cancer the prognosis has been well documented, related to the stage of the illness and other factors. The rate of development of that disease is also often known. Thus an expert armed with such data can state what the chances were of cure if the disease had been treated at various stages of its development. Even more specifically, the expert is able to say in many cases that, if the disease had been treated X years – or even Y months – earlier, the chances of a cure were Z% greater. The court will also want to know whether, at each stage, the chances of cure were greater or less than 50%. Even if the chance of cure is only 51% at a specified time, and falls to 40% a year later, on the balance of probability failure to offer treatment at the earlier stage is negligent because, at that time, the chance of a successful cure was greater than the chance of failure, whereas a year later the reverse was the case.

Case 75: Negligence but no consequential damage

A 10-year-old boy developed a tender swollen testicle and his general practitioner refused to visit him. His parents therefore took the boy immediately to the Accident and Emergency Department where torsion of the testis was diagnosed and surgery performed. At operation it was too late to save the testicle and he underwent orchidectomy.

   Although it was clearly negligent to fail to see a child with sudden onset of a painful testicle, the fact that the parents took him straight away to hospital meant that no delay had resulted from the general practitioner's negligence and thus no damage was caused. The claim was therefore abandoned.

Case 76: Carcinoma of the lung – negligence but no consequential damage

The patient injured his back on 13 July after a fall. He went to the Accident and Emergency Department where his back and chest were X-rayed. The latter showed a possible shadow. Despite a letter to his general practitioner dated 19 July requesting follow-up, none was arranged by the GP. Only on 2 December when he next attended was this abnormal result noticed, and he was sent for a further chest X-ray which showed that he had carcinoma of the lung. He was treated with chemotherapy and two attempts to resect the tumour. Unfortunately, the following year he was found to have liver metastases and he died soon afterwards.

Whilst there was clear evidence of negligence in the failure by the GP to follow up an abnormal chest X-ray which led to a 6-month delay in diagnosis, the expert evidence was that the delay in treatment did not have any significant effect on the prognosis. The case was therefore withdrawn.

Balance of probability

In a criminal case, proof of guilt has to be 'beyond all reasonable doubt'. In civil cases, including medical negligence, that degree of proof would put the claimant at a disadvantage. The proof required is 'the balance of probability' – in other words, the odds in favour of – or against – the outcome of the disease being favourable.

Case 77: Malignant melanoma – a failure to refer

A 40-year-old woman had a malignant melanoma excised in June 1997. It was found to be 8 mm deep. Two years earlier it had been seen by her general practitioner who took no action. Expert opinion was that in 1995 the lesion would only have been 4 mm deep, at which stage the chances of a 5-year cure were said to be 70%, whereas at 8 mm the chances were only 40%. Therefore, on the balance of probability, the general practitioner was not only negligent in not arranging for the lesion to be excised in 1995, but the chance of cure had been appreciably decreased as a consequence of the delay in referral.

Qualifications of a medical expert in general practice

Medical experts in general practice do not need to be senior or 'super'-practitioners sitting at the pinnacle of their profession, but rather they should be experienced and competent practitioners undertaking work to a reasonable standard. They should preferably have been in practice at the time of the incident as they must advise the judge on the standard of care at the relevant time, taking into account all the difficulties and frustrations of everyday general practice.

They will need to be principals who, preferably, were in practice at the time of the incident. Postgraduate qualifications are impressive to the judge, especially Membership (or Fellowship) of the Royal College of General Practitioners, but a whole string of qualifications will not necessarily establish the expert more than basic experience and qualifications.

The role of a medical expert

General practice experts must:

- be experienced general practitioners
- provide an unbiased opinion
- not be associated with either the defendant or the claimant
- consider all the evidence placed before them
- base their opinion on the literature and practice which were contemporary at the time of the event
- point out both the positive and the negative aspects of the case
- be consistent and rational in their opinion and prepared to discuss and defend it against criticism by other experts
- on the other hand, be prepared, if appropriate in the light of new evidence, to amend that opinion
- be willing and able to attend court and also conferences with counsel
- be able to meet the time constraints of the case
- maintain confidentiality to those instructing them.

Often there is a dispute as to what happened. It is not for the expert to decide which version of events was factually correct –

that is for the court. Thus it may be necessary for the expert to give two opinions based on the two versions of events so that the court is guided either way once it has decided which version of events it will accept.

The independence of medical experts

It is very important that medical experts advising in a case are independent and have no vested interest in the outcome. They should not be in practice in the immediate locality of the incident, nor should they be acquainted either professionally or socially with any of the parties. This independence is central to the role and credibility of the expert in a medical negligence case, whether acting on liability or causation and whether acting for the claimant or for the defendant.

Lord Woolf recently published recommendations for the improved management of all civil cases, including those involving clinical negligence, in an attempt to improve access to justice and speed up the process. The Government responded with a White Paper closely followed by the Access to Justice Act 1999 (*see* Chapter 5). The Civil Procedure Rules (1999) were published on 29 January 1999 and Part 35 (there are 51 Parts in total) deals specifically with expert witness work. The rules make it quite explicit that the duty of the expert is primarily to the court and not to those instructing him or her. In the past there have been a number of so-called 'experts' – often referred to as 'hired guns' – whose bias usually sticks out like a sore thumb. Indeed, some of them claim an expertise over a wide range. Courts will now not only have greater control in the management of experts, but will also be encouraged to appoint a joint expert to advise the court. Where possible, matters requiring expert evidence will be dealt with by a single expert. The corollary is that an expert can ask the court for guidance and directions in how to carry out their task without seeking the agreement of the parties involved. How all this will work in practice has yet to be seen.

An expert's fee should be based on the time spent on the case. It is generally held not to be appropriate for this fee to be based on the outcome, for this could affect the expert's independence, although this is not the case in the USA where both 'conditional' and 'contingency' fee arrangements may be used. A conditional fee is one where payment of the fees of lawyers and experts is only due if the party instructing succeeds, and to compensate for cases where no fees are paid an uplift is allowed of as much as 100% of the fees. A contingency fee allows lawyers to make no charges but instead to take a percentage of any damages awarded, typically 25% or 33% of the total damages, if the claimant wins.

In this country it is held by many to be unethical for experts to enter into either contingency or conditional fee arrangements, but the issue has not yet been fully decided.

Instructions to a medical expert

The first approach to an expert will be in the form of an initial letter of enquiry from the claimant's solicitor. The letter should include the name of the defendant and hospital involved, so that the expert can ensure there is no conflict of interest. Although some solicitors will anonymise the patient's name at this stage and may also not disclose the name of the general practitioners involved, it is helpful to obtain the names before agreeing to give an opinion, in case the subject of the allegation is known to the invited expert. The letter should set out the basic facts of the matter so that the expert can decide if the case falls within his or her area of expertise. Any time constraints should be mentioned, as should the quantity of documentation, so that the expert can estimate the time and hence the fee involved. The volume of papers to be read can vary considerably. Several hundred pages is not unusual – sometimes the expert will have to read the contents of two or three lever-arch files! However, the time taken often depends less on the volume of documents to be read than on the complexity of the case and the need to check the literature. There should also be mention that the expert's fees will be met by the solicitor. At present most cases are legally aided, but this may change under the new arrangements which limit the aid available for civil cases, although clinical negligence is to be treated as a special case. Usually an estimate is required by the Legal Aid Board from the expert before their approval – and hence the solicitor's undertaking – can be given.

Only after acceptance of the case should the full documentation be sent by the solicitor to the expert. Unsolicited bundles of notes are not appreciated, especially if the case is refused and the notes have to be returned at the expert's expense.

The formal instructions to the expert will include the following:

1 the claimant's proof of evidence (i.e. statement)

2 other collaborating proofs (e.g. from family and friends)
3 other supporting documents (e.g. photographs and diaries)
4 the full medical records from:
   - the general practitioner, including any computerised records
   - the hospital – including X-rays themselves as well as X-ray and pathology reports and correspondence to and from the general practitioner and other specialists
   - private practice, if any
   - district nurses
   - health visitors
   - district midwives
   - community psychiatric nurses
   - child health clinics
5 patient-held records
6 health authority complaint proceedings, if any
7 post-mortem reports
8 documentation from a Coroner's inquest
9 pleadings.

The letter of instruction should try to identify the issues in the case. It should indicate what questions the solicitor or counsel would like to have addressed by the expert and what questions – if any – the claimant has raised. However, the expert should be left free to identify and discuss any other areas of concern that arise. After all, he or she is the person best placed to identify where the standard of care has fallen below what should be expected.

Another result of the Access to Justice Act is that, in the interest of openness, all instructions to experts are disclosable to the other side. Previously this was not the case, such correspondence being privileged. Now all correspondence between experts and those instructing them is disclosable. Even verbal interactions should be noted and are technically disclosable.

The matter of whether the expert should see the claimant in order to deal with liability is controversial. On the one hand, it is important to establish what the claimant considers went wrong and to understand their version of events, but on the other hand, the expert must not be seen to be on the side of the claimant. Furthermore, the claimant and the expert may be located on opposite sides of the country to each other. Most experts generally rely on the solicitor to take a careful statement (proof of evidence) from the claimant and other possible witnesses. The expert will then proceed on the basis of that and the medical records to see if there is a case.

However, if any reports on the present condition and prognosis of the patient are required, they will often have to be based on an examination of the patient. In order to prepare these it may therefore be necessary for the claimant to be seen by the expert.

The format of the initial medico-legal report

Reports vary in their format, but the following elements must be present, although not necessarily in the order given:

- **Introduction** – a brief outline of the case including a summary of all the instructions from the solicitor (written or oral).
- **Sources and background** to the report – detailing the documents seen when preparing the report and highlighting any further documents needed. The Rules make it essential that all such documents are listed.
- **Chronology and statement of events** – a description of events as put by those instructing the expert, including a chronology of the matter. *The claimant may state a case which is contrary to the records, and in this case the expert should indicate what the claimant states, and give an opinion both on the standard of care if the judge accepts what the claimant states, and also whether the standard of care was acceptable if alternatively the medical records (and later defendant statements) are accepted.*
- **The medical records** – a review of the medical records highlighting any discrepancies that may indicate areas of *factual* dispute.
- **The standard of care** – which may include a brief outline of the medical issues and a glossary and explanation of technical terms.
- **Opinion** – including a discussion of the issues. If there is to be a range of possible opinions, these should each be listed and the expert should state, with reasons, which he or she prefers, always remembering it is for the judge to decide where facts are disputed.
- **Conclusions**.
- **Causation** – this may be dealt with either in detail or briefly, depending on whether the expert feels able to comment – often general practitioners will deal with liability and leave causal issues to specialists.
- **References** to any contemporaneous literature, with copies provided where possible, upon which the expert has relied in making the report.

- **Qualifications** and a brief curriculum vitae of the expert establishing his competence to comment.
- **Declaration**.

A statement of truth at the end of the report is required. The minimum is of the form 'I believe that the facts I have stated in this report are true and that the opinions I have expressed are correct.' However, following the Woolf Report into litigation, both the Academy of Experts and the Expert Witness Institute recommend that all reports should conclude with a declaration along the following lines:

> I understand that my primary duty in written reports and giving evidence is to the court rather than the party that instructed me.
>
> I have endeavoured in my report and opinion in this matter to be accurate and to consider all relevant issues concerning the case, including any matters which I have knowledge of or of which I have been made aware, that might adversely affect the validity of my report.
>
> I have indicated the sources of all the information that I have relied upon.
>
> I have not, without forming an independent view, included or excluded anything which has been suggested to me by others, including those instructing me.
>
> I will notify those instructing me immediately (confirmed in writing) if for any reason my report requires correction or qualification.
>
> I understand that my report, subject to any corrections before swearing as to its contents, will form the evidence to be given under oath and that I may be cross-examined on the contents of my report by a cross-examiner assisted by a medical expert. Further, I may be the subject of adverse criticism by the judge if the court concludes that I have not taken reasonable care in trying to meet the standards set out above.
>
> I confirm that I have not entered into any arrangement where the amount of payment of my fees is in any way dependent on the outcome of the case.
>
> This report, which consists of 7 pages, has been prepared from the documents and sources referred to above.

In an expert's report it is very helpful if the paragraphs are numbered so that the solicitor, claimant and counsel can easily refer to any paragraphs that they wish to discuss.

In many cases the expert's initial medical report will indicate that there is no case in liability that he or she can identify, or alternatively, it is unlikely on the evidence presented that the case will succeed. In a large survey of cases it was found that over half did not proceed beyond this stage for those reasons. A good expert report can therefore minimise the costs to claimants if they are funding themselves (currently uncommon) or to the Legal Aid Board. It will also greatly relieve the stresses that proceedings bring to both the claimant and the defendant.

En passant, experts will often have to learn to live without knowing the outcome of many of the cases for which they have prepared a preliminary report. Solicitors do not always notify the expert when a case is halted – this is regrettable as experts are usually interested in the outcome of the cases in which they act, and in any event welcome the opportunity to close their file. Wise experts make sure that they have a system for ensuring that they are paid for work they have done, and many submit a fee note with the preliminary report.

The expert for the defence

Almost all general practitioners are members of one of the defence societies. Each of these usually relies on their particular firm of solicitors for all their cases. The defence societies also generally have their own 'in-house' team of experts.

The defendant practitioner's proof of evidence will be based on his or her contemporaneous records and on his or her usual practice. Often the practitioner has little recollection of the events due to the passage of time, although sometimes the event was one which was memorable. This is one of the reasons why good notes are valuable. Other than this, the format and process of preparing reports for the defence are much the same as those used to prepare reports for the claimant.

Dealing with further evidence

As the case progresses further evidence will emerge. At each stage the expert will need to review this and consider how it fits with his or her opinion. In particular, the defence will forward a document (the defence) stating why they do not feel that there is a case. There may also be subsequent witness statements from the defendants which will allow a fuller version of events from this perspective to be seen.

All such documents will have to be read and considered carefully. It is quite proper for the expert to amend his or her opinion in the light of such evidence. The expert will then advise the solicitor as to whether or not he or she has amended his or her opinion and, if so, how.

Finally, once the factual statements are exchanged, the expert will finalise his or her report for exchange with the other side and, at this time, will see the advice of the other experts – if he or she has not already done so. They should be considered carefully. Often the experts are in broad agreement about the standard of care, but sometimes there is argument about this. It is important to consider carefully what is said by the other experts and, of course, to consider the references used to support their view.

Conferences with counsel

Conferences between the medical experts and legal advisers are useful exercises, although they can be time-consuming. They occur in probably about 25% of cases, and in all of the cases that go to court. Initially these conferences are held by the claimant team prior to service of the claim in order to decide if the case can proceed and, if so, to finalise the Statement of Claim. Later, there may be further conferences to consider the defence witness statements and the exchanged expert opinions, in preparation for trial. These conferences are also an opportunity for counsel to weigh the factual basis of the evidence and to test the expert evidence, as well as an opportunity for the lawyers to assess the competence of the experts as witnesses.

A useful benefit in cases that are to proceed no further is that these conferences can provide explanation – and catharsis – for the claimants. This may allow them to move on from what has undoubtedly been a harrowing experience.

The meeting of experts

The Access to Justice Act presumes that there will usually be discussion by the experts instructed by both sides to focus on the issues in the case. Rule 35 now refers to 'discussions between experts' rather than to meetings, and this presumably allows for video-conferencing or even telephone conferences.

The objectives of such discussions can be summarised as follows:

- to identify the relevant issues
- where possible to reach an agreement
- where not possible, to state the issues which are agreed, those where agreement has not been reached and to set out the reasons for such disagreement.

The outcome of such discussions is only binding if all parties agree to this. The importance of keeping a record of what was said in discussion is extremely important. At the discussions the factual basis of the matter is not for consideration, as this will be for the court to decide. It is important that the experts should not enter the discussion with an entrenched opinion, and should feel free to adjust their views if a compelling argument is made.

In this way, many issues which have previously been areas of contention between experts on the two sides may no longer be contentious. Thus both the time of the court and that of the experts, can be saved. The judge can now be directed to issues where there is no agreement, rather than being distracted by areas where all are in accord.

Parties to the action are not present at the meetings between experts, although sometimes the solicitors may insist on being present – as is their right. The objective is that these meetings will avoid the need for much oral expert evidence, although only time will show if this succeeds and if it allows a just exploration of all the complex issues.

Case 78: A meeting of experts – focusing on the issues

The patient was a 53-year-old lorry driver who smoked 40 cigarettes per day and had a body mass index of 31. However, he was otherwise fit and well and had not seen a doctor for 10 years. He suffered a pain in his chest and left shoulder whilst driving. The pain was so bad he had to stop his lorry. The pain went off after about half an hour. The next day he suffered another attack of pain in the lower chest, causing him to rub his chest. This lasted over an hour. When he got home, the general practitioner was called and administered GTN spray. This did not relieve the pain. The general practitioner nevertheless diagnosed the cause of the pain as non-cardiac, although without reaching a formal diagnosis. A week later the patient collapsed with a fatal arrhythmia. At an experts' meeting it was not possible to agree whether the administration of GTN spray could be used to discount a cardiac aetiology for the pain, nor could the criteria for referral of chest pain be agreed. Both parties did, however, agree on causation, it being conceded that admission to hospital would have led to the correct diagnosis and, on the balance of probability, have averted the death. The matter therefore went to trial on liability alone.

At the trial the experts for the claimant indicated that, in their view, acute chest pain in a 53-year-old male smoker who was overweight should be considered to be cardiac in origin, and referral was mandatory, unless an alternative diagnosis could be made with a degree of certainty. The evidence of the defendant general practitioner's expert did not stand up to cross-examination. The defence then conceded the case before the trial was completed and substantial damages of £80 000 were paid.

The trial

Only a very small proportion – 1 to 2% – of civil negligence cases will come to trial as it is the intention of the Access to Justice Act to make trials even less common than they are now, and wherever possible to avoid experts attending by reaching agreement beforehand. The court will in future be able to direct that evidence on a particular issue is to be given by one expert only, and where there are a number of disciplines relevant to that issue a leading expert in the dominant discipline should be identified as a single expert. He or she has to prepare the general part of the report and be responsible for annexing or incorporating the contents of any reports from experts in other disciplines. It is hoped that the parties will agree to a common expert, but failing this the court will be able to choose from a mutually agreed list of possible experts.

For a variety of reasons the great majority of cases will be discontinued by the claimant before the case gets to court, or will have been settled by the defence when it is clear that the doctor cannot be defended. Of the cases that do come to trial, the majority do so because the factual evidence cannot be resolved and the judge will have to decide whose version of events is to be preferred. In cases of alleged medical negligence, medical issues are seldom the reason for the case going that far.

Most experts' experience of trials will be limited. Cross-examination by opposing counsel is always a challenge. To meet it, experts must be confident in the opinion that they have formed and be aware of the evidence behind that opinion.

At the trial the factual evidence of the claimant and their witnesses will be given first, followed by the claimant's experts who will be taken through their opinion. Sometimes their written opinion is accepted and only the most salient points will need to be brought out by the claimant's counsel. The defence barrister will then cross-examine the expert. The expert must listen very carefully to what is being put to them by counsel and then answer honestly. Experts who refuse to consider any view other than their own and who do not try to maintain a fair and unbiased attitude will rapidly be discredited. Sometimes the defence barrister will, in their cross-examination, introduce hypothetical alternatives to which different interpretations and/or standards might apply. The expert must be prepared to say 'I do not know' when challenged with such a hypothesis.

A recent case, *Matthews v Tarmac Bricks & Tiles Ltd*, went to appeal and was heard before Lord Woolf, who commented that it had some general significance as it was the first to take into account the new Civil Procedure Rules. The main reason for the appeal was that the case was heard in the absence of the defendant's medical experts, who were unavailable. They were unable to give any reason for this inability to attend.

Lord Woolf pointed out that a court cannot fix dates to suit the convenience of the doctors alone and give this priority over other considerations. Furthermore, he said that although it may have been preferable to have them present, he was not persuaded that the judge in the case could not make up his mind on the written reports. The solicitors were at fault for failing to place early enough before the court the true nature of the problems with regard to the attendance of the medical experts.

This illustrates the necessity of a medical expert ensuring, when he or she embarks on a case, that he or she will be able to fulfil all of the tasks required and to do so reasonably promptly.

The cost of litigation

Although not directly relevant to the involvement of general practitioners, it is helpful to understand the basic principles underlying the way in which the cost of a medical negligence suit has to be calculated.

In most cases the quantum (amount) of damages awarded is based on a Tariff which lists the range likely to be awarded for specific injuries and/or death. Contrary to the impression given by the media, the average award is only between £5000 and £10000 – which is often less than half the total costs of the case.

If the claimant succeeds in his or her case, the defendant general practitioner – via their own defence organisation – will have to pay:

- damages for the injuries caused
- all of the costs incurred by the claimant, including those of the solicitor and the medical experts
- their own costs, including the fees of their solicitor and their medical experts
- the fees for the barristers on both sides if the case goes to trial
- the expenses of the medical experts and other witnesses attending the trial.

Note that all of the above costs are subject to approval – known as 'taxation' – by a court official.

On the other hand, if the claimant loses the case, he or she will have to pay the defendant's costs. However, when the case is legally aided – as a very large proportion of medical negligence cases are – the defence costs are not reimbursed. (A claimant who is legally aided when suing a doctor for medical negligence has been likened to a man given a free lottery ticket – if he wins he makes quite a bit of money, and if he loses, it has not cost him anything.)

Because the costs of mounting a medical negligence case are usually very high, few claimants who are not eligible for legal aid will pursue their claim. Their solicitor will usually advise them that success can never be guaranteed, however strong their case may seem, and that if they lose their case, they will be faced with a large bill – not only their own costs but also those of the defendant. Furthermore, in most cases the damages awarded will often be a lot less than the costs incurred.

This approach to litigation is also reflected by the defence in legally aided cases. The defence societies have to weigh the potential costs of mounting a defence – even if they win – against the lesser costs of the case settled earlier on, even allowing for the damages they will also have to pay. By and large, the earlier the settlement, the less the cost. In addition, once the case gets to court, the costs increase at a very rapid rate.

For these reasons, attempts will frequently be made by the solicitors involved to settle the case before it gets to court. The vigour with which the solicitors on the two sides pursue their negotiations will depend on the strength of their respective cases, as they see it at the time.

Not infrequently, the case may get as far as the date of the trial – 'at the door of the court', as it is called – when the two parties will agree a settlement. This will then be formally approved by the judge without any witnesses being called.

The outcome of a trial is always potentially problematical.

Case 79: Cardiac arrest – funding the litigation

Sometimes fate plays a hand. A wife telephoned her general practitioner at 8.45 a.m. because her husband had collapsed with acute chest pain. The general practitioner accepted the call but decided to complete his morning surgery before visiting. At 10.45 a.m. the wife phoned again to say her husband was worse and the general practitioner promised to come as soon as possible. By 11.30 a.m. he had still not arrived, so the wife telephoned 999 and an ambulance arrived within five minutes. Whilst the ambulance technician was examining him he had a cardiac arrest and despite attempts to resuscitate he was pronounced dead on arrival at the hospital at 11.50 a.m.

His widow was on limited widows benefit and so received legal aid to pursue a claim in clinical negligence against the general practitioner. The defence disputed the content of the telephone calls, claiming that the first was to request a routine visit for a man who was generally unwell, and the second was to ask when the GP was likely to attend.

It was four years before the claim came to court (not unusual in these cases) and seven days before the trial the widow herself died. Her son wished to pursue the claim for his father, but as he was earning a good salary he could not obtain legal aid. He was advised that whilst the claim was a strong one, there was no guarantee that it would succeed, and if he lost he would be liable not only for his own legal expenses but also for those of the GP's defence society. He therefore decided to abandon the claim. The defence society was still left with all of the expenses incurred prior to the abandonment of the claim.

Professional witnesses (be they expert witnesses or witnesses with regard to facts) who have agreed to attend a Civil Court on a specified date or dates are entitled to a cancellation fee – provided that they have negotiated this with the solicitor in advance. A cancellation fee is also payable when the case is settled a few days before the hearing, but again only if the cancellation fee has been agreed in advance. Sometimes a subpoena requiring the expert to attend court is issued. This is not because the expert is distrusted, but it serves to protect the expert from a conflict of claims upon his or her time.

Professional bodies

As litigation becomes more prevalent and the need for experts expands, bodies have been established whose aim is to maintain the standards of experts, represent their views and facilitate training. The training is directed not at their areas of expertise but at their understanding of the legal process and thus how they can contribute to the management of cases.

Particularly eminent in this field are the Academy of Experts (who require prospective members both to provide references with regard to the quality of their work and also to sit an examination) and the Expert Witness Institute (who have similar entrance requirements). The UK Register of Expert Witnesses also supports its members in various ways, and the aspiring expert would be well advised to seek the advice of one of these organisations on the availability of training.

CHAPTER ELEVEN

Fatal Accident Inquiries in Scotland

John R Griffiths

In Scotland, the investigation and prosecution of alleged or apparent crime has for centuries been the responsibility of the Procurator Fiscal, a legally qualified official who acts quite independently of the police, the courts and local authorities and is answerable only to the Crown Office and the Lord Advocate. The Fiscal's jurisdiction has naturally expanded to include the investigation of sudden, suspicious or unexplained deaths, the circumstances of which, whilst they might not found criminal proceedings, could none the less justifiably give rise to public concern.

Accordingly, Fiscals were given statutory authority at the end of the nineteenth century to pursue inquiries into such deaths by the Fatal Accident Inquiry (Scotland) Act 1895 (which essentially dealt with accidents at work) and the Fatal Accidents and Sudden Deaths Inquiry (Scotland) Act 1906 (which provided wider powers, particularly in relation to the investigation of sudden and unexpected deaths). The passage of this latter Act reflected in part a growing concern with the number of deaths from general anaesthesia, and it remains an interesting anomaly that there is still a requirement issuing from a Crown Office direction of so many years ago that doctors should report on a special Form, F89, certain deaths associated with the provision of medical care. This category still includes deaths which occur following the administration of an anaesthetic. Until the passing of the Fatal Accidents and Sudden Deaths Inquiry (Scotland) Act 1976, Fatal Accident Inquiries were regulated under these two statutes. The singular feature of such inquiries was that they were heard before a jury of seven. In many cases the jury would be persuaded by the sheriff to return a formal verdict, although from time to time they would add a 'rider' criticising medical care, particularly if a young child's death was the cause of the inquiry.

The Fatal Accidents and Sudden Deaths Inquiry (Scotland) Act 1976

With the implementation of The Fatal Accidents and Sudden Deaths Inquiry (Scotland) Act 1976 ('The Act'), the following four significant changes were effected:

1 that the sheriff would now sit alone without a jury
2 that the Lord Advocate was given powers to make extensive rules – which he did (*see* The Fatal Accidents and Sudden Deaths Inquiry Procedure (Scotland) Rules 1977 ('The Rules'))
3 that mandatory inquiries into the deaths of persons in legal custody was brought specifically within the jurisdiction of the statute, and
4 that the jurisdiction was extended in effect to cover the off-shore oil industry by including deaths arising in the area covered by the Continental Shelf Act 1964.

The Act has only 10 Sections, and its Rules are also very short. Briefly, the Act provides as follows:

(a)   Sections 1 to 3 – Application of the Act
Mandatory inquiries apply to deaths arising from the course of employment or of persons in legal custody. **Section 1(1)(a).** 'Discretionary' inquiries are held where it appears to the Lord Advocate 'to be expedient in the public interest' to hold such an inquiry into deaths which are 'sudden, suspicious or unexplained' or which have occurred 'in circumstances such as to give rise to serious public concern'. The 'medical FAIs' largely fall into the last category, although police surgeons and prison medical officers may be involved in deaths of those in custody, including suicides.
(b)   When a relevant death is reported to the Procurator Fiscal, he will wherever possible instruct a post-mortem; thereafter he will take steps to recover documentation

including, where appropriate, hospital and general practitioner records. He will also obtain statements known as 'precognitions' from witnesses, and it should be noted that the Fiscal has the power to cite witnesses for precognition, under penalty of fine or imprisonment.

Section 2. Having concluded his investigation the Fiscal then submits a report to Crown Office where, in the case of a 'discretionary' inquiry, the decision is taken as to whether or not a Fatal Accident Inquiry should be held. Whilst the decision remains one for Crown Office, considerable weight is given to the views of the deceased's family or next of kin.

When the decision has been taken to hold an inquiry, then the Fiscal applies to the sheriff, who makes an order fixing a time and place for the inquiry and grants warrant to cite relevant witnesses and to recover relevant documents or other information.

The Fiscal then intimates the time and place to the next of kin and other interested parties and publically advertises this information.

Section 3. It is at this point that a doctor, who has earlier been precognosed, will know for certain that the inquiry is proceeding and if the Fiscal gives intimation of the inquiry directly to the doctor – as opposed to simply citing him as a witness – the doctor would be well advised, if he has not already done so, to seek advice from his medical defence organisation. It may be that the circumstances of the doctor's involvement are such (e.g. a fatal overdose) that he should be legally represented at the inquiry for, whilst strictly such a doctor always remains a 'witness', in practice, where there has been an obvious medical error, or criticism of the medical care is made, the doctor requires to be defended.

(c)   Section 4 – Conduct of the inquiry

Section 4 of the Act provides for the conduct of the inquiry. It is of course the Fiscal's inquiry. He principally adduces the evidence and leads it. If the Fiscal is aware that a doctor is legally represented, he will make available to the doctor's solicitor, prior to the inquiry, copies of all the documents on which he intends to rely, including the post-mortem report, medical records and reports from independent experts, where these have been sought. It is of course essential for the doctor's lawyer to have this information to be able to prepare for the case properly.

The parties that have a right to appear at an FAI are the wife or husband or nearest known relative of the deceased, the employer, an HSE Inspector and 'any other person who the sheriff is satisfied has an interest in the Inquiry ...'. Plainly doctors, whose care of the deceased may be criticised at the inquiry, have such an 'interest'. Not only may such persons appear, but they may adduce evidence. On a practical note, at the very commencement of the inquiry the sheriff will always ask the lawyers in the well of the court to introduce themselves and state who they are representing. Whilst of course the whole point of the inquiry is that it should be public, the sheriff does have power where any person under the age of 17 years is in any way involved in the inquiry to restrict publicity in respect of that person.

It is also open to the sheriff at his own instance or at the request of the Procurator Fiscal or of any other party to take advantage of the assistance of an assessor who has special knowledge of any of the issues at stake. Last but not least, **Section 4(7)** provides that 'the procedure and powers of the sheriff to deal with contempt of court and to enforce the attendance of witnesses at the inquiry shall be as nearly as possible those applicable in an Ordinary Civil Cause brought by the sheriff sitting alone.'

(d)   One must always have regard to the possibility of criminal proceedings in the context of an FAI and it is worth noting that **Section 5** provides that the examination of a witness or haver at the inquiry will not be a bar to criminal proceedings being taken against him. **Section 5(2)** provides a safeguard in that no witness shall be compellable to answer any question tending to show he is guilty of any crime or offence, and it is not uncommon for the Procurator Fiscal or a solicitor representing a party to ask the sheriff to issue the appropriate warning. Rarely are prosecutions taken after Fatal Accident Inquiries, but it has happened.

(e)   Section 6 – The sheriff's determination (judgement)
This is the nub of the matter. At the conclusion of the evidence and after submissions made by the Fiscal and on behalf of the parties represented, the sheriff has to make a determination. There are five heads under **Section 6(1)(a)**

to **(e)** under which he can make a determination, two of them being mandatory, namely **Section 6(1)(a)** 'Where and when the death and any accident resulting in a death took place') and **Section 6(1)(b)** ('The cause or causes of such death and any accident resulting in the death'). The latter three are discretionary heads. They are **Section 6(1)(c)** ('The reasonable precautions, if any, whereby the death and the accident resulting in the death might have been avoided'). **Section 6(1)(d)** ('The defects, if any, in any system of working which contributed to the death or any accident resulting in the death') and **Section 6(1)(e)** ('Any other facts which are relevant to the circumstances of the death'). It is under these heads that the sheriff may make findings critical of the deceased's medical care, if the evidence supports such criticism and 'Reasonable precautions' under 6(1)(c) 'whereby ... the death *might* have been avoided', could have been, for example, immediate admission of the patient to hospital at the conclusion of a house call by a GP, or alternatively the GP's arranging to review the patient in, say, 3 hours' time.

'Defects ... in any system of working' under 6(1)(a) would be the relevant head in a case of a fatal overdose of a drug where there was no system for checking the dosage in place.

'Any other facts which are relevant to the circumstances of the death ...' 6(1)(e) is obviously a 'catch-all' provision which sheriffs do utilise – for example, in a case where a doctor may have made no notes of a particular consultation. Whilst this failure may not justify a finding under 6(1)(c) or (d), it enables a sheriff, none the less, to criticise a doctor for his shortcomings in perhaps a more general context.

Section 6(2) provides that evidence need not be corroborated.

The provisions of **Section 6(3)** are interesting, namely 'that the determination of the sheriff shall not be admissible in evidence or be founded on in any judicial proceedings of whatever nature arising out of the death or out of any accident from which the death resulted.' The sheriff's determination itself may therefore not be used in civil action for damages subsequent to an FAI *but* the sworn testimony given by the witnesses which will be enshrined in the transcript of the evidence may be extremely useful to a pursuer in a civil claim and will be admissible in further proceedings.

However, the General Medical Council have ruled that they *will* take into account the sheriff's determination. Increasingly, complaints are being made to the GMC following on from FAIs. Given the powers which the GMC has to reprimand a doctor, or to suspend his or her membership or erase him or her from the Register, it obviously becomes very important indeed for a doctor to make the best showing possible at an FAI.

The Fatal Accidents and Sudden Deaths Inquiry Procedures (Scotland) Rules 1997

The Rules deal with some matters of procedure in greater detail, and examples are listed below.

- **Rule 6** empowers the sheriff to inspect any land, premises, article or other thing which he or she considers desirable for the purposes of the inquiry.
- **Rule 7** deals with representation.
- **Rule 7(2)** provides that any person may appear on his or her own behalf or be represented by an advocate or a solicitor or with the leave of the sheriff by any other person.
- **Rule 9** empowers a sheriff to adjourn an inquiry at any time.
- **Rule 10** allows for the production and admission of written evidence by way of affidavit, but only if all persons who appear or are represented at the inquiry agree to its admission or the sheriff considers that its admission will not result in unfairness.
- **Rule 11** deals with the mechanics of the issuing of the sheriff's determination. Anyone who appeared or was represented at the inquiry is allowed to inspect it free of charge during the period of three months after the date when the determination is made. As a matter of practice the determination is sent out to the parties by the Sheriff Clerk – in my experience free of charge.
- **Rule 12(2)** provides that if an assessor is appointed, his or her appointment shall not affect the admissibility of expert evidence.
- **Rule 14** is important because it enables a party to obtain a copy of the transcript within a period of up to *three months* after the date of the sheriff's determination.
- **Rule 17** gives the sheriff very wide dispensing powers at his or

her discretion to relieve any person from the consequences of any failure to comply with the provision of the Rules.

Remedies

There is no appeal as such against a sheriff's determination. However, in a case where it is thought that the sheriff has come to an unreasonable conclusion – where, for example, there may be no evidence to sustain his view – an aggrieved party may seek to have the determination judicially reviewed in the Court of Session. There have been at least two reported cases of determinations which have been successfully judicially reviewed.

General comments on Fatal Accident Inquiries

What then is the importance and true function of Fatal Accident Inquiries? There would appear to be some disagreement amongst judges. The then Lord President (Scotland's senior judge) said in a case on appeal (*Black v Scott Lithgow Ltd*)[1]

> There is no power in this Section to make a finding as to fault or to apportion blame between any persons who might have contributed to the accident. This is in contrast to Section 4(7) of the 1895 Act which gave power to the Jury to set out in its verdict the person or persons, if any, to whose fault or negligence the accident was attributable. It is plain that the function of the Sheriff to Fatal Accident Inquiries is different to that which he is required to perform at a Proof in a civil action to recover damages, his examination and analysis of the evidence is conducted with a view only to setting out in his determination the circumstances to which this sub-section refers insofar as this can be done to his satisfaction. He has before him no record or other written pleading. There is no claim for damages by anyone and there are no grounds of fault upon which his decision is required. The Inquiry is normally held within a relatively short time after the accident – in this case the evidence was heard within about eight months after the death of the deceased. It provides the first opportunity to canvas matters relating to precautions which might have avoided the death or

any defects in any system of working which contributed to it at a stage when these issues have not been clearly focused by the parties to any future litigation which may arise and it is not uncommon as happened in the present case to find questions being asked about the possible precautions or defects which are not the subject of averments in the subsequent action of damages.

That view would appear to place a limit on the sheriff's powers under Sections 6(1)(c) to (e) of the Act, but it is not a view necessarily shared by the sheriffs themselves. An experienced Glasgow sheriff in *FAI: Mildred Allan* in 1985 said:

It seems to me that Fatal Accident Inquiries may be regarded as having two essential purposes and one important corollary. The essential purposes are the enlightenment of those legitimately interested in the death, i.e. the relatives and dependants of the deceased as to the cause of death and of any accident resulting from the death and the enlightenment of the public at large including the relatives as to whether any reasonable steps could or should have been taken whereby the death might have been avoided so that lessons may be learned or at least the attention of further enquirers directed into ways whereby practices may have contributed to the death can be improved. The provision in Section 6(1)(c) empowering the Sheriff to make determinations as to reasonable precautions whereby the death might have been avoided and the provision that evidence need not be corroborated gives the Sheriff a very wide power to make determinations but the summary nature of the proceedings including the lack of written pleadings which give advance notice of any line of criticism must make the Court cautious of drawing too sweeping conclusions from the evidence which may be incomplete. The provisions of Section 6(1)(e) are still wider and in my view entitle and indeed oblige the Court to comment upon and where appropriate make recommendation to any matter which has been legitimately examined in the course of the Inquiry as the circumstances surrounding the death if it appears to be in the public interest to make such a comment or recommendation. The corollary of these procedures is the accessibility to legitimately interested parties of the evidence made available to and adumbrated in the course of the Inquiry. The availability of such evidence enables those legitimately interested parties, if so advised, to establish negligence or other culpability in the ordinary courts which by their procedure of written pleadings which give advanced notice of particular allegations are well suited to dealing fairly and fully with such matters: hence no doubt the provision that the Sheriff's determination of a Fatal Accident Inquiry may not be founded upon in any such subsequent proceedings.

In practice, sheriffs are inclined to the latter view and will not shrink from criticising doctors where they believe the evidence to justify such criticism. It is therefore very important for doctors in Scotland, whether they work in hospitals or as general practitioners, to be fully aware of the significance of Fatal Accident Inquiries, of the need to seek advice, assistance and perhaps legal representation for such inquiries, and to bear in mind that the most worrying consequence of criticism at an FAI may not be the immediate publicity in the media, or a civil claim for damages, but a complaint to the General Medical Council to which the unfortunate doctor must answer.

Case reference

1   Black v Scott Lithgow Ltd (1990) *Scots Law Times*: 612.

Further reading

Carmichael IHP (1993) *Sudden Deaths and Fatal Accident Inquiries* (2e). W Green & Sons, Edinburgh.

CHAPTER TWELVE

Civil procedure in Scotland

Fiona MF Paterson

Introduction

The aim of this chapter is to provide the medical practitioner with an overview of civil rather than criminal procedure in the Scottish Court of Session and Sheriff Court. Scotland is divided geographically into six Sheriffdoms, each presided over by a member of the judiciary known as the Sheriff Principal. Within most Sheriffdoms, there are several Sheriff Courts with a bench of between five and 20 Sheriffs. Civil business within the Sheriff Court is divided into three Courts. Actions in which the claimant or pursuer seeks damages from his opponent, the defender, of £1500 or less are dealt with in the Small Claims Court. Those with a value of between £1500 and £5000 are heard in the Summary Cause Court and finally, a claim with a value of more than £5000 is dealt with in the Ordinary Cause Court. In practice, the three courts run simultaneously in one building with two or more sheriffs sitting at once. As most claims involving allegations of medical negligence have a value greater than £5000 and are raised in the Ordinary Court, it is the Ordinary Cause procedure which is explored here.

The Court of Session sits only in Edinburgh. Very broadly, it is divided into the Outer House (in which actions are raised) and the Inner House (in which appeals are heard). Unlike the Sheriff Courts, it has jurisdiction for the whole of Scotland. Until relatively recently, only Counsel (known as barristers in England and Wales and advocates in Scotland) had the right to present cases in the Court of Session, unlike the Sheriff Court where solicitors have a right of audience as well. However, solicitors may now acquire the title 'Solicitor Advocate' and appear in the Court of Session after sitting various written and oral tests.

How do pursuers decide where to raise an action?

As there is no financial limit on cases which can be raised in the Sheriff Court, a pursuer has a choice between raising an action in either court. However, he will often select the Court of Session in an action of medical negligence despite the additional cost of Counsel's involvement. The advantages of raising an action in the Court of Session are that advocates are able to bring additional expertise to the presentation of the case, parties have longer to prepare their cases as the procedure is much lengthier and the Court of Session judiciary has greater experience of complex medical evidence. The disadvantages are the additional costs and the longer wait the parties face before the final resolution of the case. In practice, the decision will often be based on the funding available to the Pursuer and his solicitor's familiarity or lack of familiarity with the Court of Session.

Civil procedure in the Court of Session

All actions in the Court of Session are commenced with a document known as a Summons being served on the Defenders. Service is affected by posting the Summons by recorded delivery post or by Sheriff Officers delivering it to the Defender's home or place of business. The Summons is prepared by the Pursuer's solicitors and Counsel. It sets out the factual allegations and legal case against the Defender. Most importantly, it also indicates the sum sued for! Once it is served the action commences.

If a Defender wishes to defend an action he has to lodge a document in Court known as Defences and send a copy to the Pursuer's solicitor.

The Summons and Defences form the written basis of parties' cases. The law of evidence in Scotland dictates that only matters stated in the Summons and Defences can be referred to during the final hearing of evidence in the case. The philosophy underpinning the whole system is one of 'fair notice'. Consequently, if either party tries to introduce evidence which is not referred to in the Summons or Defences during the final hearing, the Judge may decide not to hear that evidence.

It is recognised that at the time the Summons and Defences are prepared parties' investigations into the claim may not yet be complete. In a medical negligence action usually these investigations will involve obtaining an expert opinion on the actions of the doctors and the outcome of those actions as opposed to the underlying pathology. Naturally, it would be very unfortunate if parties were not able to make use of the investigations they undertake after the Summons and Defences are lodged, so the Court allows a period known as an 'adjustment period' during which both sides are allowed to expand upon the allegations in the Summons and the Defences. The two documents are combined into a document known as an 'Open Record' and adjustments are marked on it and exchanged between parties. Usually, a Court will only allow this process to continue for three to six months. The Record then *'closes'*. The litigants then have to let the Court know what sort of hearing they wish to have in order to dispose of the case. Between the Record closing and any hearing, neither the Pursuer or Defender can make further additions or alterations to their case without the leave of the Court. In practice, such additions, or amendments as they are known, are allowed, unless the party seeking the amendment does so very shortly before a hearing. The Judge may then decide that to allow the amendment could cause prejudice to the other party.

There are four different types of hearing:

- a 'Procedure Roll Debate'
- a 'Proof'
- a 'Proof Before Answer'
- and a 'Jury Trial'.

A case can proceed directly to any of the four hearings once the Record has closed. The first one, a procedure roll debate, is a hearing on legal arguments only. No evidence is heard. A Judge sits alone and has to decide whether the case is bad in law. If it is, he has the option to dismiss the action there and then. The Pursuer would then have to re-raise the action. However, this is a very unusual step in an action involving allegations of medical negligence or personal injuries. Judges tend to take the view that the individual parties should not be penalised in such a drastic manner merely because the legal presentation of the case has been poor. Although many procedure roll debates are fixed by the Court they are often cancelled as the party who is being criticised alters their case to correct any presentational weaknesses. If the procedure roll debate proceeds and the Judge decides not to dismiss the case, it proceeds to a proof, or a proof before answer or a jury trial.

To anyone apart from a lawyer or a Judge, a proof or a proof before answer is essentially the same. A Judge sits alone and hears the evidence from both parties. Usually witnesses appear for both sides. Once the Judge has heard the witnesses and Counsels' submissions, he makes a decision on whether there has been negligence and if so, whether the negligence caused the Pursuer harm. If the Judge decides that there has been negligence which has harmed the Pursuer, he will also make a finding on the damages which should be awarded to the Pursuer. A court order known as a decree is granted by the Judge ordaining the Defender to pay the Pursuer damages. If however, the Judge finds there has been no negligence, he grants decree of absolvitor. Either type of decree brings the case to an end.

The final type of hearing is known as a jury trial and involves a jury rather than a Judge making the decisions outlined above in light of the evidence led before them. However, a Judge hears the case with the jury and grants decree in accordance with their findings.

Normally, the entire procedure will take between 18 and 24 months. However, the Court of Session does provide 'a fast track procedure' known as the 'Optional Procedure' which is slightly shorter. Very few medical negligence actions are raised under this procedure.

Civil procedure in the Sheriff Court: ordinary cause rules

Unsurprisingly, the procedure in the Sheriff Court is broadly similar to that in the Court of Session although the terminology is a little different in places. The action is commenced by a document known as an 'Initial Writ' being served by the Pursuer on the Defender. Its format is almost identical to the Court of Session Summons. Defences are then lodged by the Defender if he wishes to defend the action. Again a Record is prepared incorporating the Summons and Defences.

A period of eight weeks only is allowed for adjustment of the pleadings. Solicitors for the Pursuer and Defender then have to attend a hearing in Court before the Sheriff – this is known as an 'Options Hearing'. The purpose of the hearing is to allow the

Sheriff to 'seek to secure the expeditious progress of the (case) by ascertaining from the parties the matters in dispute and information about any other matter...'. In practice, the Sheriff after reading the pleadings and hearing solicitors' submissions decides whether the parties require further time to adjust their cases, or he closes the Record and fixes a debate, proof or proof before answer. There are no jury trials held in the Sheriff Court. The comments made above regarding amendments in the Court of Session apply here too.

The procedure may only take between six months and a year. However, a great deal will depend on the Court's location. Sheriff Courts based in cities such as Edinburgh, Glasgow, Dundee or Aberdeen inevitably have more cases passing through them than those in more rural areas. Consequently, several months can pass between a Sheriff allowing a hearing and it taking place.

In both the Court of Session and the Sheriff Court, actions can be 'sisted' which means they are temporarily frozen procedurally. The most common reasons for a party asking the Court to grant a sist are a pending application to The Scottish Legal Aid Board, outstanding inquiries or negotiations. Usually, the length of the sist is at the discretion of the parties which can lead to lengthy delays in procedure.

Table of legal cases

Table of statutes and statutory instruments

Index